episode 25:
Dominica's Heart

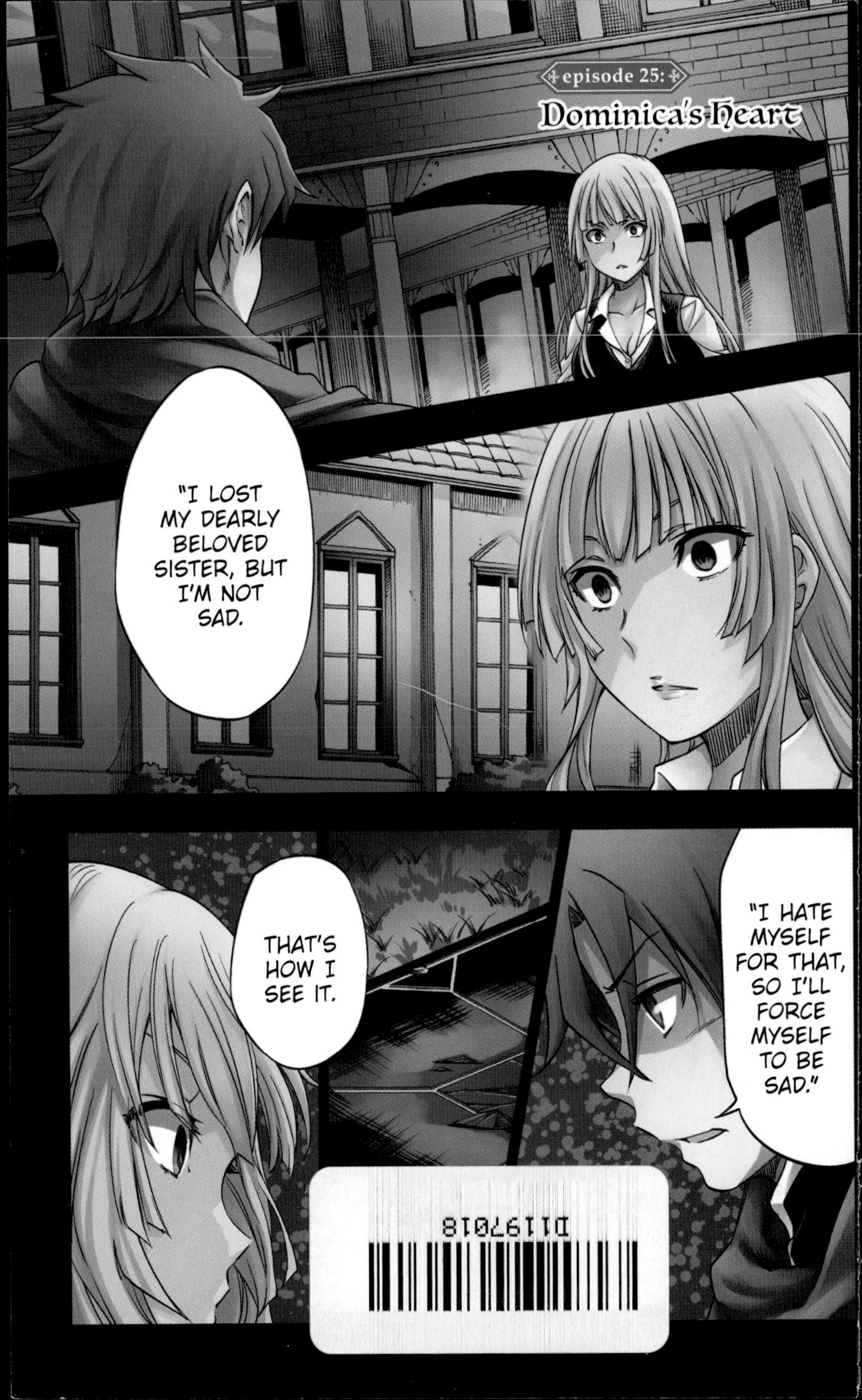
"I LOST MY DEARLY BELOVED SISTER, BUT I'M NOT SAD.
"I HATE MYSELF FOR THAT, SO I'LL FORCE MYSELF TO BE SAD."
THAT'S HOW I SEE IT.

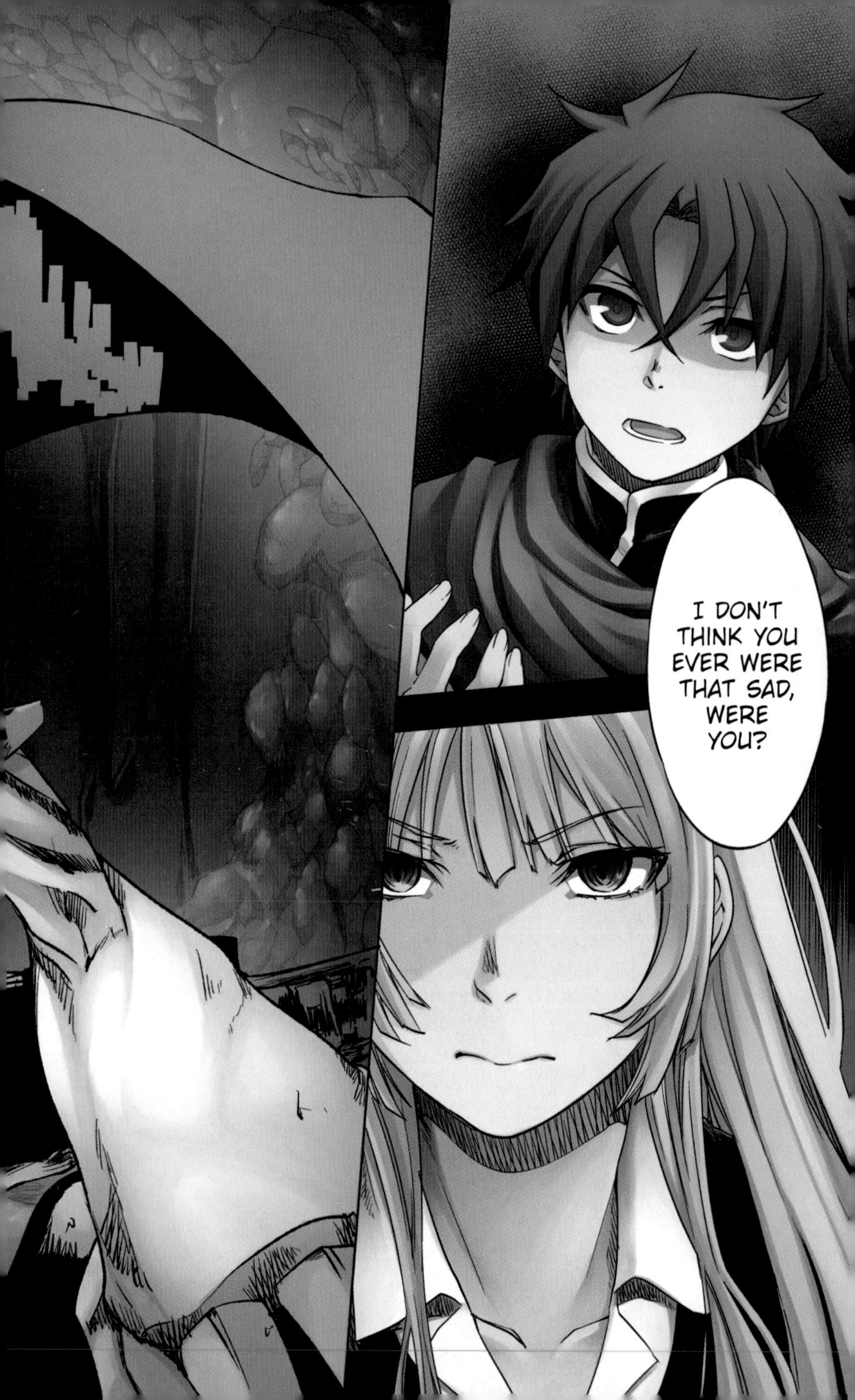
I DON'T THINK YOU EVER WERE THAT SAD, WERE YOU?

CHAIKA: THE COFFIN PRINCESS

IV

ORIGINAL STORY
ICHIROU SAKAKI

ART
SHINTA SAKAYAMA

CHARACTER DESIGN
NAMANIKU ATK
(NITROPLUS)

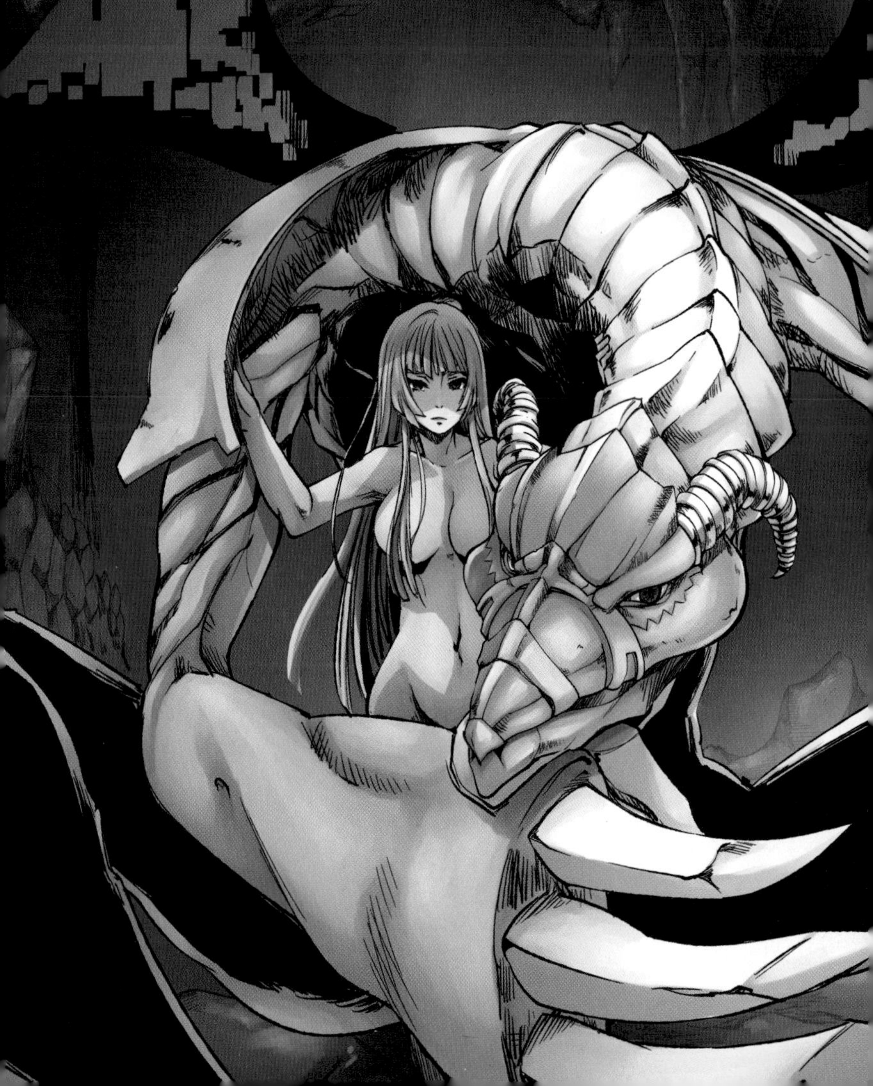

CONTENTS

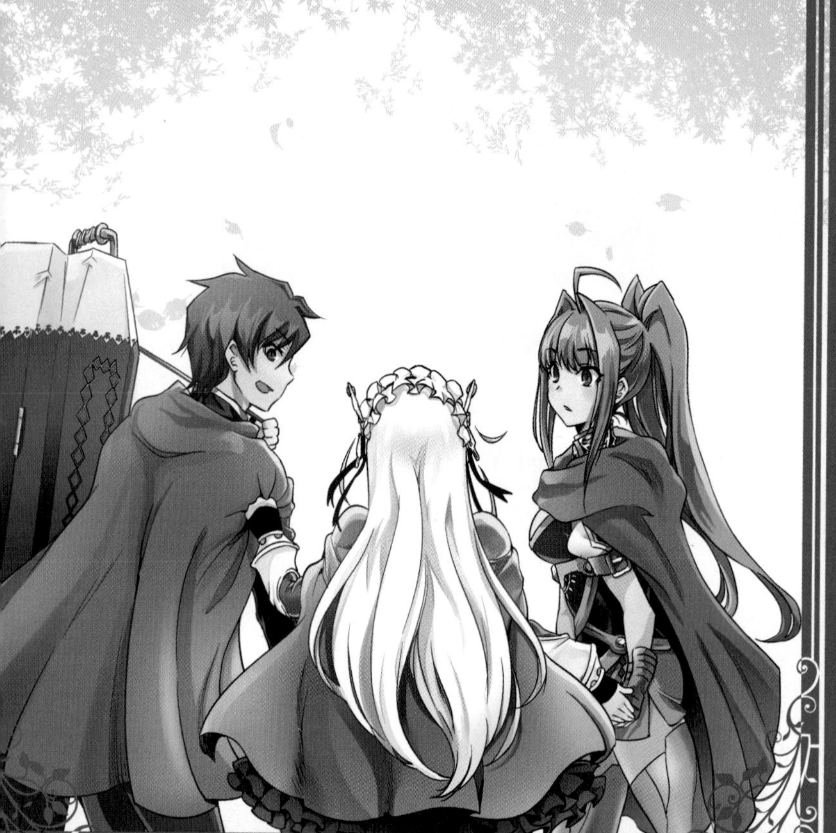

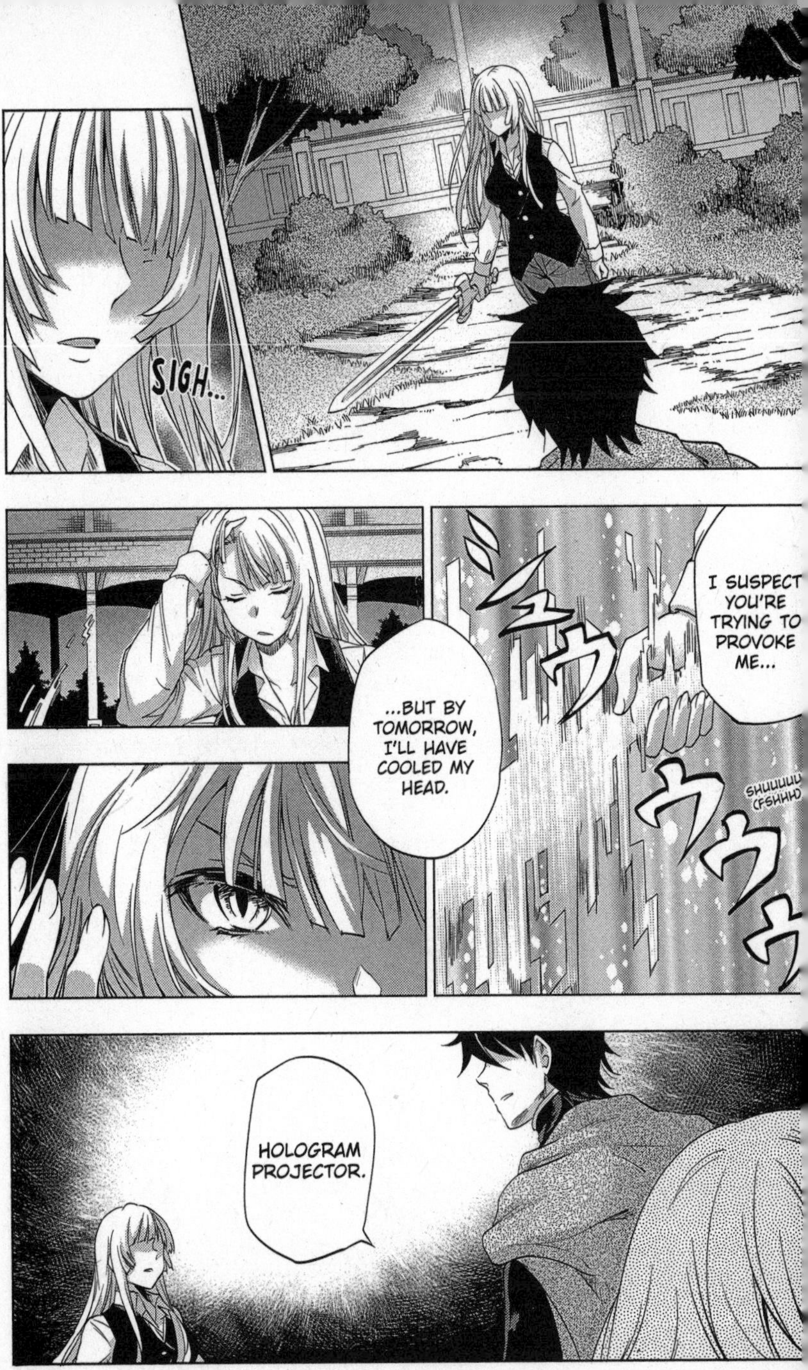
SIGH...
I SUSPECT YOU'RE TRYING TO PROVOKE ME...
シュウウウウ
SHUUUUU (FSHHH)
...BUT BY TOMORROW, I'LL HAVE COOLED MY HEAD.
HOLOGRAM PROJECTOR.

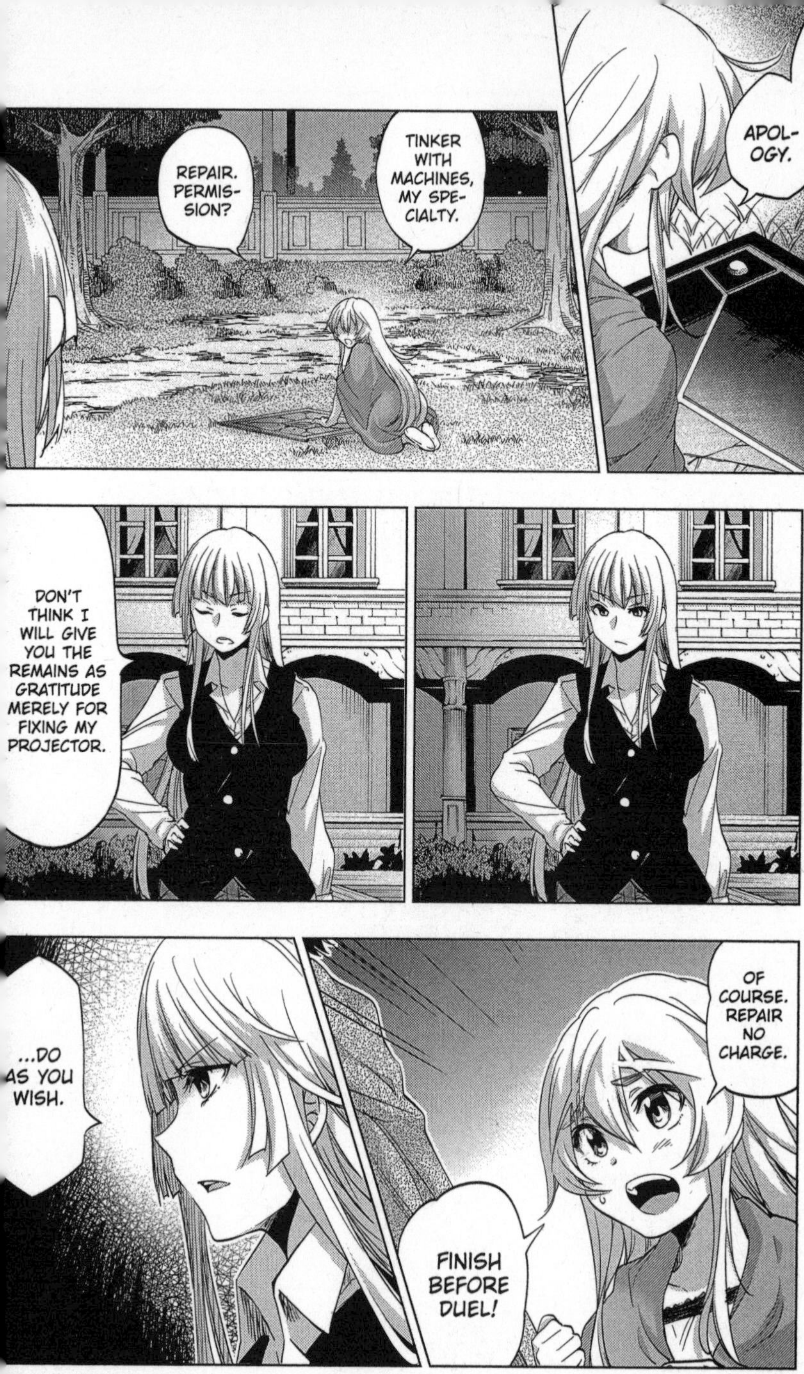
I FIX.
APOLOGY.
TINKER WITH MACHINES, MY SPECIALTY.
REPAIR. PERMISSION?
DON'T THINK I WILL GIVE YOU THE REMAINS AS GRATITUDE MERELY FOR FIXING MY PROJECTOR.
OF COURSE. REPAIR NO CHARGE.
FINISH BEFORE DUEL!
...DO AS YOU WISH.

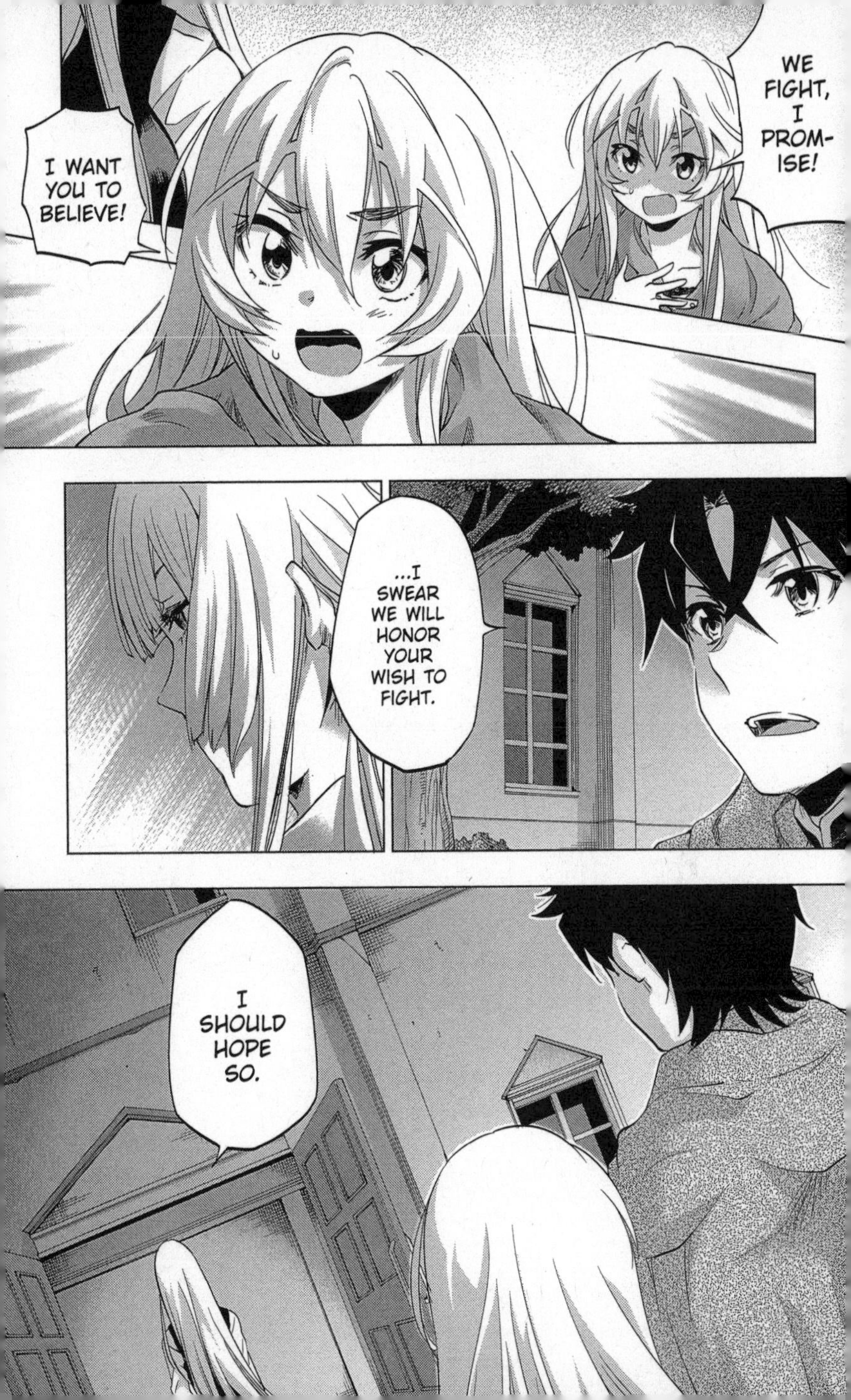
WE FIGHT, I PROMISE!
I WANT YOU TO BELIEVE!
...I SWEAR WE WILL HONOR YOUR WISH TO FIGHT.
I SHOULD HOPE SO.

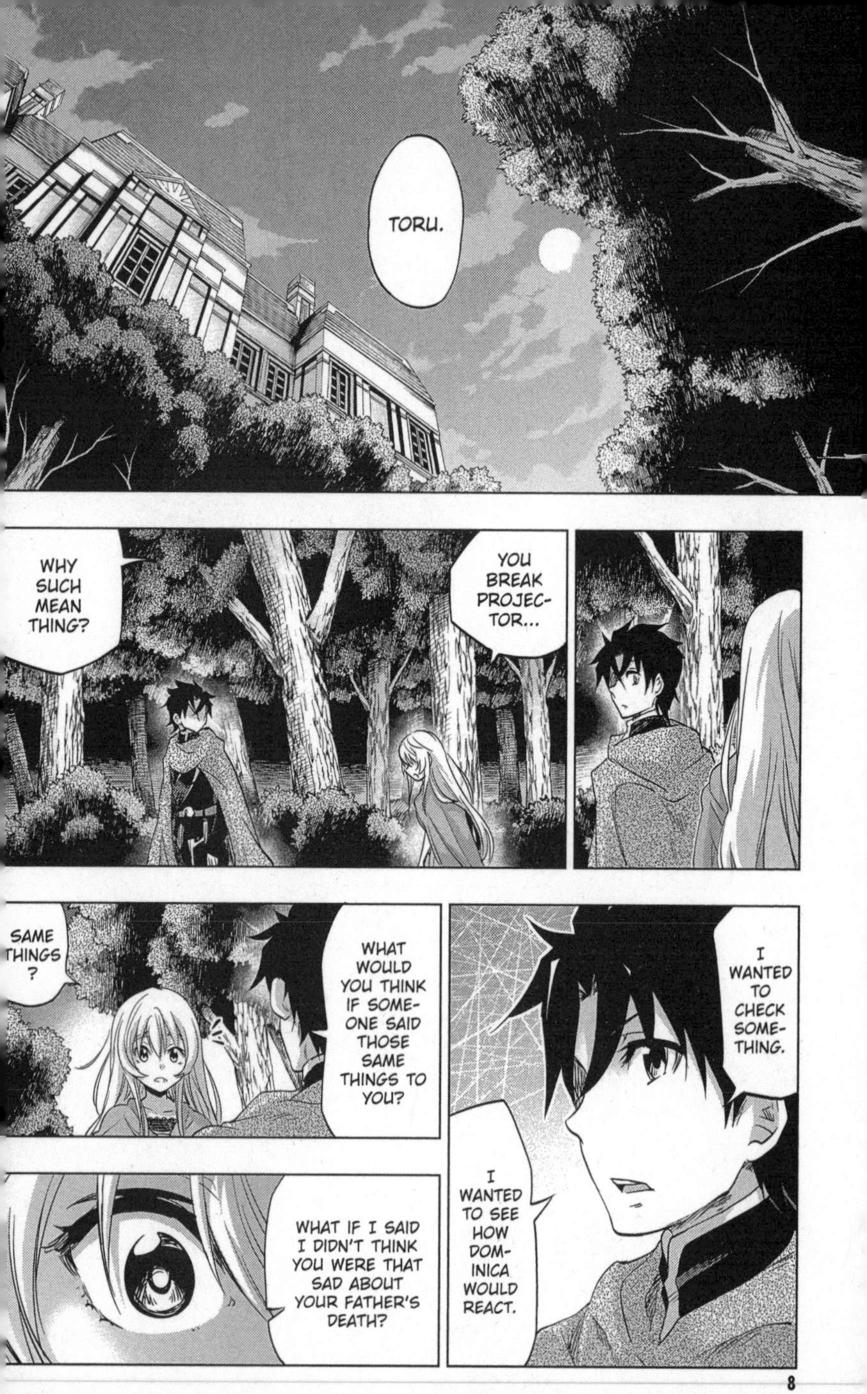
TORU.
YOU BREAK PROJECTOR...
WHY SUCH MEAN THING?
I WANTED TO CHECK SOMETHING.
I WANTED TO SEE HOW DOMINICA WOULD REACT.
WHAT WOULD YOU THINK IF SOMEONE SAID THOSE SAME THINGS TO YOU?
SAME THINGS?
WHAT IF I SAID I DIDN'T THINK YOU WERE THAT SAD ABOUT YOUR FATHER'S DEATH?

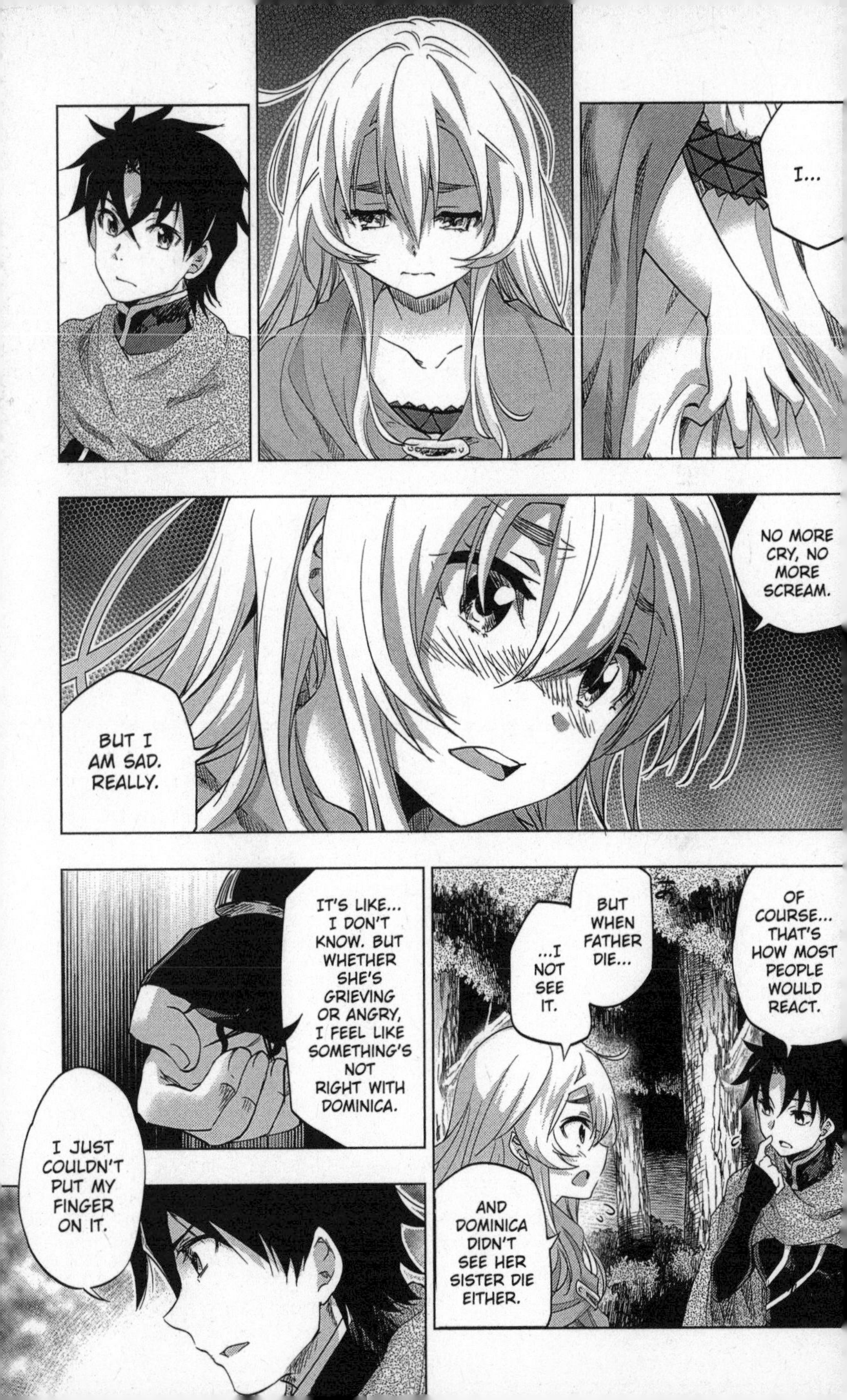
I...
NO MORE CRY, NO MORE SCREAM.
BUT I AM SAD. REALLY.
OF COURSE... THAT'S HOW MOST PEOPLE WOULD REACT.
BUT WHEN FATHER DIE...
...I NOT SEE IT.
AND DOMINICA DIDN'T SEE HER SISTER DIE EITHER.
IT'S LIKE... I DON'T KNOW. BUT WHETHER SHE'S GRIEVING OR ANGRY, I FEEL LIKE SOMETHING'S NOT RIGHT WITH DOMINICA.
I JUST COULDN'T PUT MY FINGER ON IT.

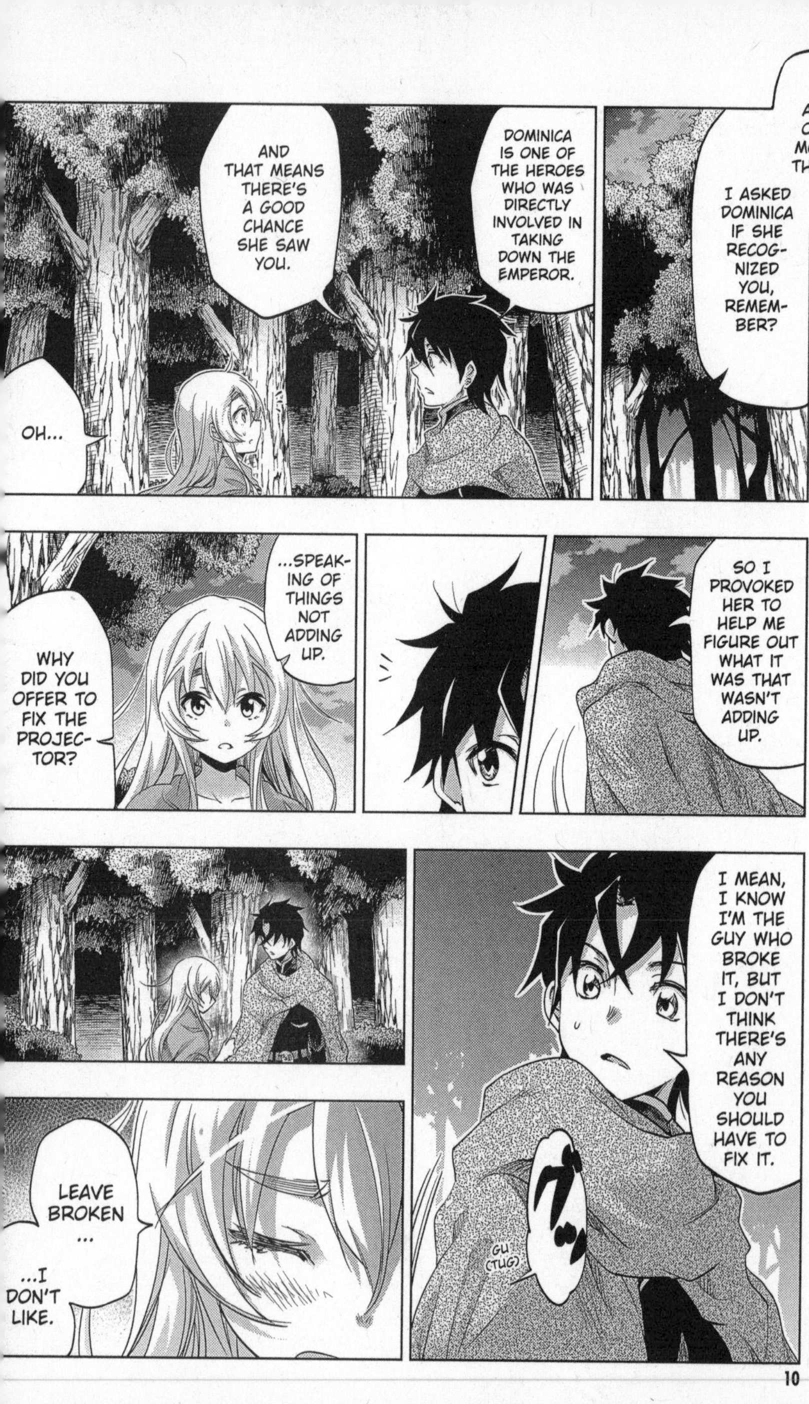

AND ONE MORE THING.
I ASKED DOMINICA IF SHE RECOGNIZED YOU, REMEMBER?
DOMINICA IS ONE OF THE HEROES WHO WAS DIRECTLY INVOLVED IN TAKING DOWN THE EMPEROR.
AND THAT MEANS THERE'S A GOOD CHANCE SHE SAW YOU.
OH...
SO I PROVOKED HER TO HELP ME FIGURE OUT WHAT IT WAS THAT WASN'T ADDING UP.
...SPEAKING OF THINGS NOT ADDING UP.
WHY DID YOU OFFER TO FIX THE PROJECTOR?
I MEAN, I KNOW I'M THE GUY WHO BROKE IT, BUT I DON'T THINK THERE'S ANY REASON YOU SHOULD HAVE TO FIX IT.
GU (TUG)
LEAVE BROKEN ...
...I DON'T LIKE.

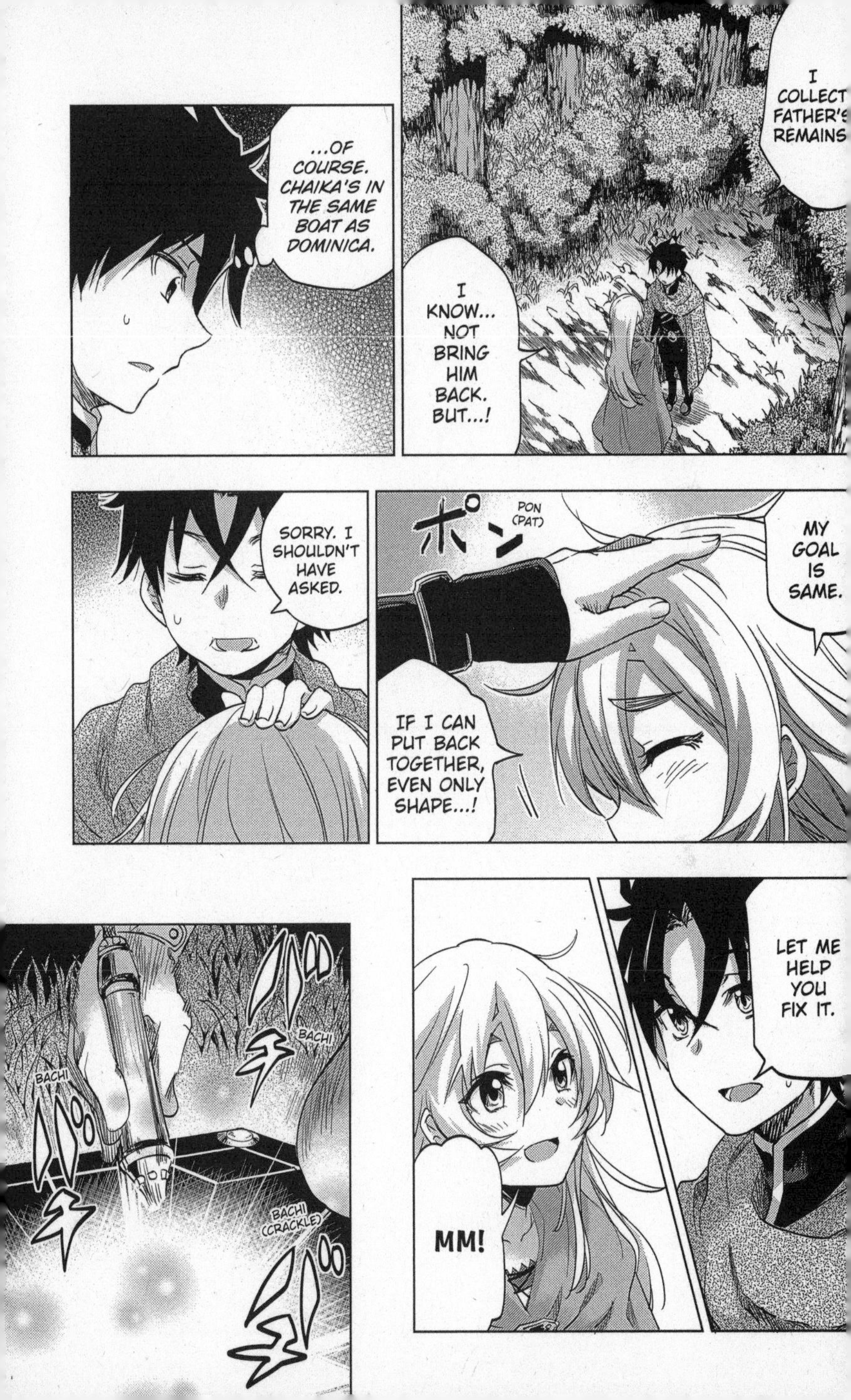
I COLLECT FATHER'S REMAINS
I KNOW... NOT BRING HIM BACK. BUT...!
...OF COURSE. CHAIKA'S IN THE SAME BOAT AS DOMINICA.
MY GOAL IS SAME.
ポン
PON (PAT)
IF I CAN PUT BACK TOGETHER, EVEN ONLY SHAPE...!
SORRY. I SHOULDN'T HAVE ASKED.
LET ME HELP YOU FIX IT.
MM!
BACHI
BACHI
BACHI (CRACKLE)

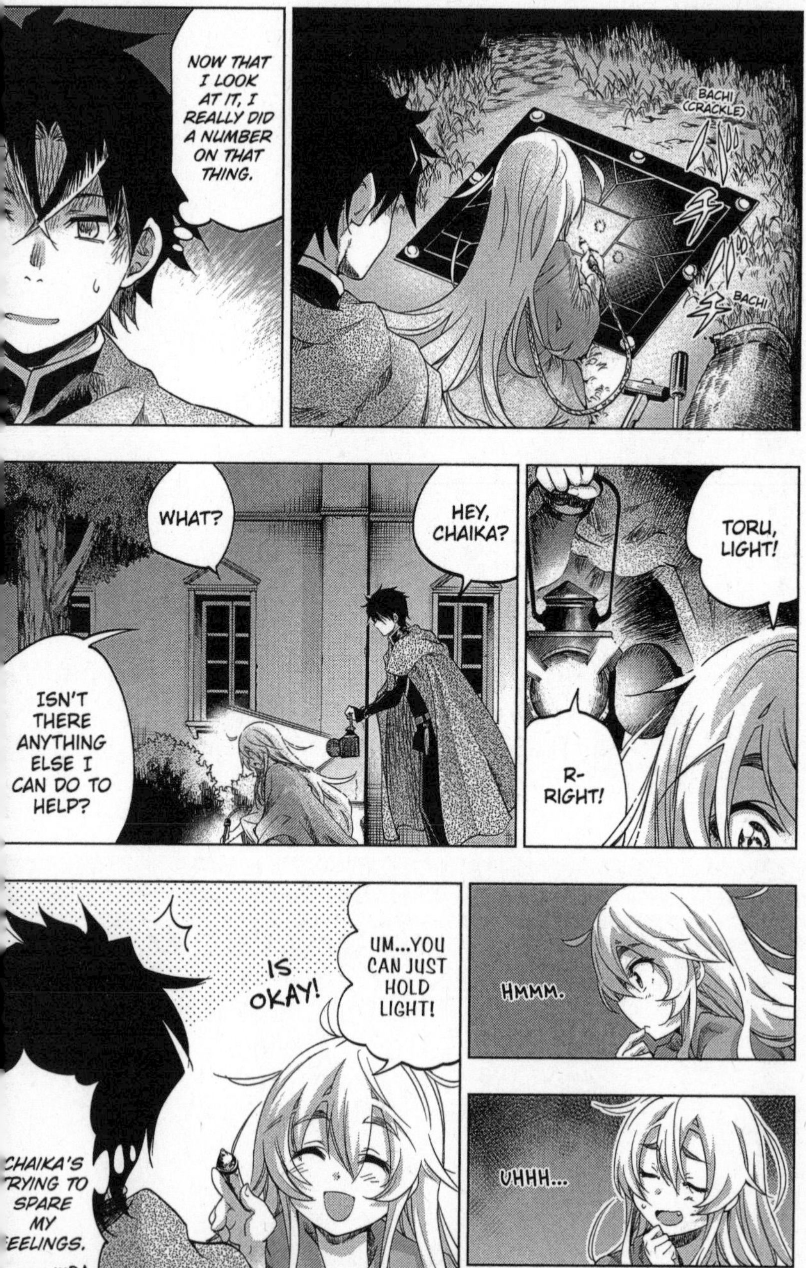
BACHI (CRACKLE)
BACHI
NOW THAT I LOOK AT IT, I REALLY DID A NUMBER ON THAT THING.
TORU, LIGHT!
R-RIGHT!
HEY, CHAIKA?
WHAT?
ISN'T THERE ANYTHING ELSE I CAN DO TO HELP?
HMMM.
UHHH...
UM...YOU CAN JUST HOLD LIGHT!
IS OKAY!
CHAIKA'S RYING TO SPARE MY EELINGS.
HAT KINDA HURTS...

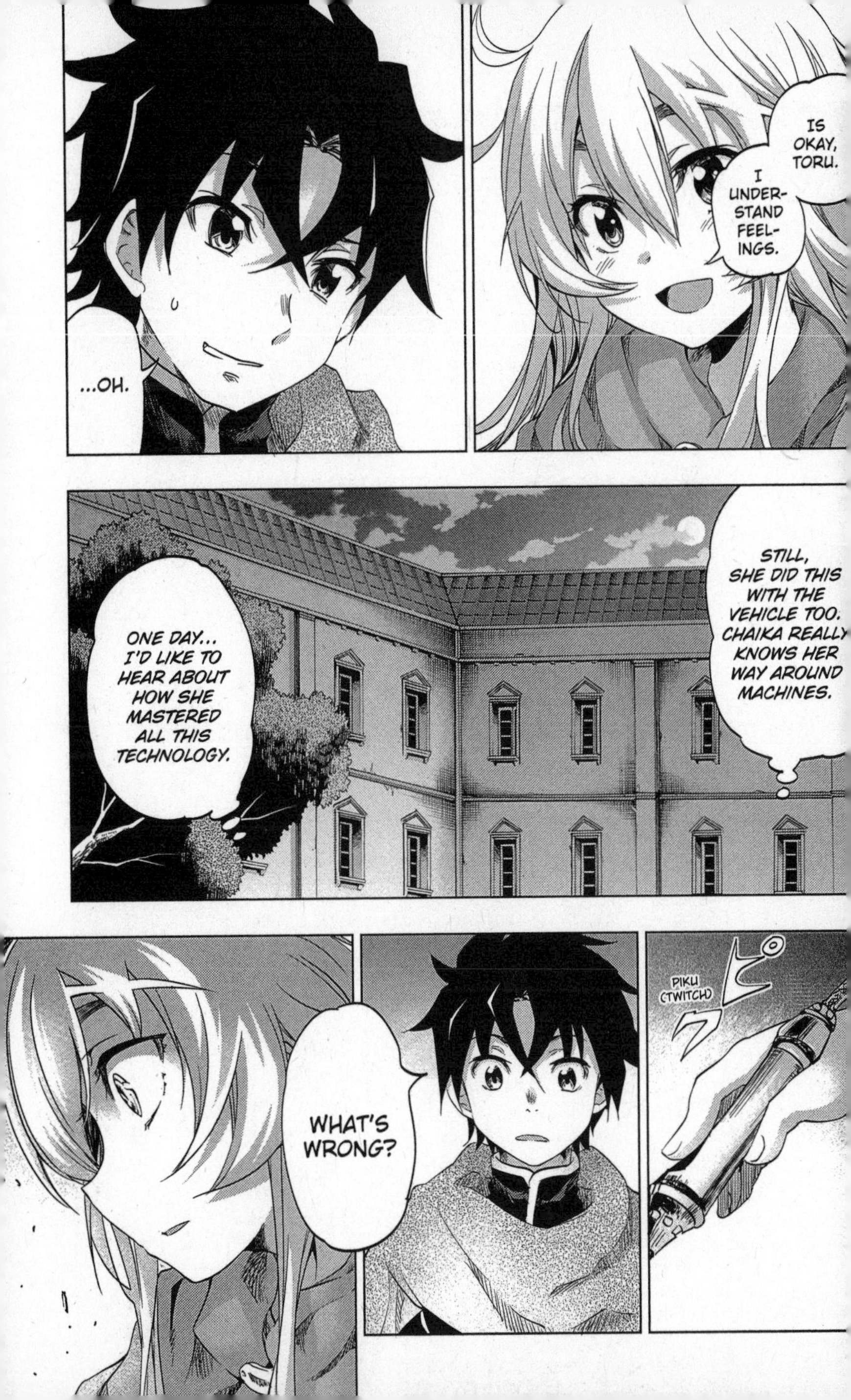
IS OKAY, TORU.
I UNDERSTAND FEELINGS.
...OH.
STILL, SHE DID THIS WITH THE VEHICLE TOO. CHAIKA REALLY KNOWS HER WAY AROUND MACHINES.
ONE DAY... I'D LIKE TO HEAR ABOUT HOW SHE MASTERED ALL THIS TECHNOLOGY.
PIKU (TWITCH)
WHAT'S WRONG?

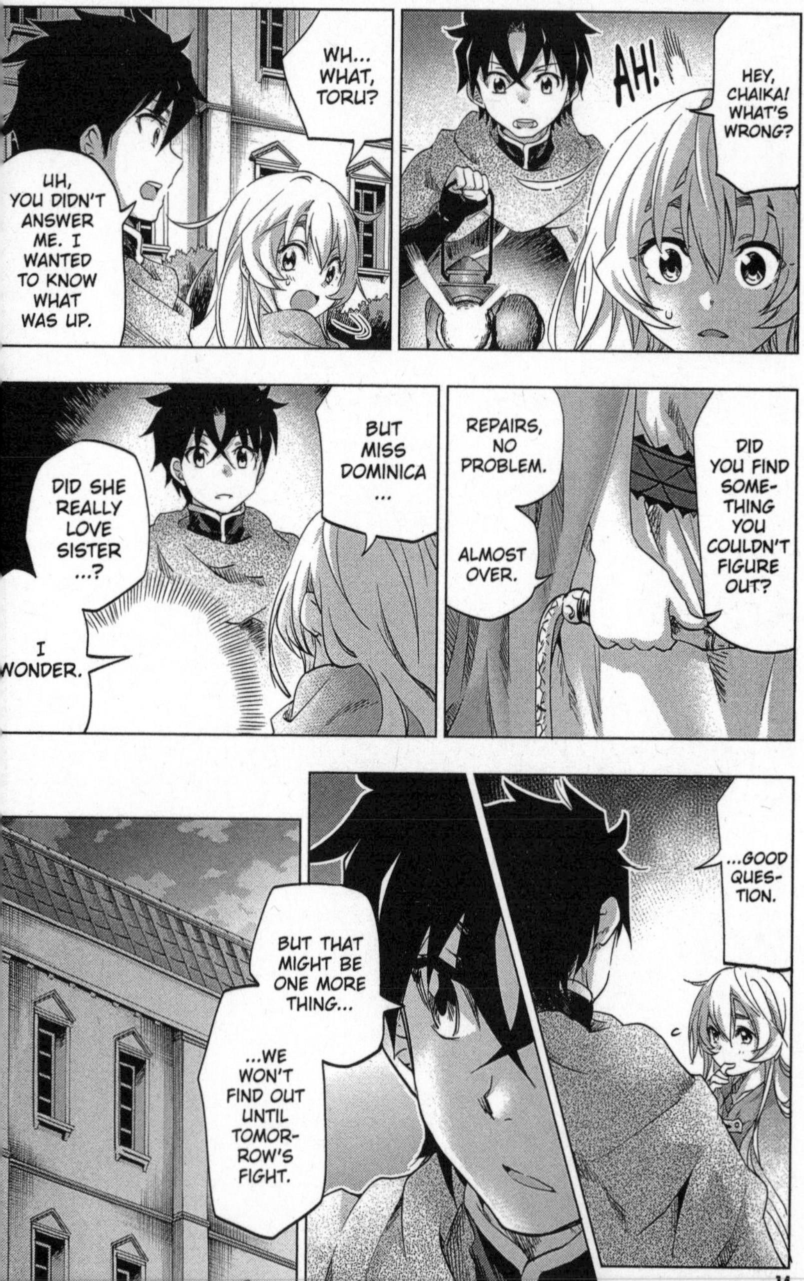
AH!
HEY, CHAIKA! WHAT'S WRONG?
WH... WHAT, TORU?
UH, YOU DIDN'T ANSWER ME. I WANTED TO KNOW WHAT WAS UP.
DID YOU FIND SOME-THING YOU COULDN'T FIGURE OUT?
REPAIRS, NO PROBLEM.
ALMOST OVER.
BUT MISS DOMINICA ...
DID SHE REALLY LOVE SISTER ...?
I WONDER.
...GOOD QUES-TION.
BUT THAT MIGHT BE ONE MORE THING...
...WE WON'T FIND OUT UNTIL TOMOR-ROW'S FIGHT.

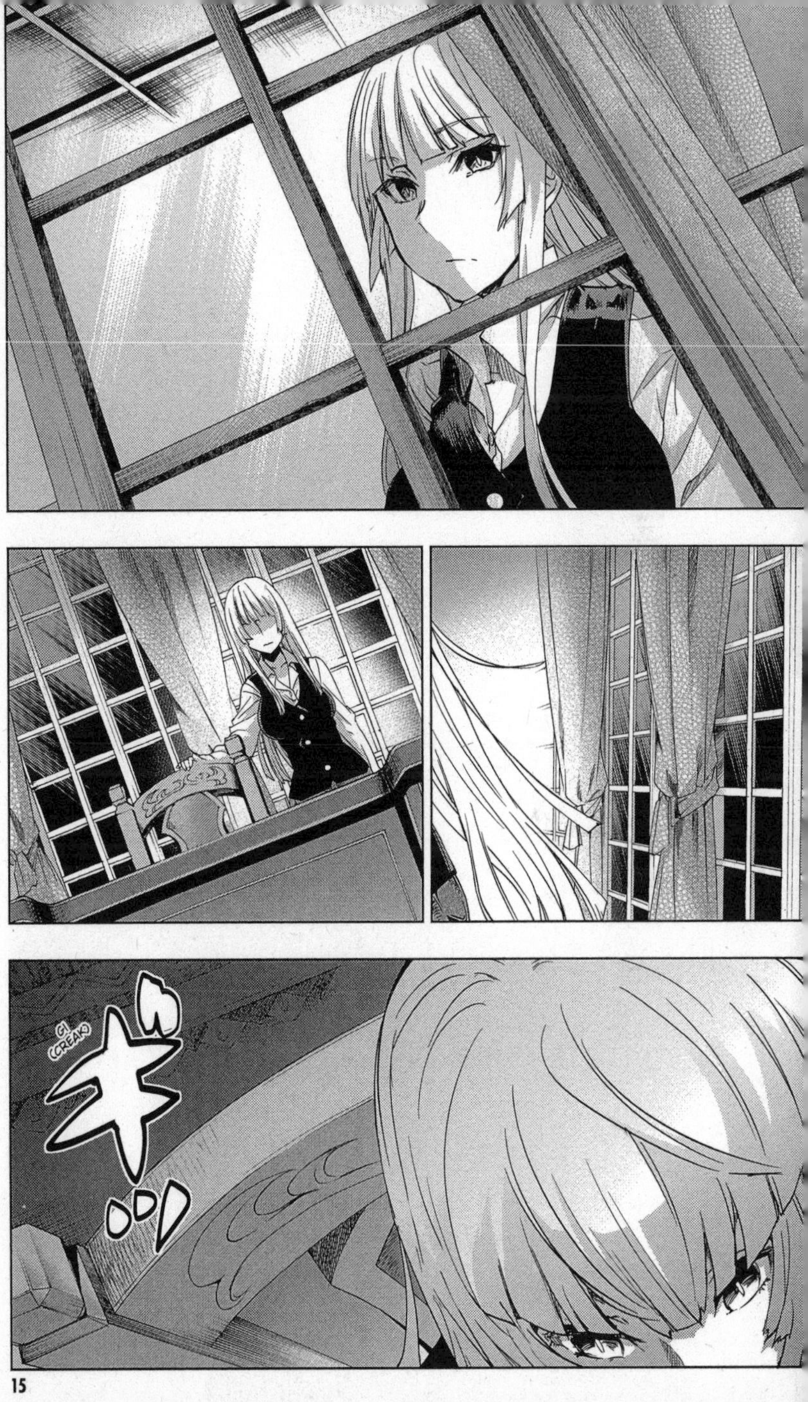
GI
(CREAK)

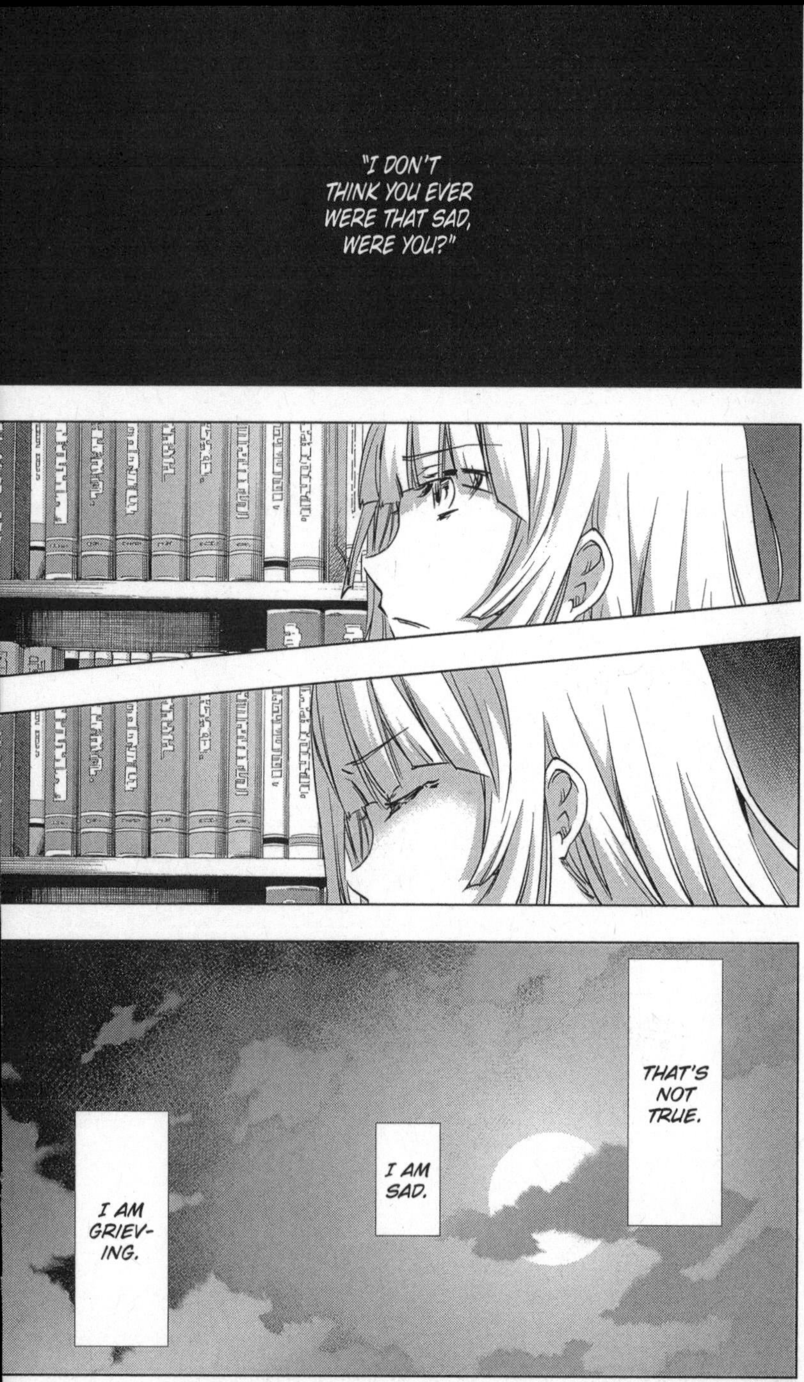
"I DON'T THINK YOU EVER WERE THAT SAD, WERE YOU?"
THAT'S NOT TRUE.
I AM SAD.
I AM GRIEV-ING.

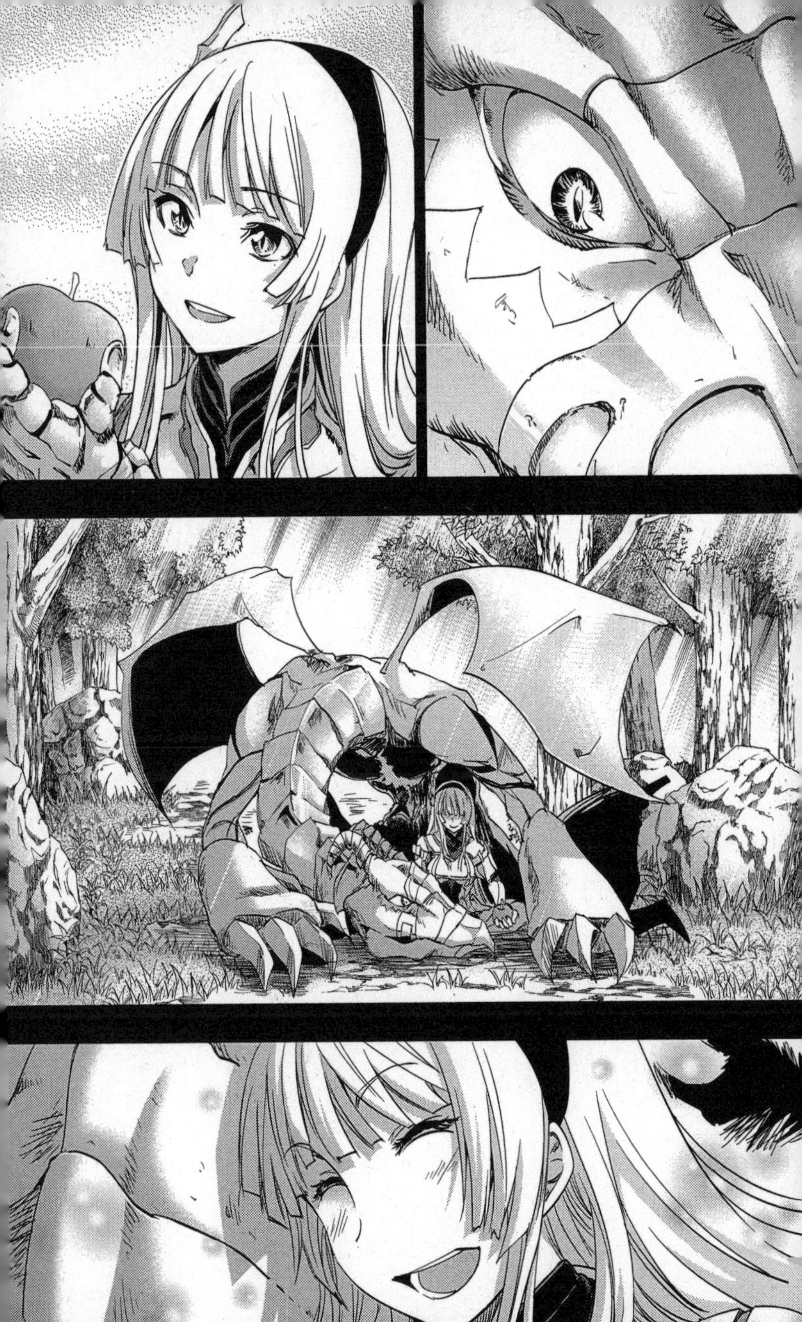

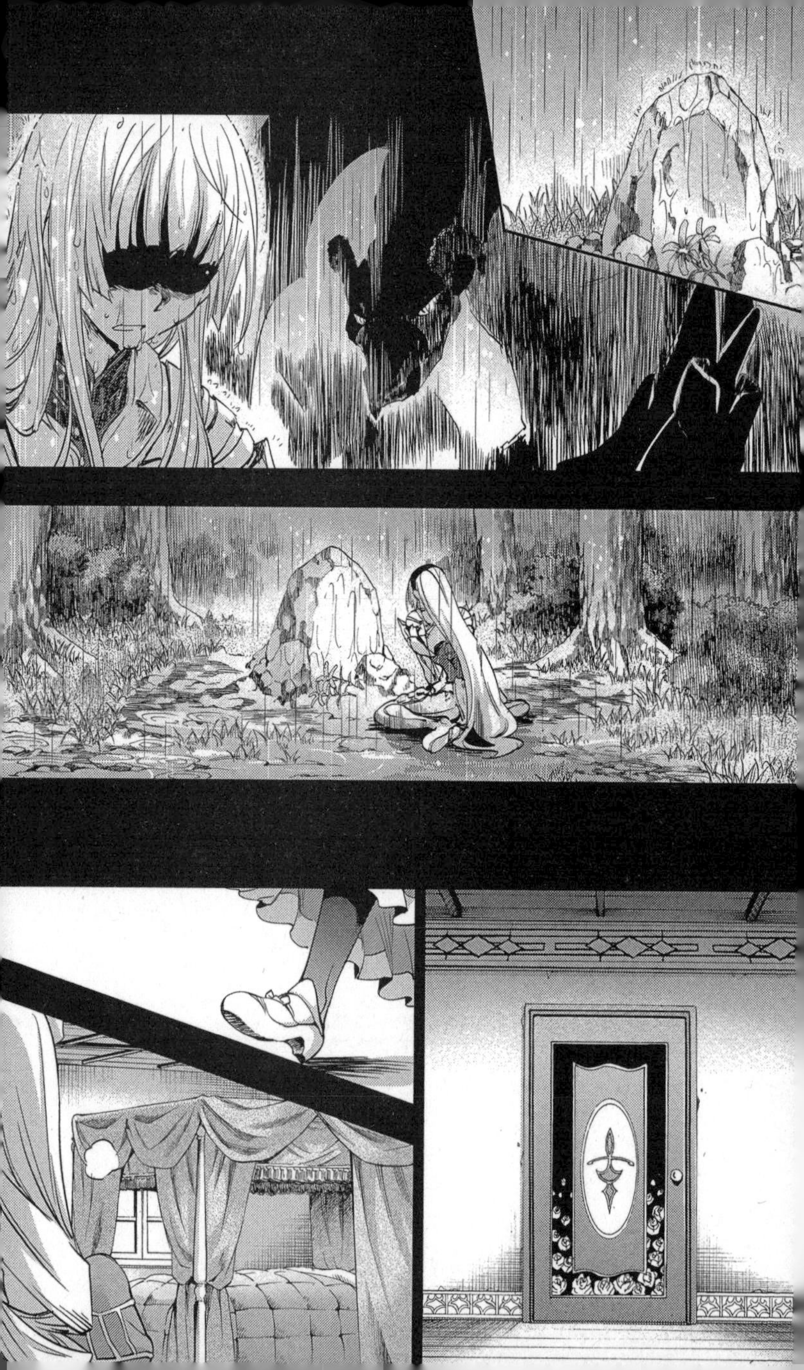

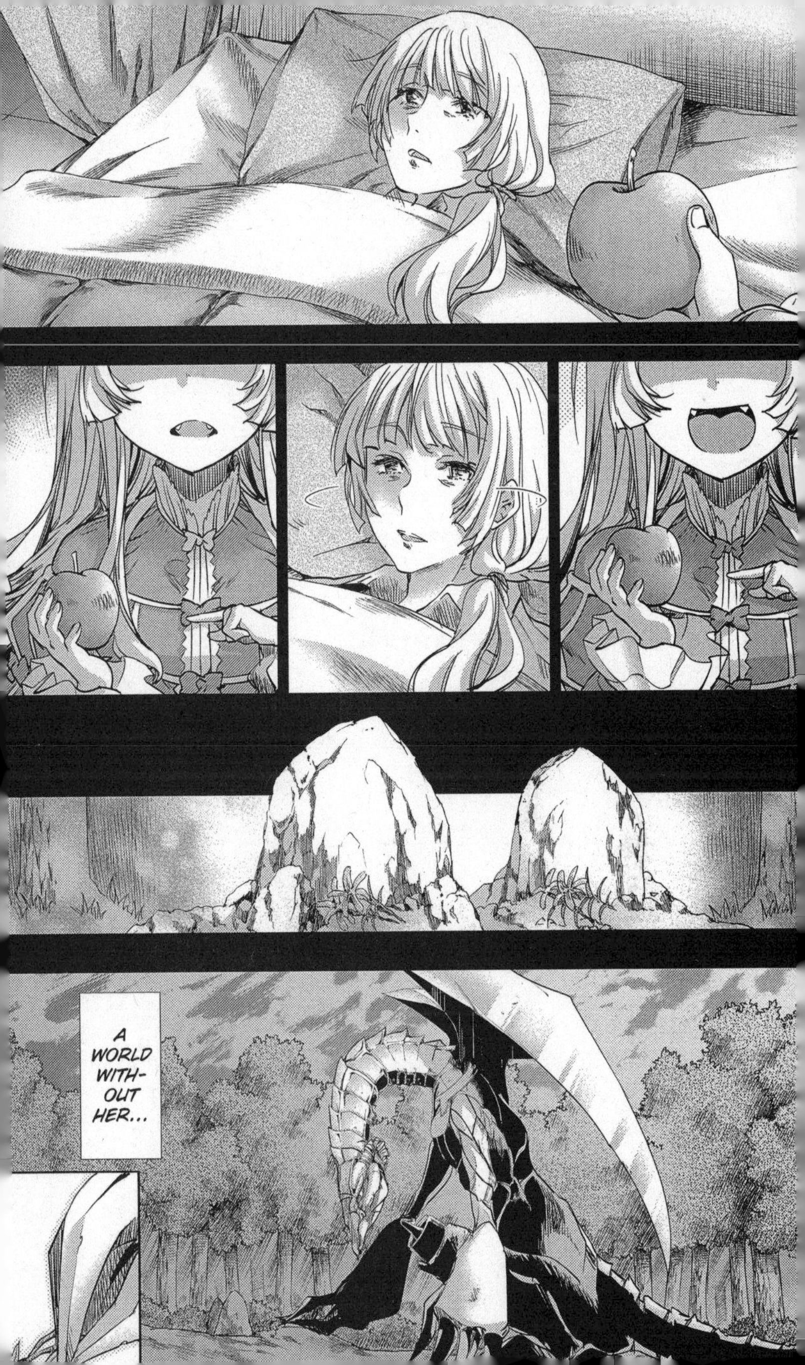
A WORLD WITH-OUT HER...

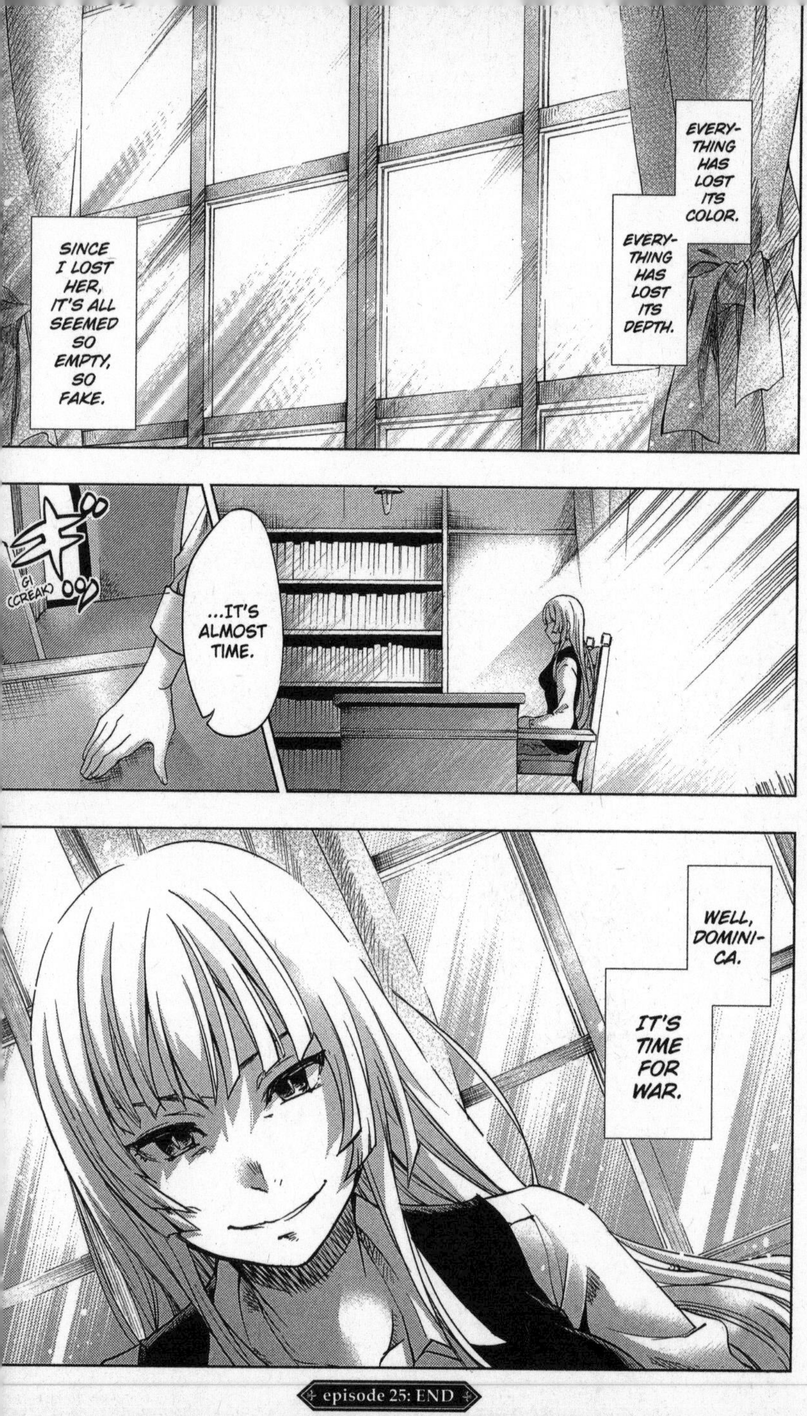
EVERYTHING HAS LOST ITS COLOR.
EVERYTHING HAS LOST ITS DEPTH.
SINCE I LOST HER, IT'S ALL SEEMED SO EMPTY, SO FAKE.
...IT'S ALMOST TIME.
GI (CREAK)
WELL, DOMINICA.
IT'S TIME FOR WAR.

episode 25: END

CHAIKA: THE COFFIN PRINCESS

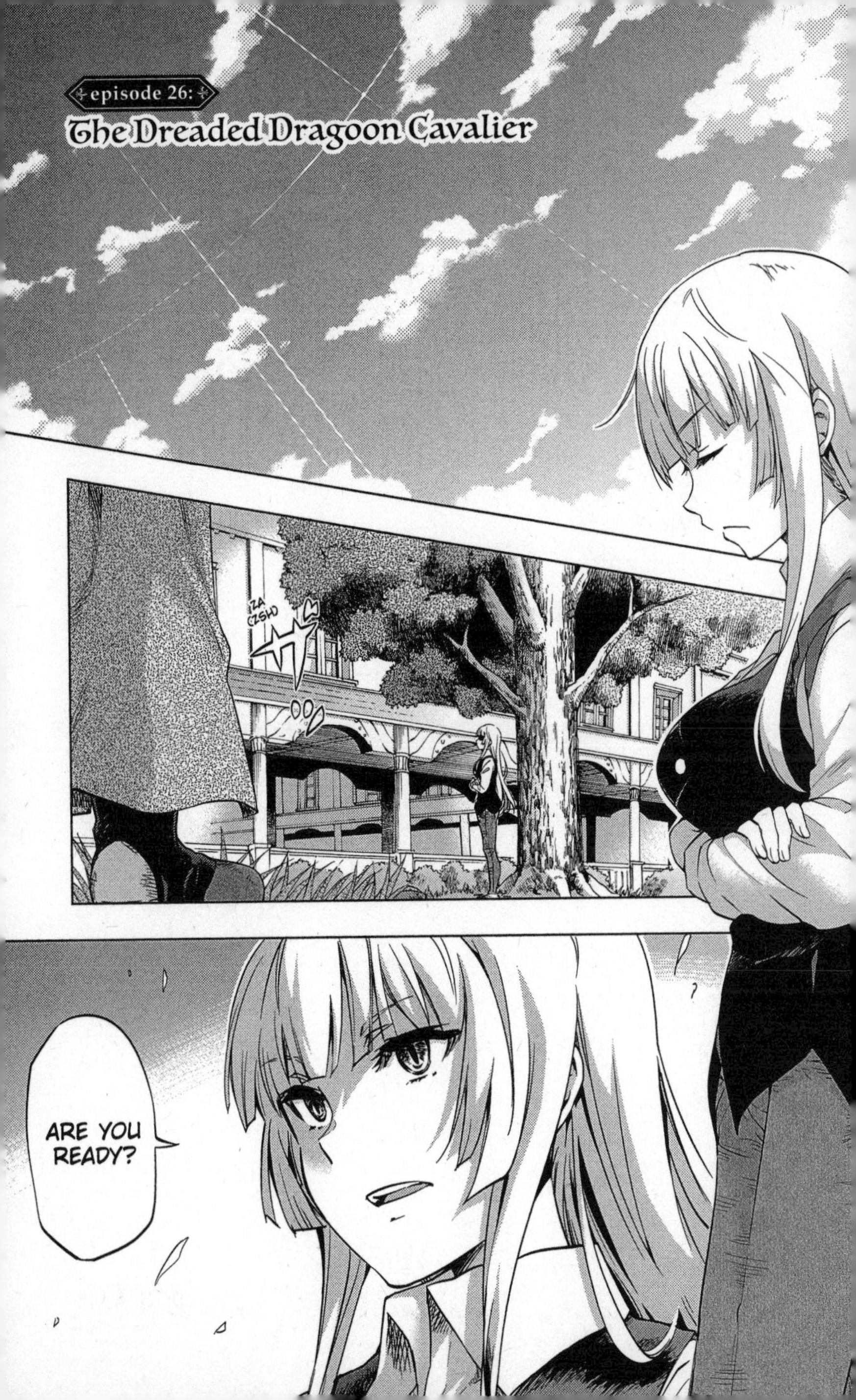
episode 26:
The Dreaded Dragoon Cavalier
ZA (ZSH)
ARE YOU READY?

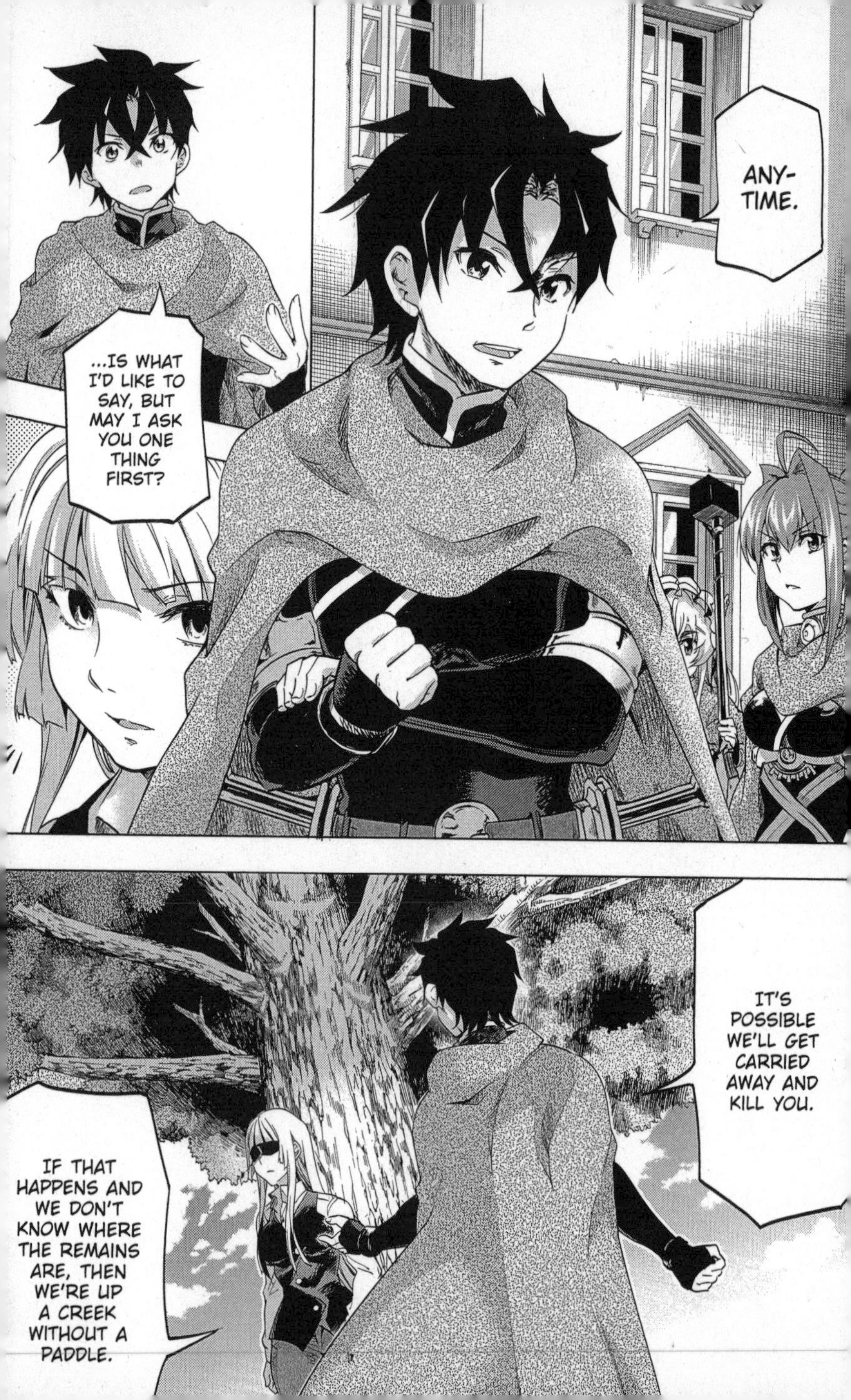
ANY-TIME.
...IS WHAT I'D LIKE TO SAY, BUT MAY I ASK YOU ONE THING FIRST?
IT'S POSSIBLE WE'LL GET CARRIED AWAY AND KILL YOU.
IF THAT HAPPENS AND WE DON'T KNOW WHERE THE REMAINS ARE, THEN WE'RE UP A CREEK WITHOUT A PADDLE.

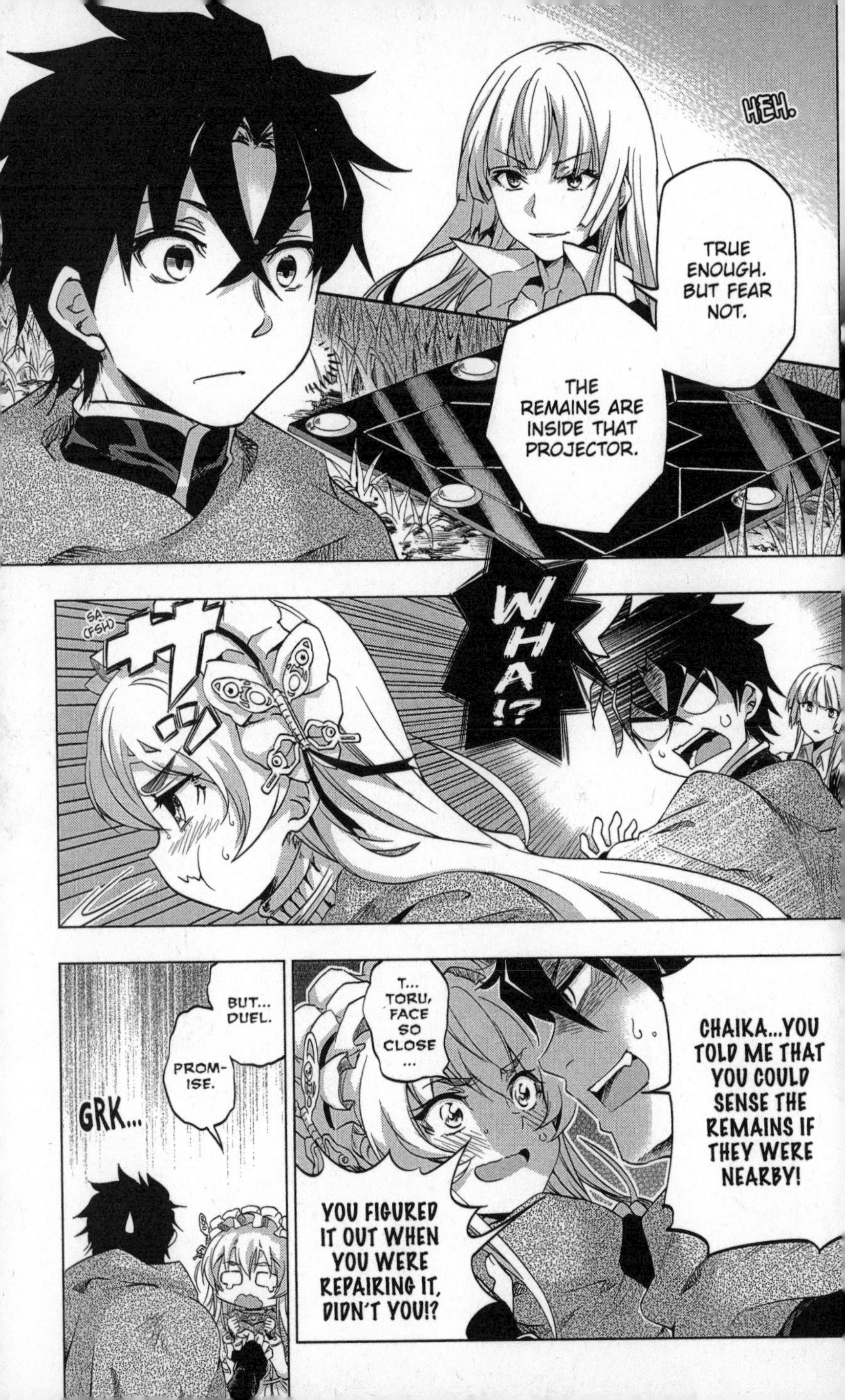
HEH.
TRUE ENOUGH. BUT FEAR NOT.
THE REMAINS ARE INSIDE THAT PROJECTOR.
WHA!?
SA (FSH)
CHAIKA...YOU TOLD ME THAT YOU COULD SENSE THE REMAINS IF THEY WERE NEARBY!
T... TORU, FACE SO CLOSE ...
YOU FIGURED IT OUT WHEN YOU WERE REPAIRING IT, DIDN'T YOU!?
BUT... DUEL.
PROM-ISE.
GRK...

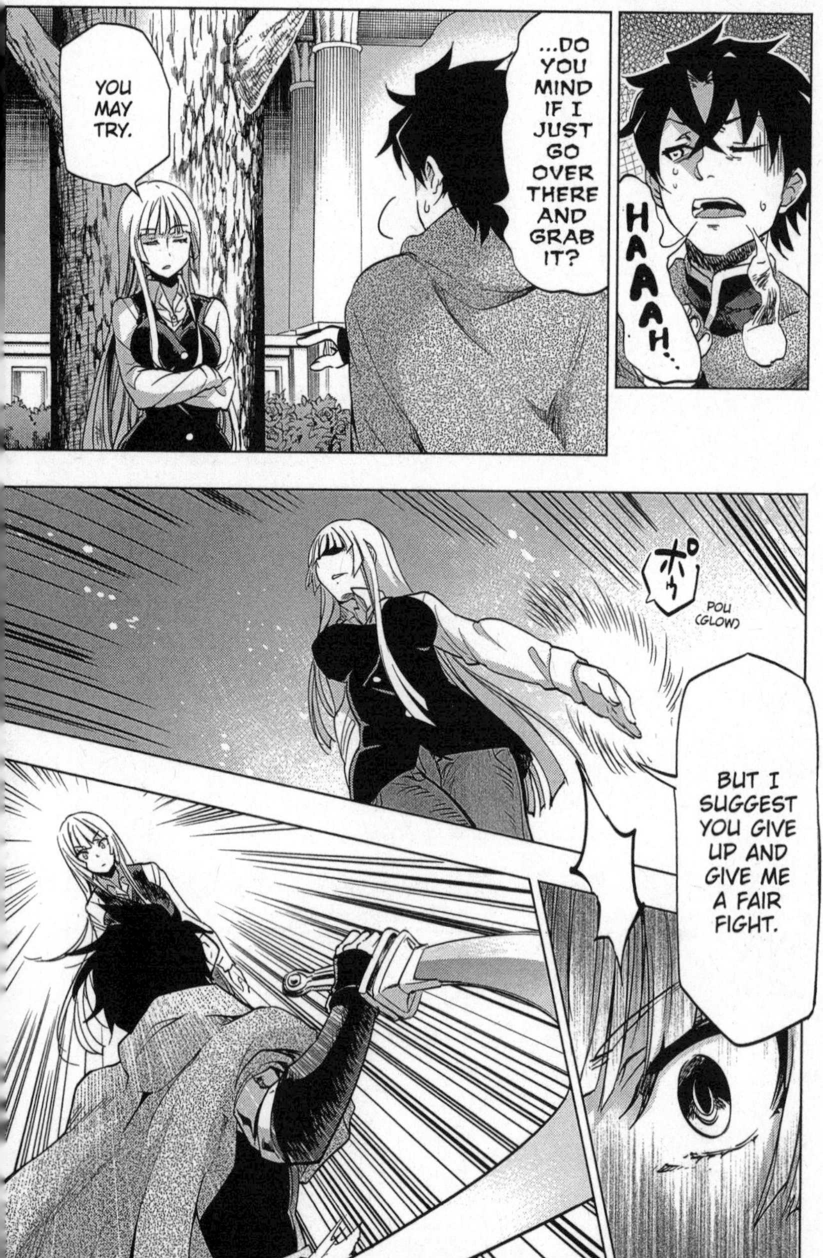
HAAAAH...
...DO YOU MIND IF I JUST GO OVER THERE AND GRAB IT?
YOU MAY TRY.
POU (GLOW)
BUT I SUGGEST YOU GIVE UP AND GIVE ME A FAIR FIGHT.

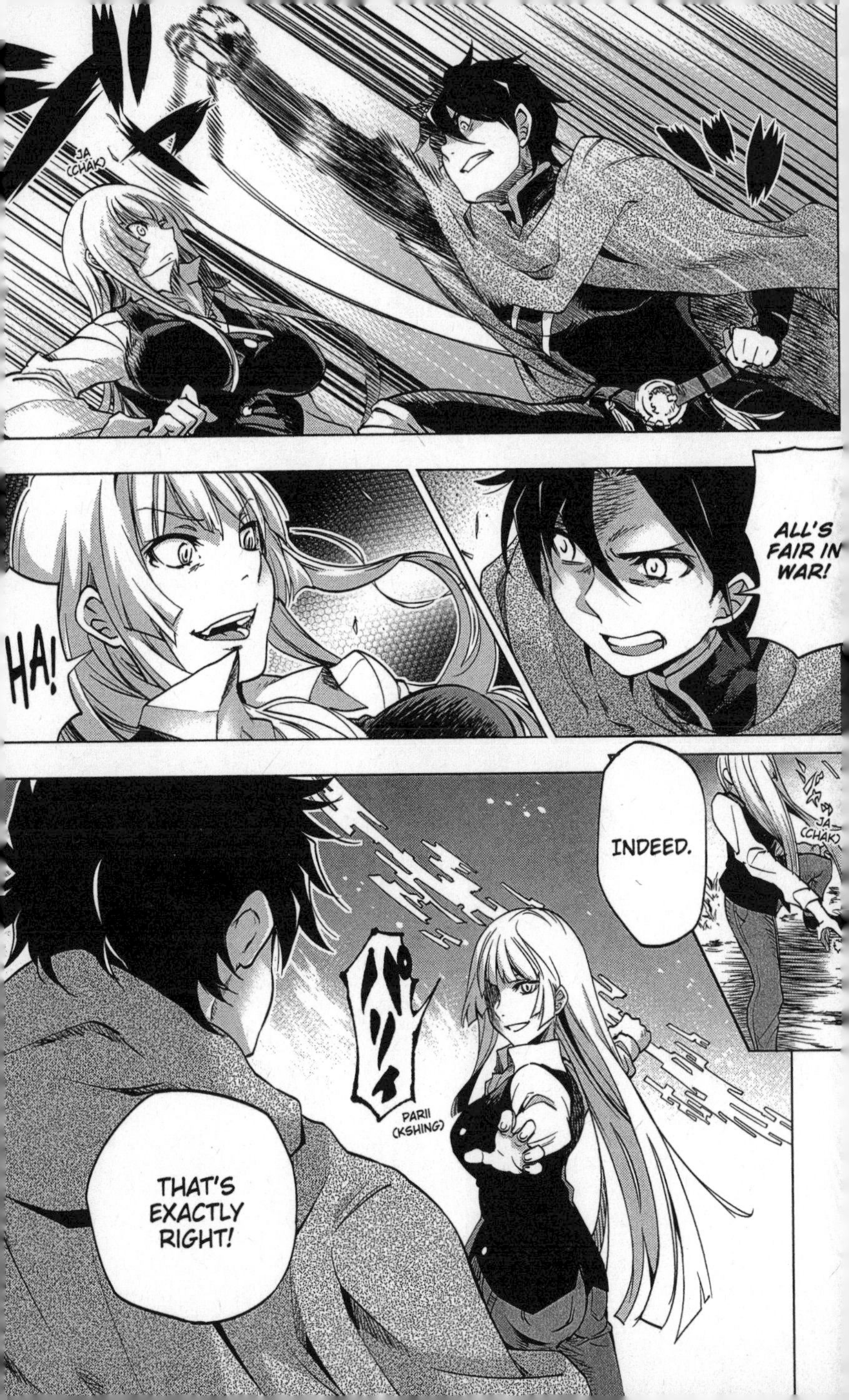
JA (CHAK)
ALL'S FAIR IN WAR!
HA!
INDEED.
JA (CHAK)
PARII (KSHING)
THAT'S EXACTLY RIGHT!

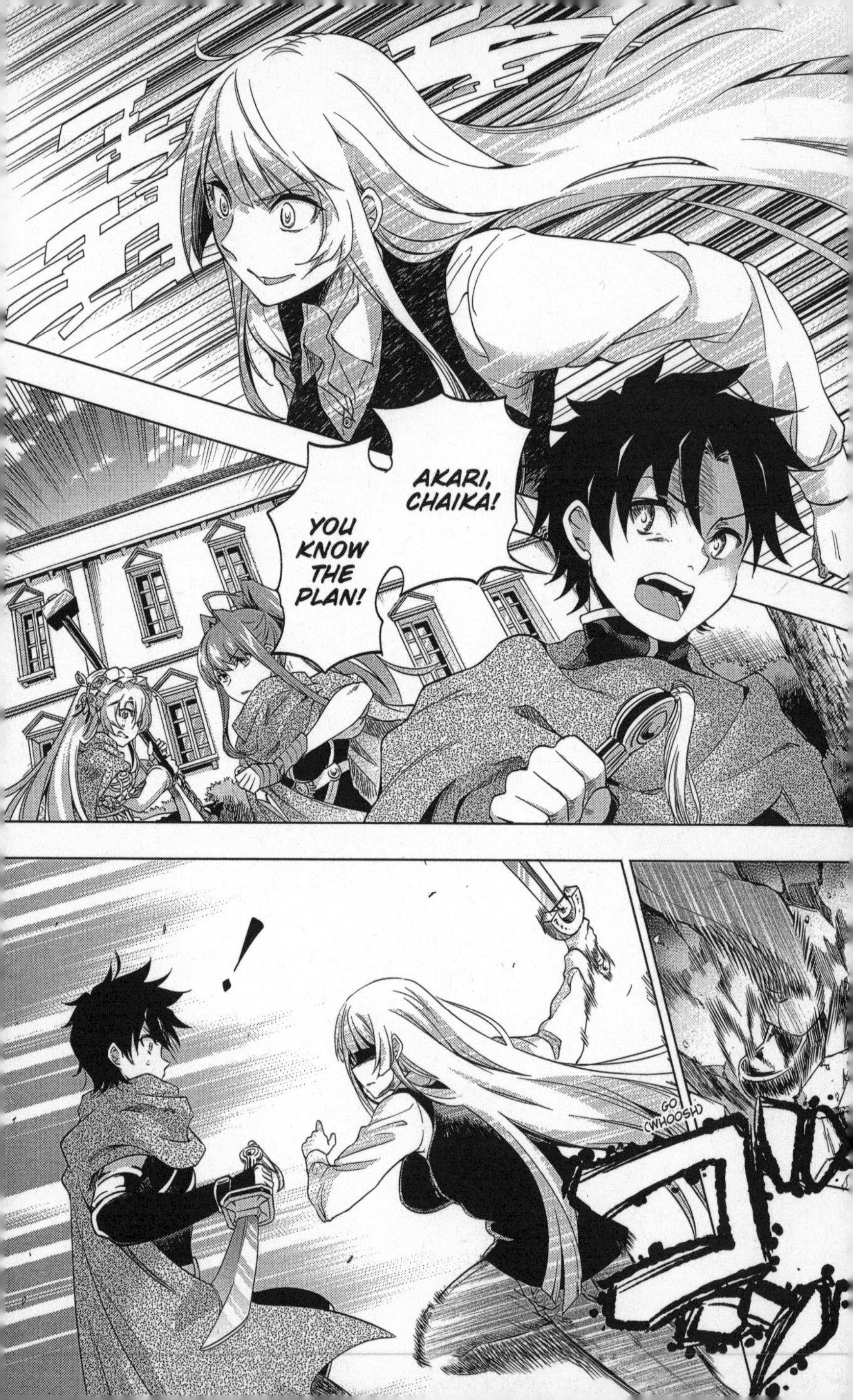
AKARI, CHAIKA!
YOU KNOW THE PLAN!
!
GO (WHOOSH)

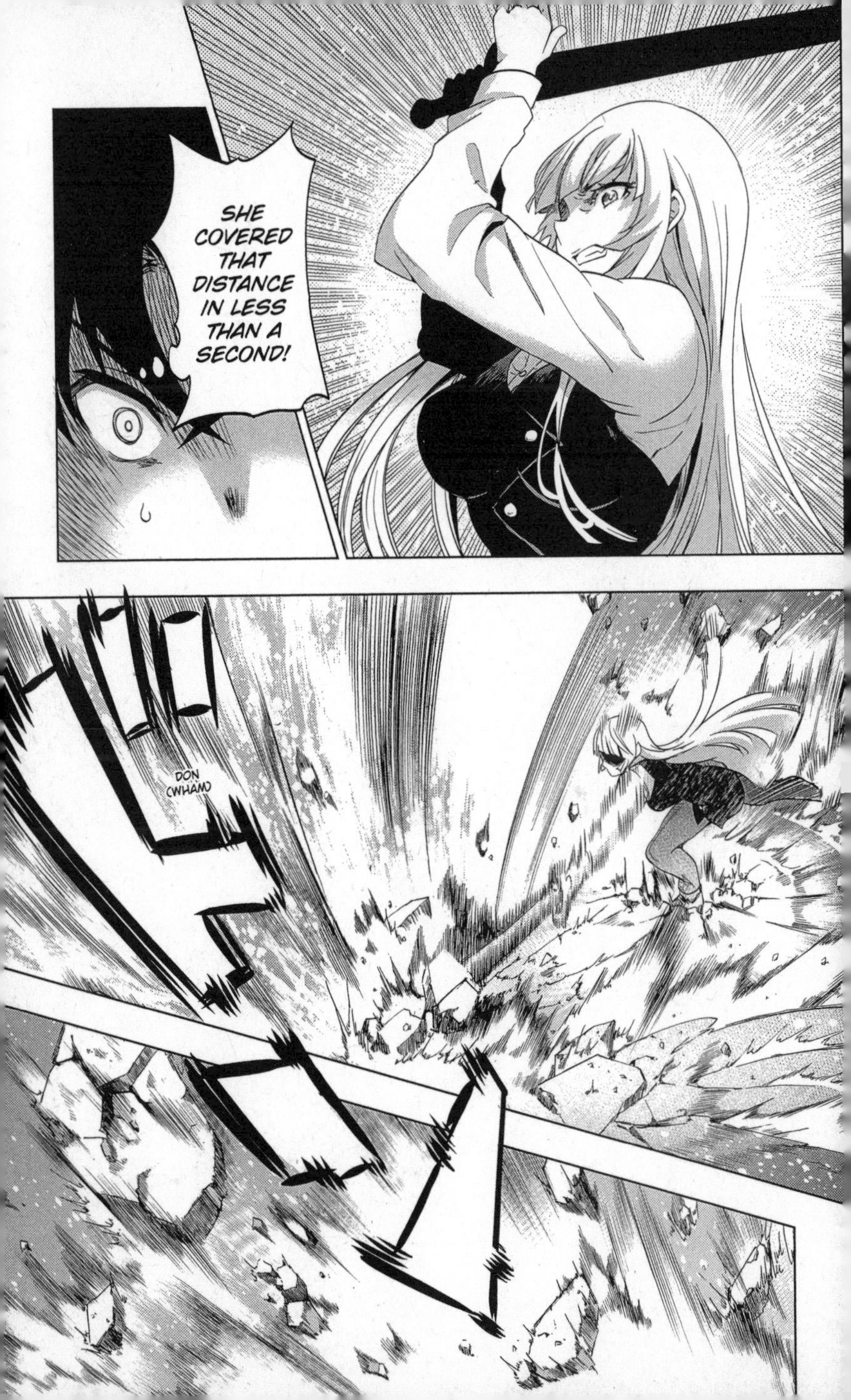
SHE COVERED THAT DISTANCE IN LESS THAN A SECOND!
DON (WHAM)

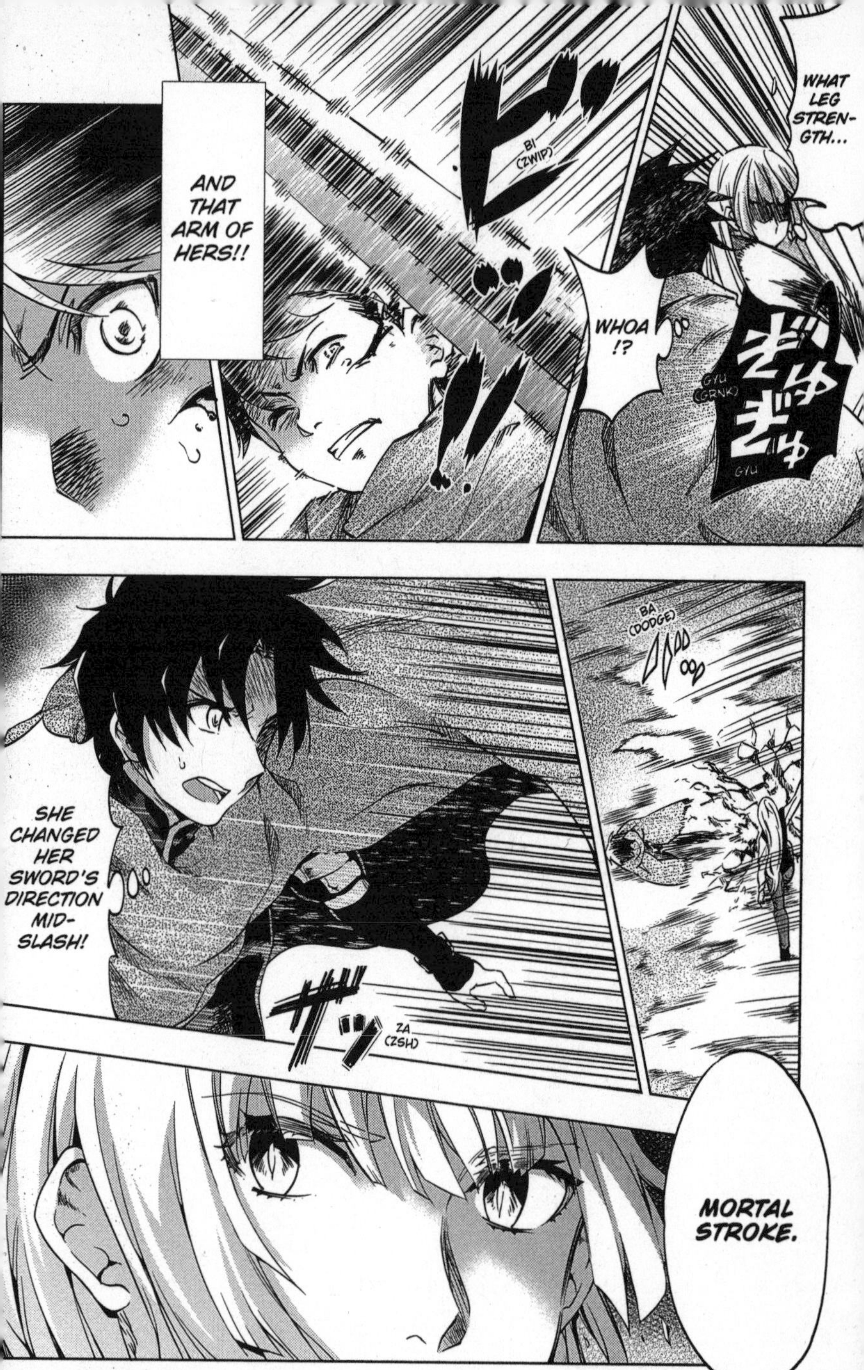
WHAT LEG STRENGTH...
GYU (GRNK)
GYU
WHOA!?
BI (ZWIP)
AND THAT ARM OF HERS!!
BA (DODGE)
SHE CHANGED HER SWORD'S DIRECTION MID-SLASH!
ZA (ZSH)
MORTAL STROKE.

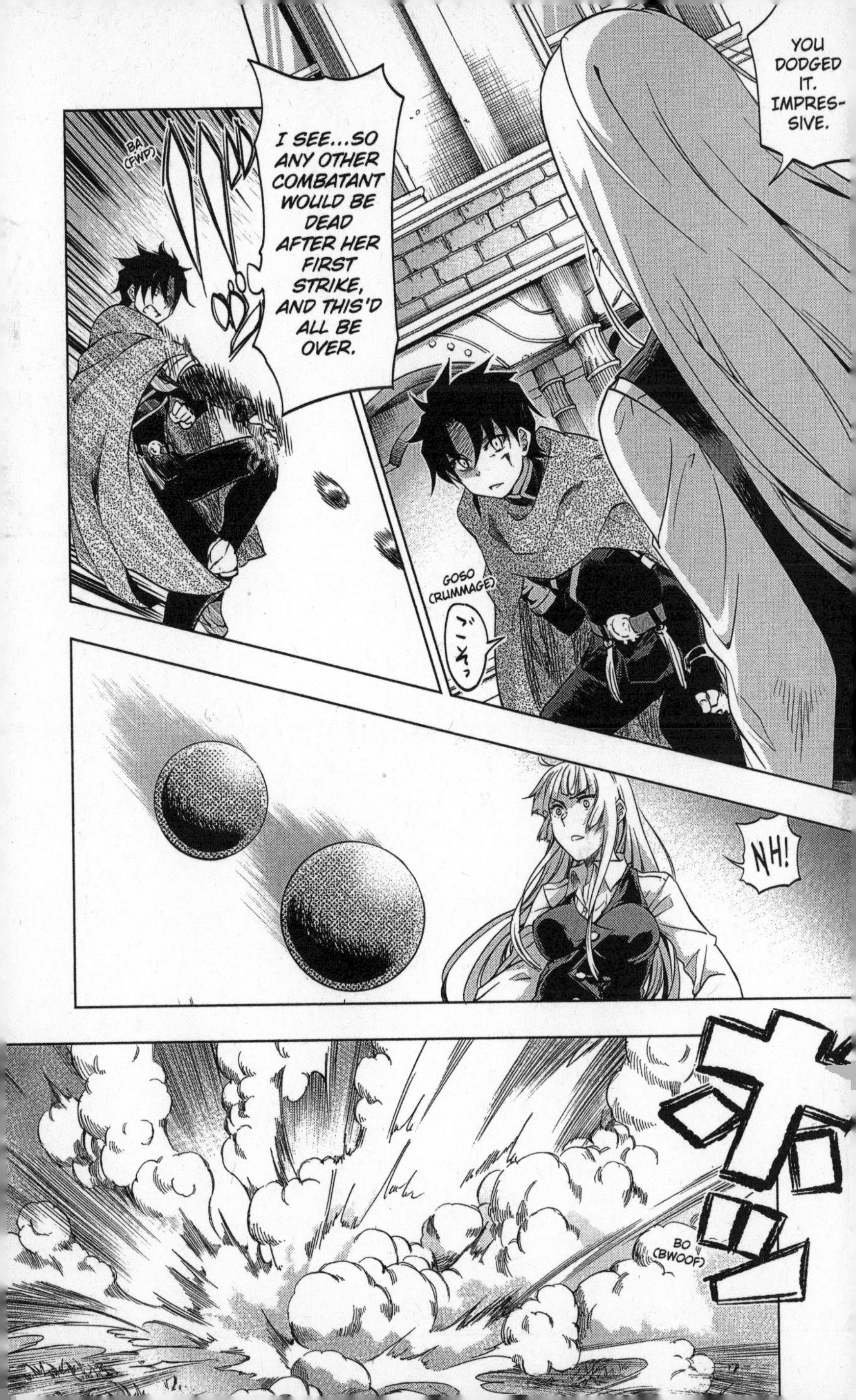
YOU DODGED IT. IMPRESSIVE.
I SEE...SO ANY OTHER COMBATANT WOULD BE DEAD AFTER HER FIRST STRIKE, AND THIS'D ALL BE OVER.
GOSO (RUMMAGE)
ごそっ
BA (FWP)
NH!
BO (BWOOF)

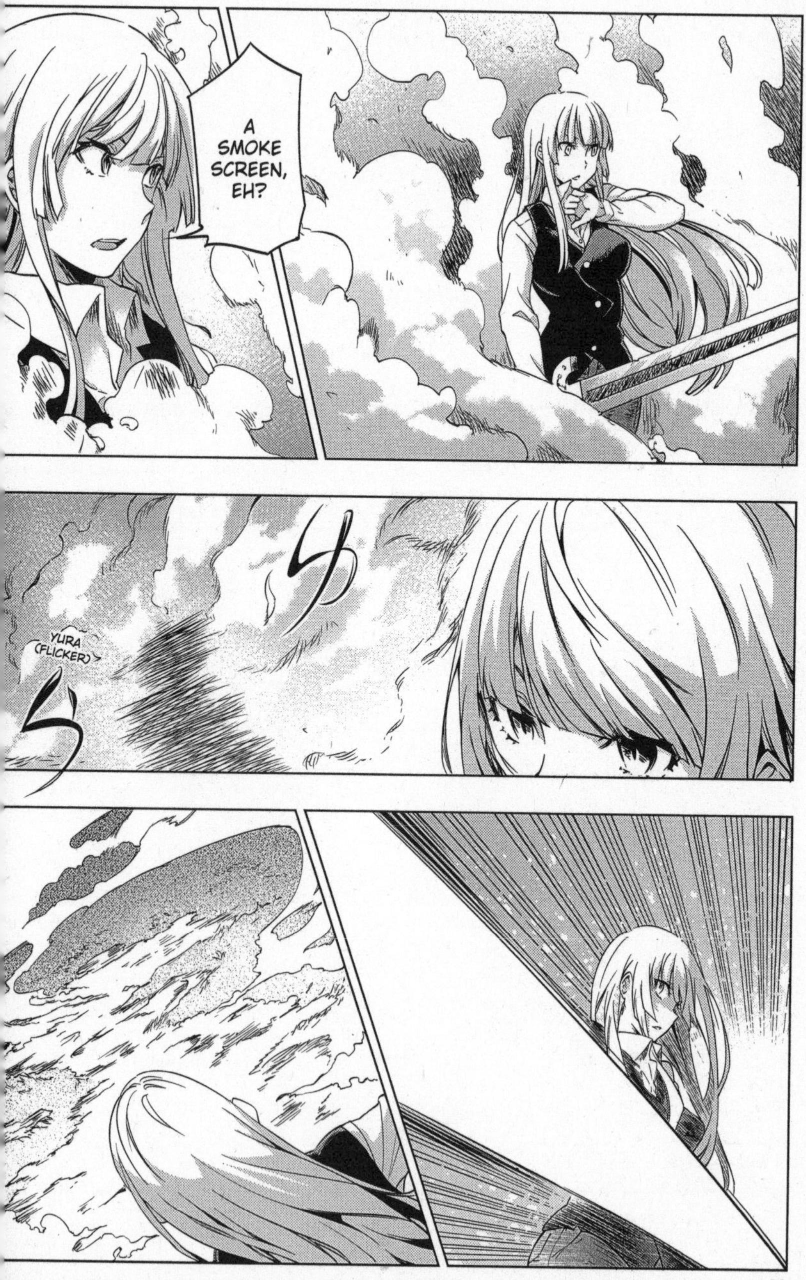
A SMOKE SCREEN, EH?
YURA (FLICKER)

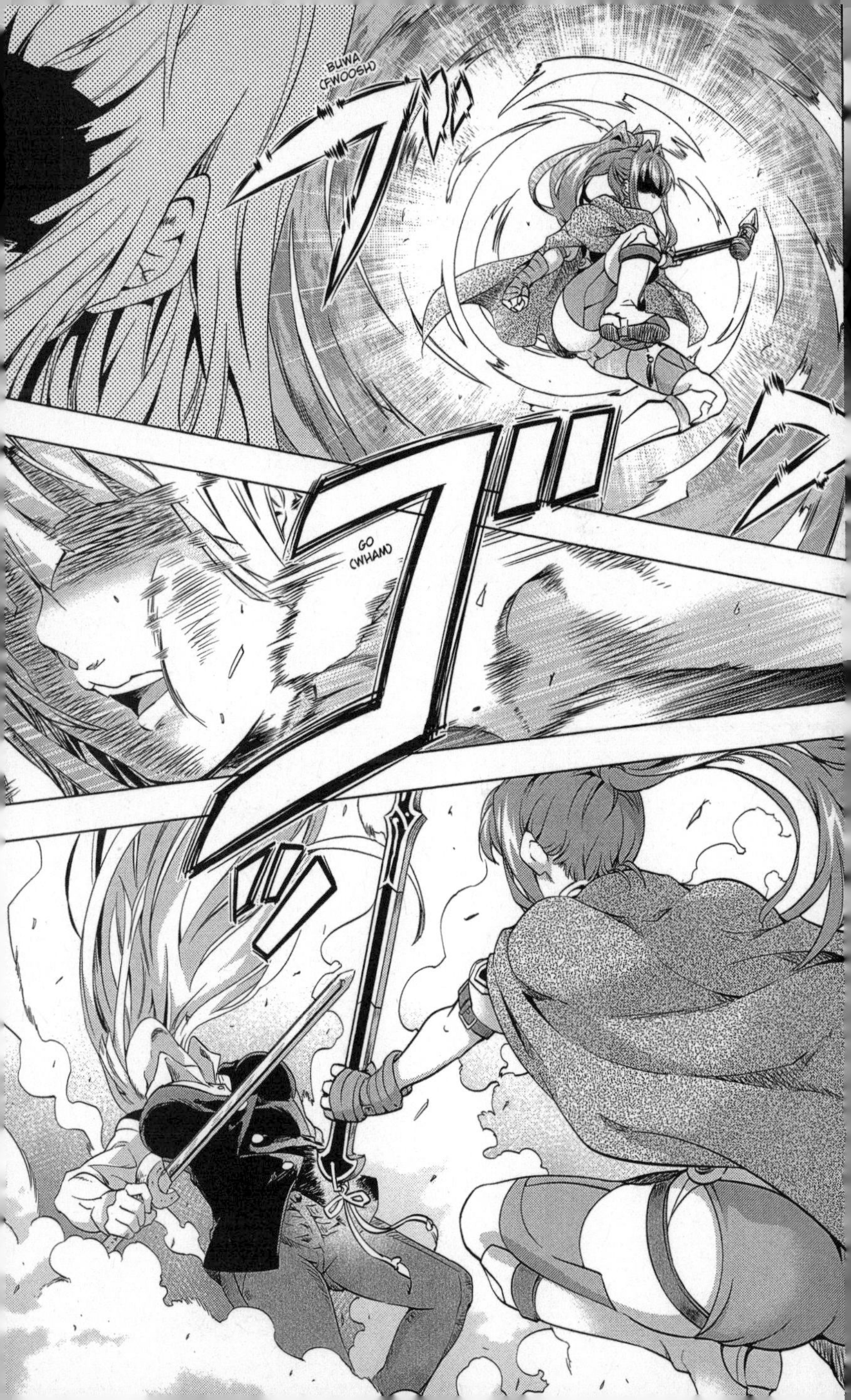
BUWA
(FWOOSH)
GO
(WHAM)

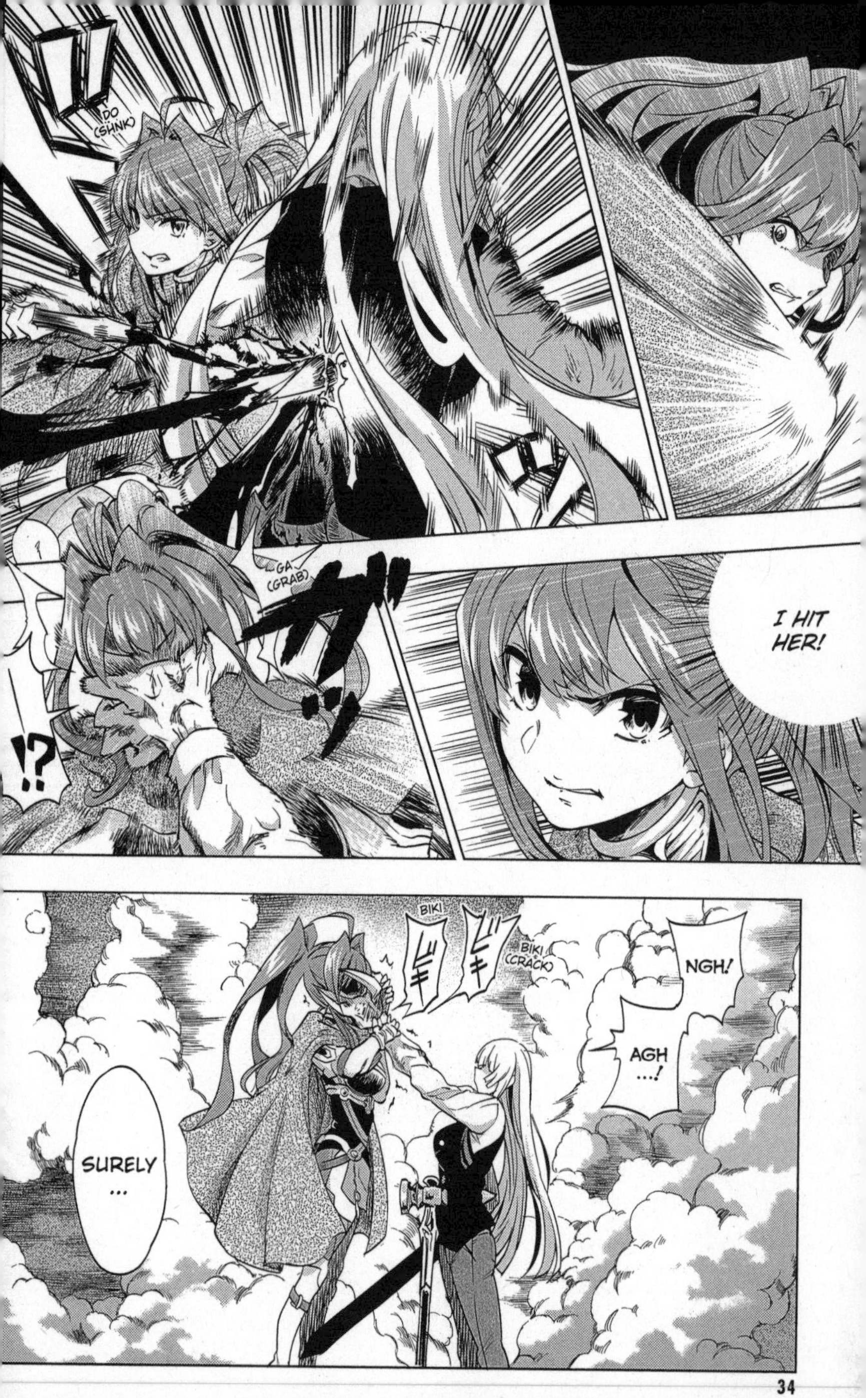
DO (SHNK)
I HIT HER!
GA (GRAB)
!?
NGH!
BIKI
BIKI (CRACK)
AGH ...!
SURELY ...

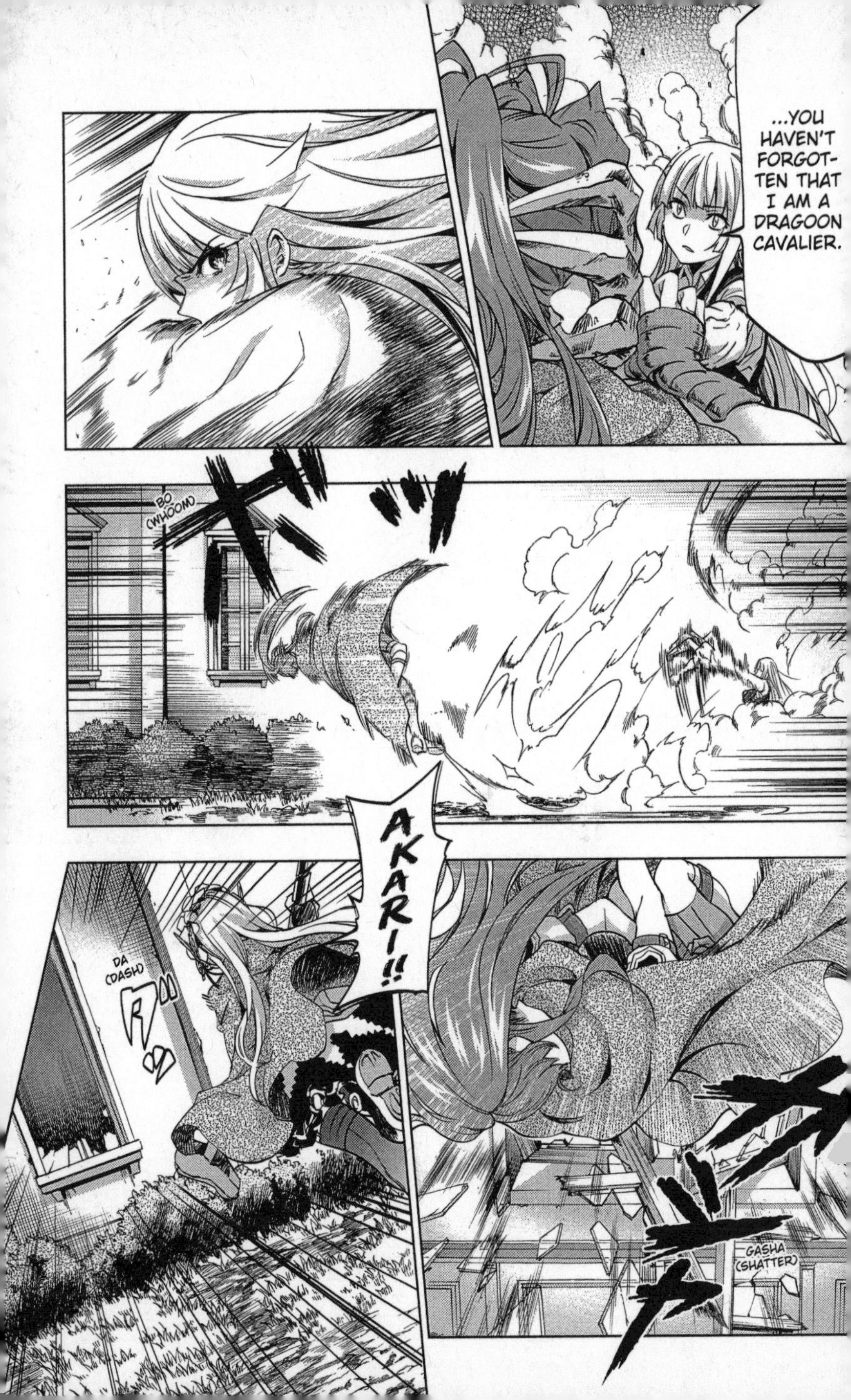
...YOU HAVEN'T FORGOT-TEN THAT I AM A DRAGOON CAVALIER.
BO (WHOOM)
AKARI!!
GASHA (SHATTER)
DA (DASH)

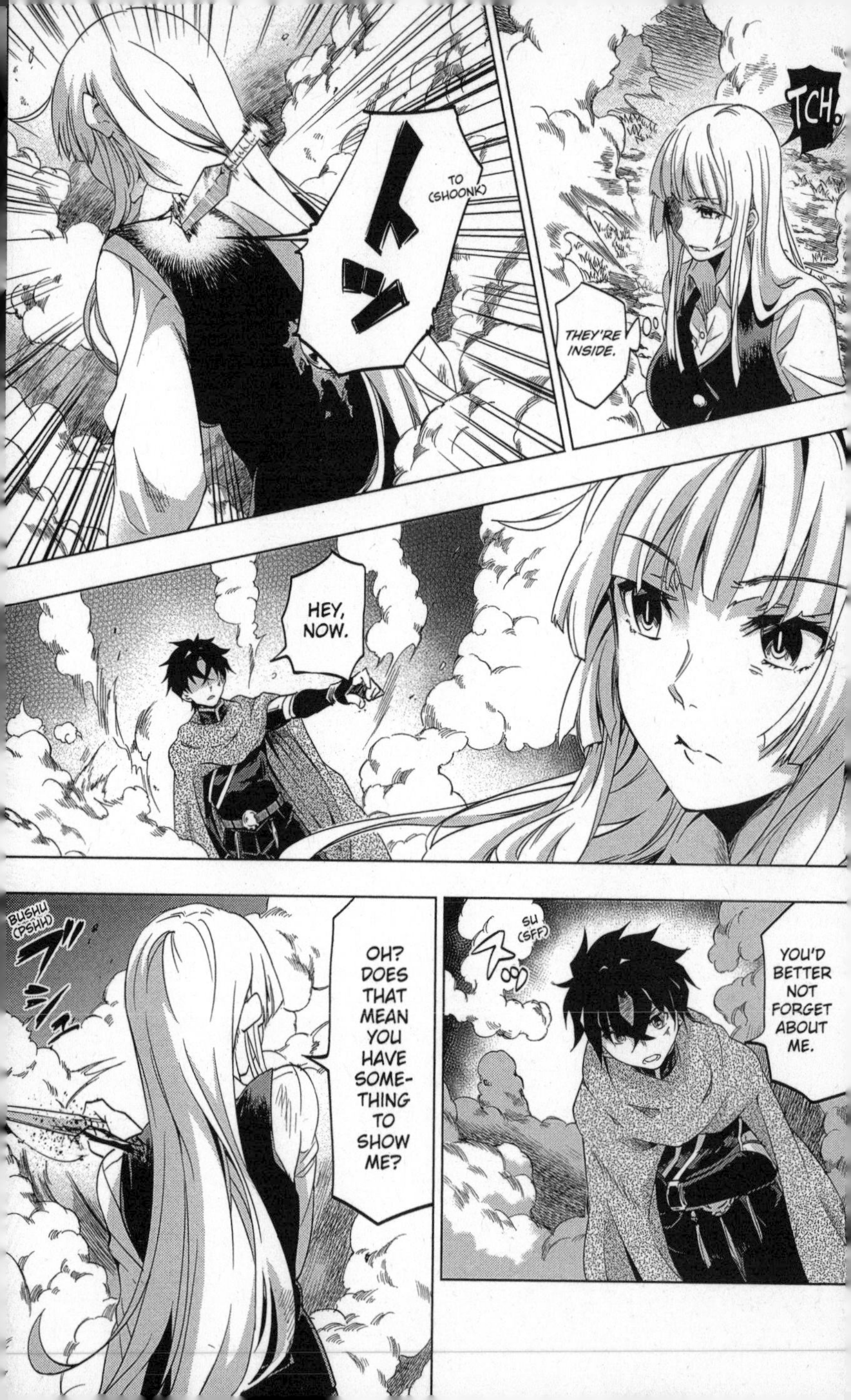
TCH.
THEY'RE INSIDE.
TO (SHOONK)
HEY, NOW.
SU (SFF)
YOU'D BETTER NOT FORGET ABOUT ME.
BUSHU (PSHH)
OH? DOES THAT MEAN YOU HAVE SOMETHING TO SHOW ME?

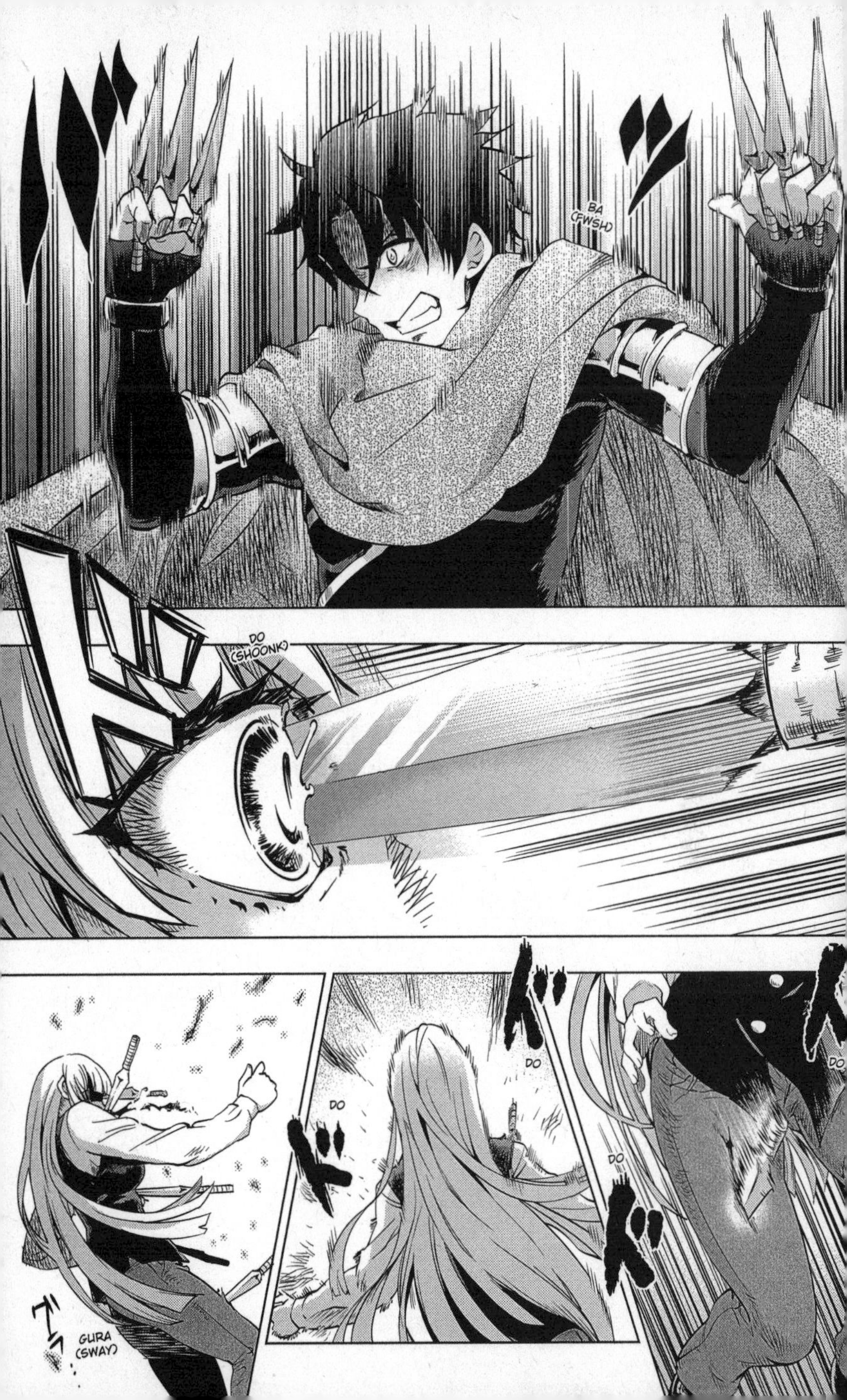
BA (FWSH)
DO (SHOONK)
DO
DO
DO
DO
GURA (SWAY)

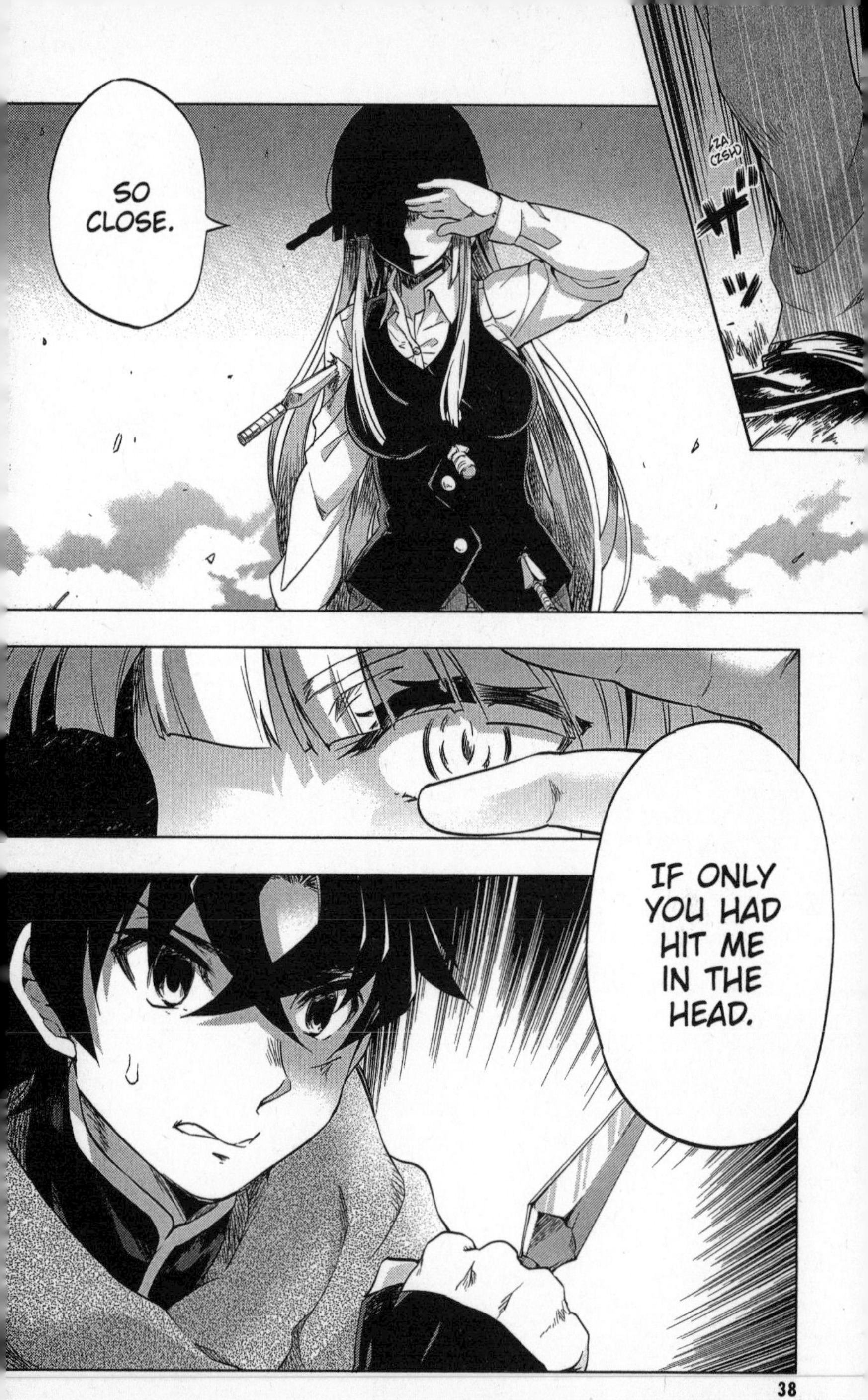
(ZA ZSH)
SO CLOSE.
IF ONLY YOU HAD HIT ME IN THE HEAD.

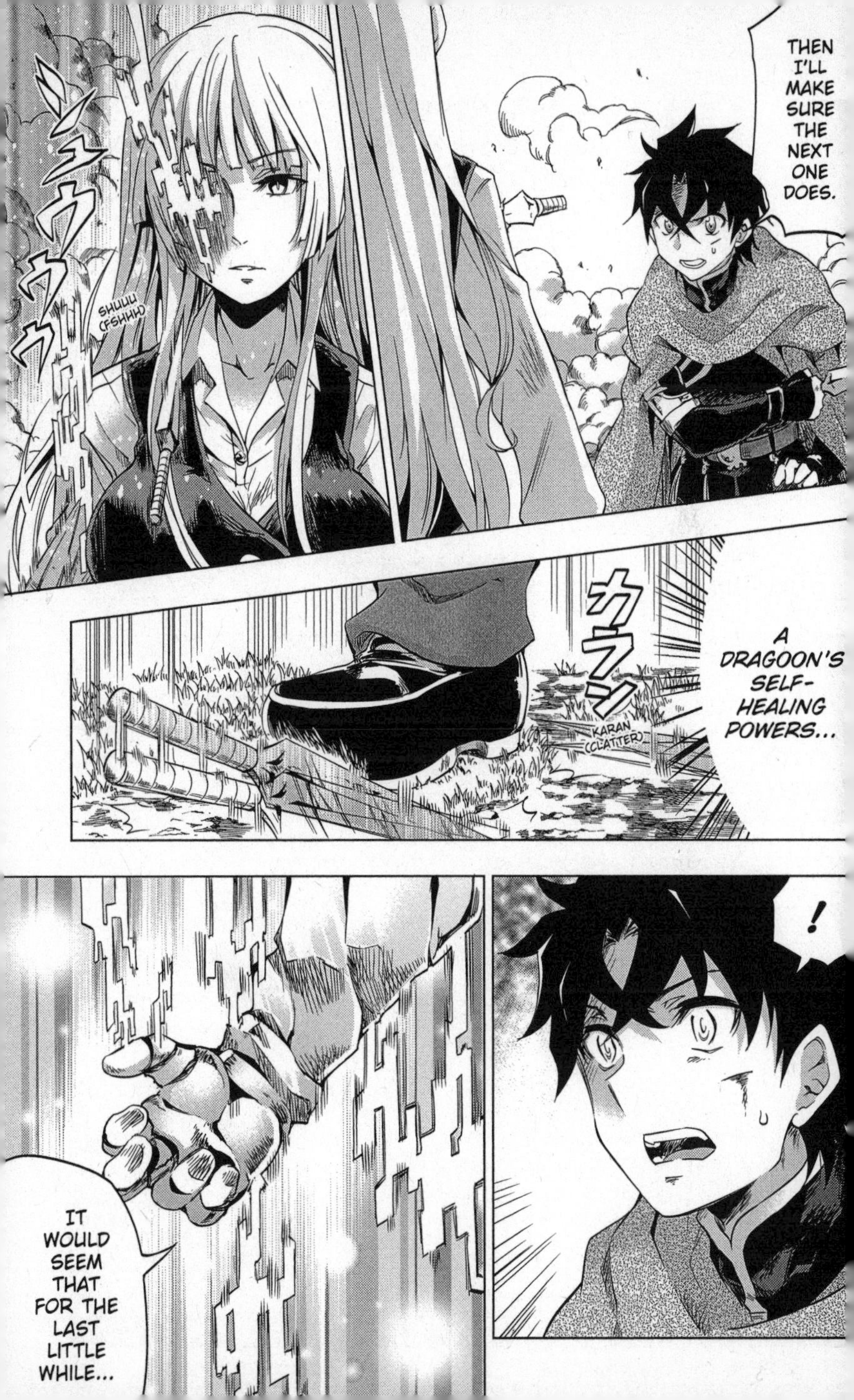
THEN I'LL MAKE SURE THE NEXT ONE DOES.
シュウウウ
SHUUU (FSHHH)
カラン
KARAN (CLATTER)
A DRAGOON'S SELF-HEALING POWERS...
!
IT WOULD SEEM THAT FOR THE LAST LITTLE WHILE...

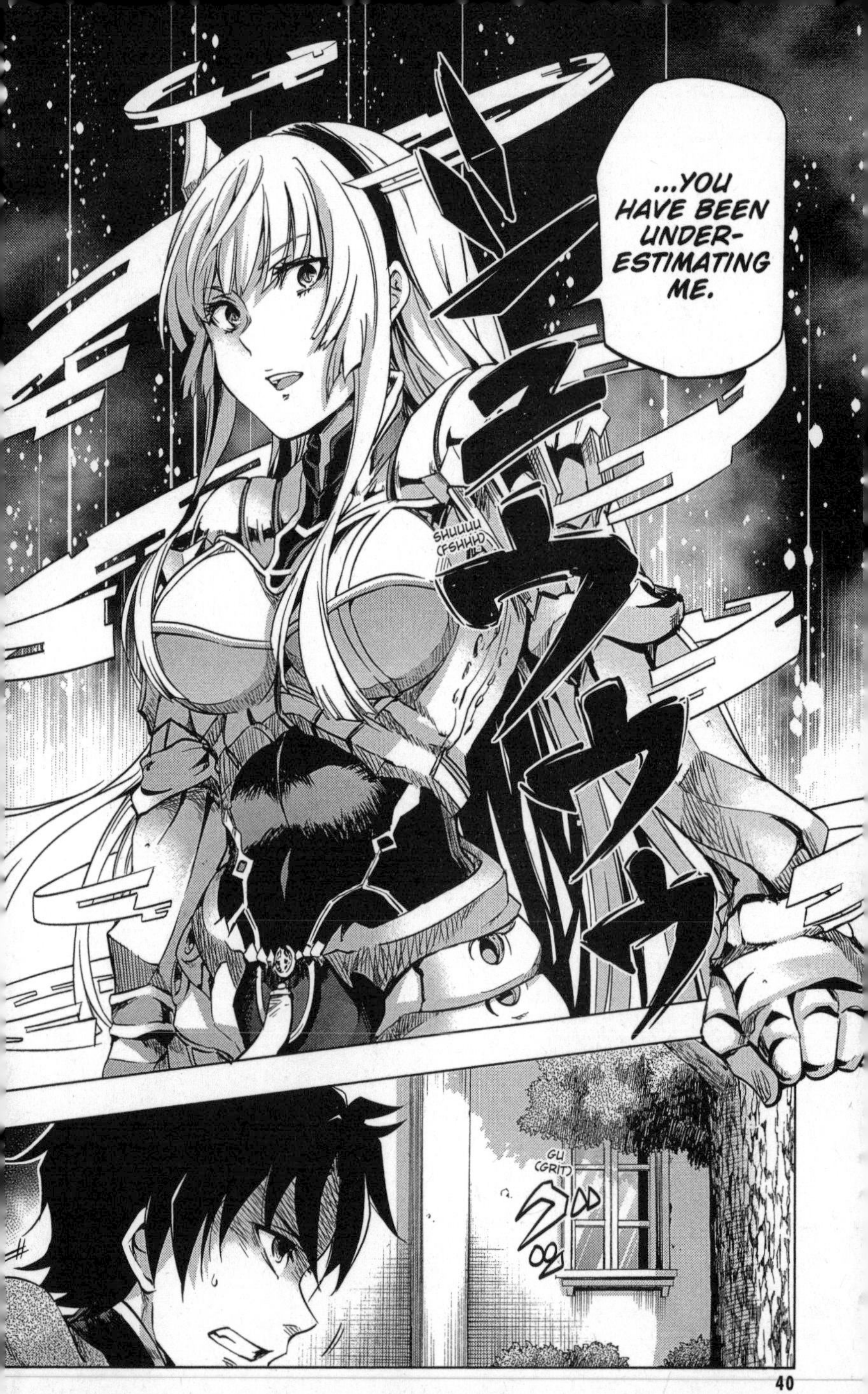
...YOU HAVE BEEN UNDER-ESTIMATING ME.
SHUUUU (FSHHH)
GU (GRIT)

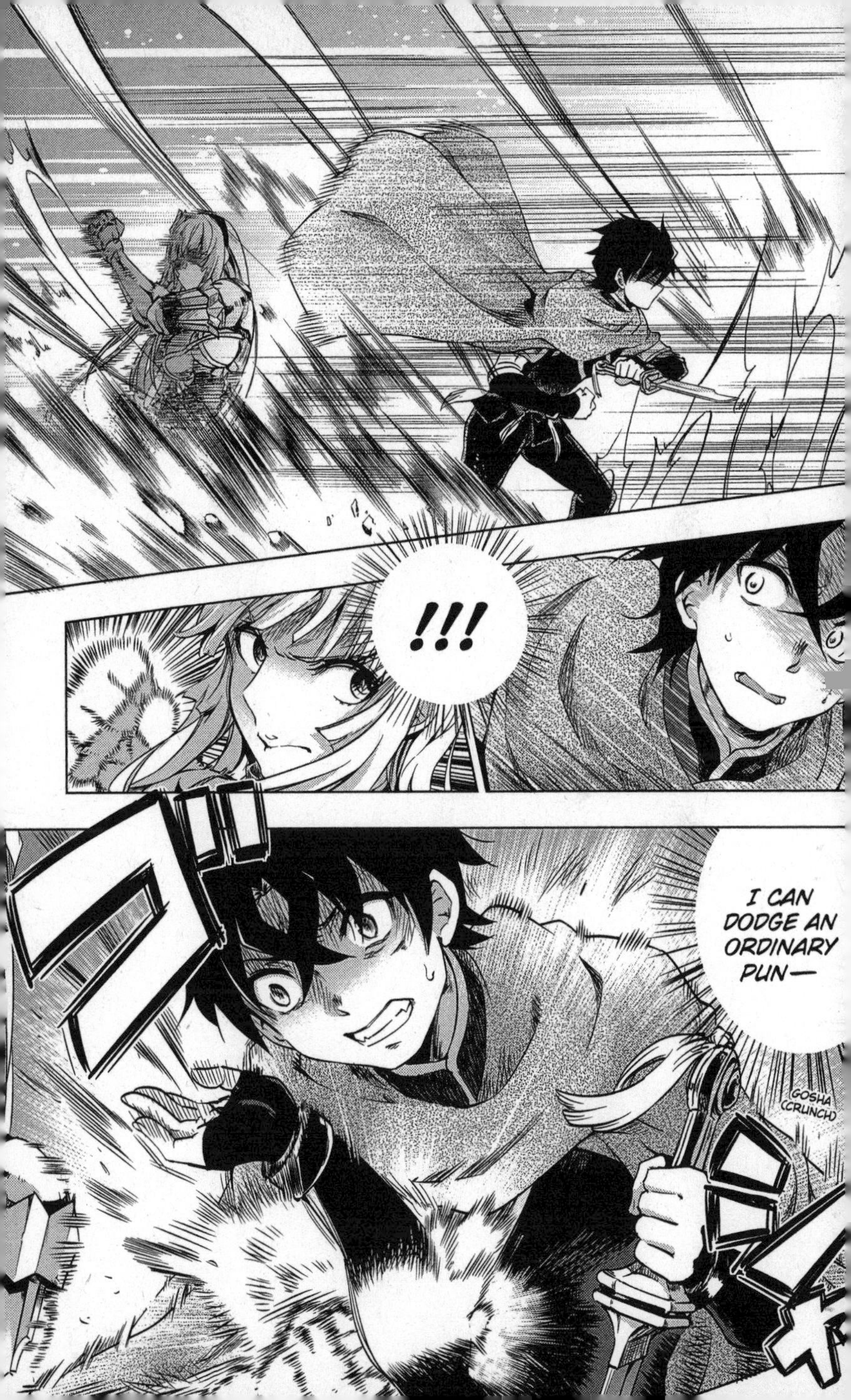
!!!
I CAN DODGE AN ORDINARY PUN—
GOSHA (CRUNCH)

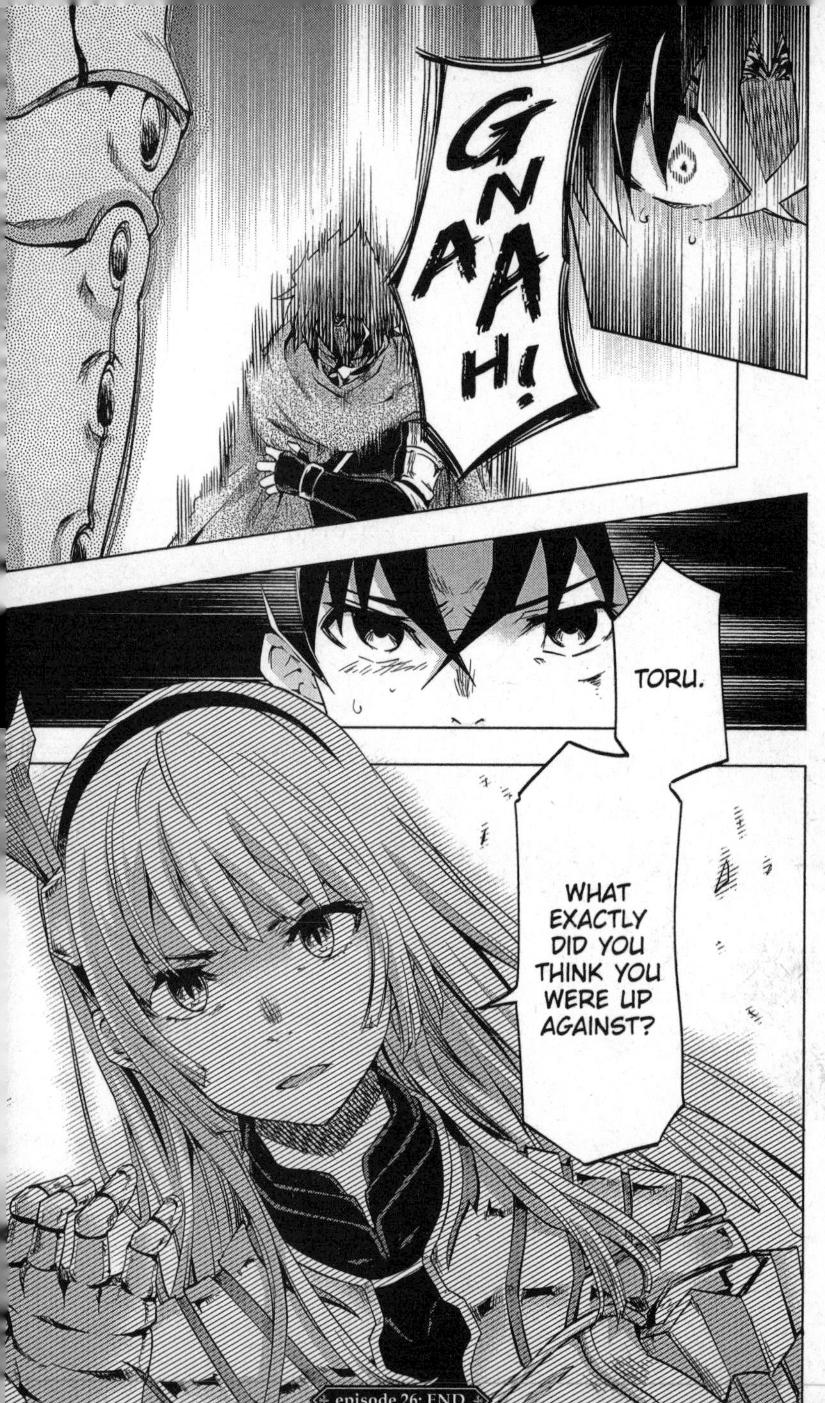
GNAAH!
TORU.
WHAT EXACTLY DID YOU THINK YOU WERE UP AGAINST?

episode 26: END

CHAIKA: THE COFFIN PRINCESS

episode 27: Dominica's Joy

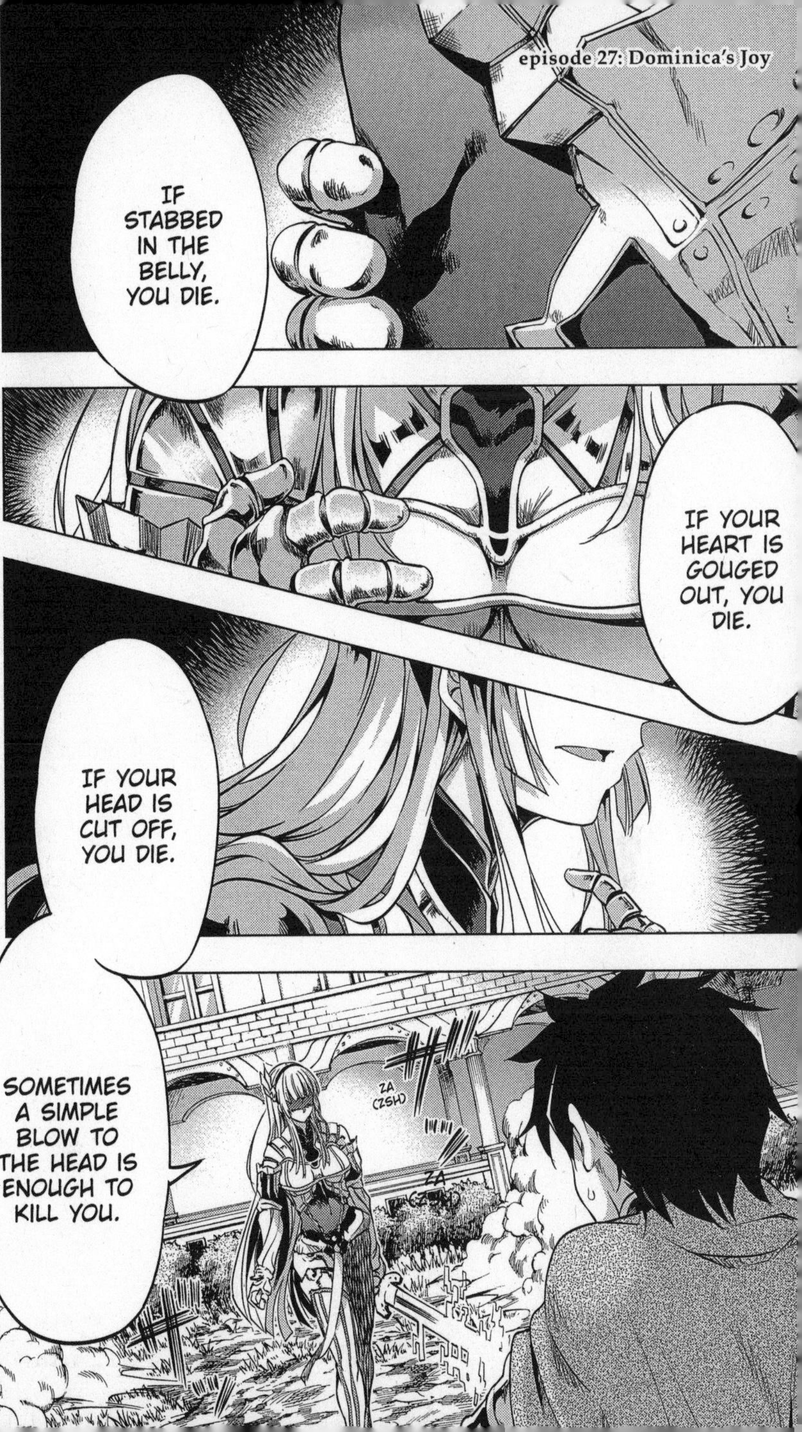
IF STABBED IN THE BELLY, YOU DIE.
IF YOUR HEART IS GOUGED OUT, YOU DIE.
IF YOUR HEAD IS CUT OFF, YOU DIE.
SOMETIMES A SIMPLE BLOW TO THE HEAD IS ENOUGH TO KILL YOU.
ZA (ZSH)
ZA (ZSH)

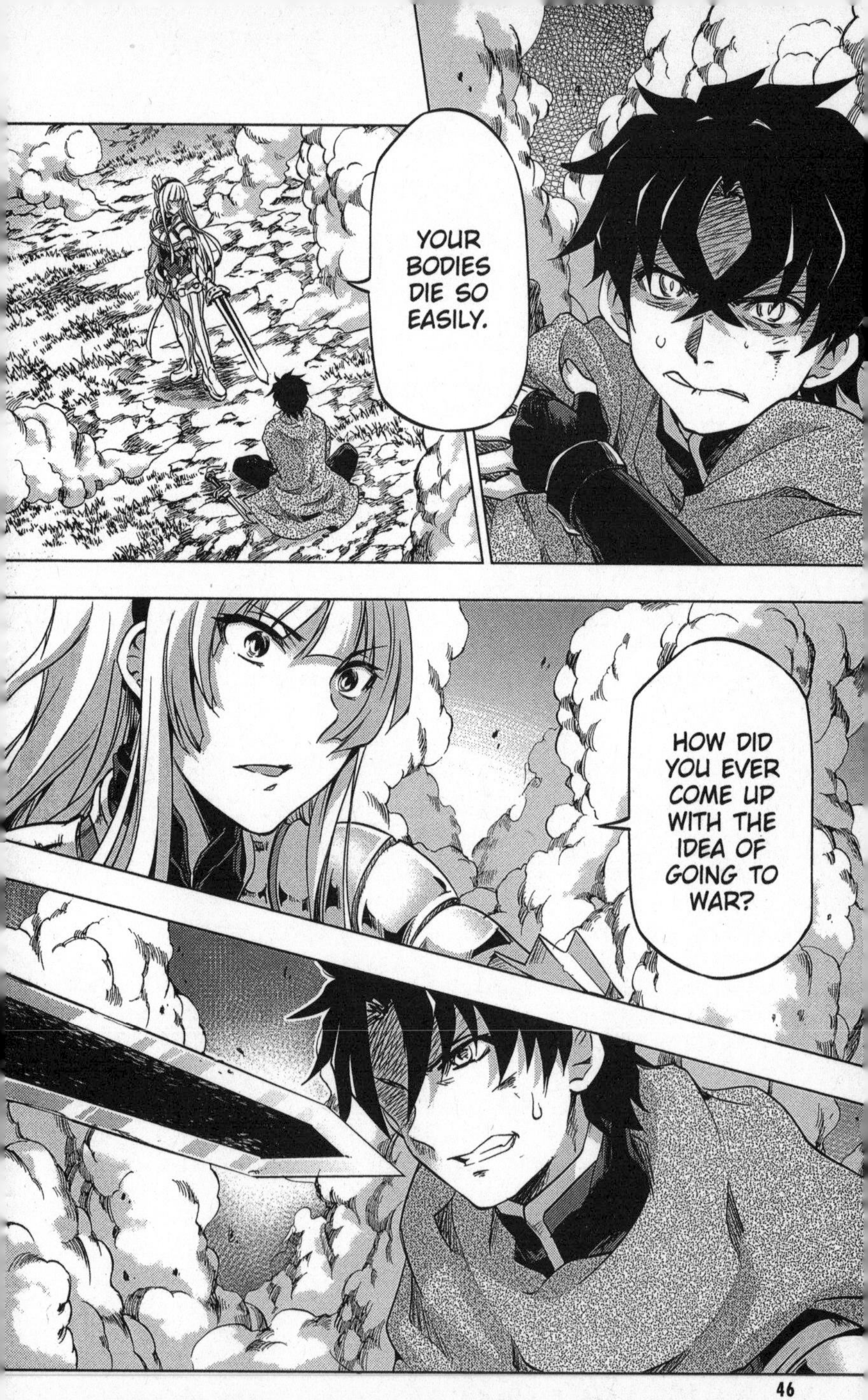
YOUR BODIES DIE SO EASILY.
HOW DID YOU EVER COME UP WITH THE IDEA OF GOING TO WAR?

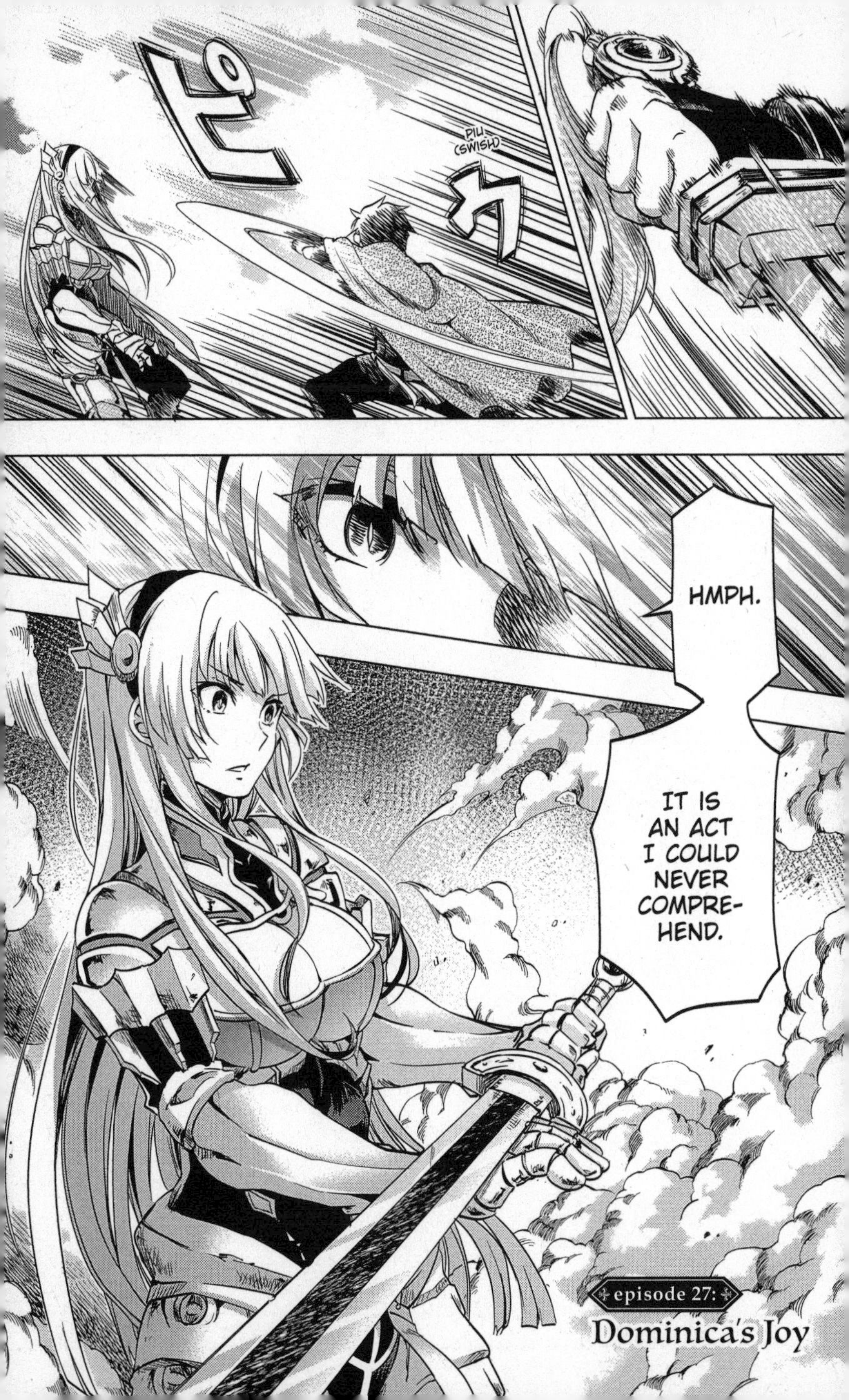
PIU (SWISH)
HMPH.
IT IS AN ACT I COULD NEVER COMPREHEND.
episode 27:
Dominica's Joy

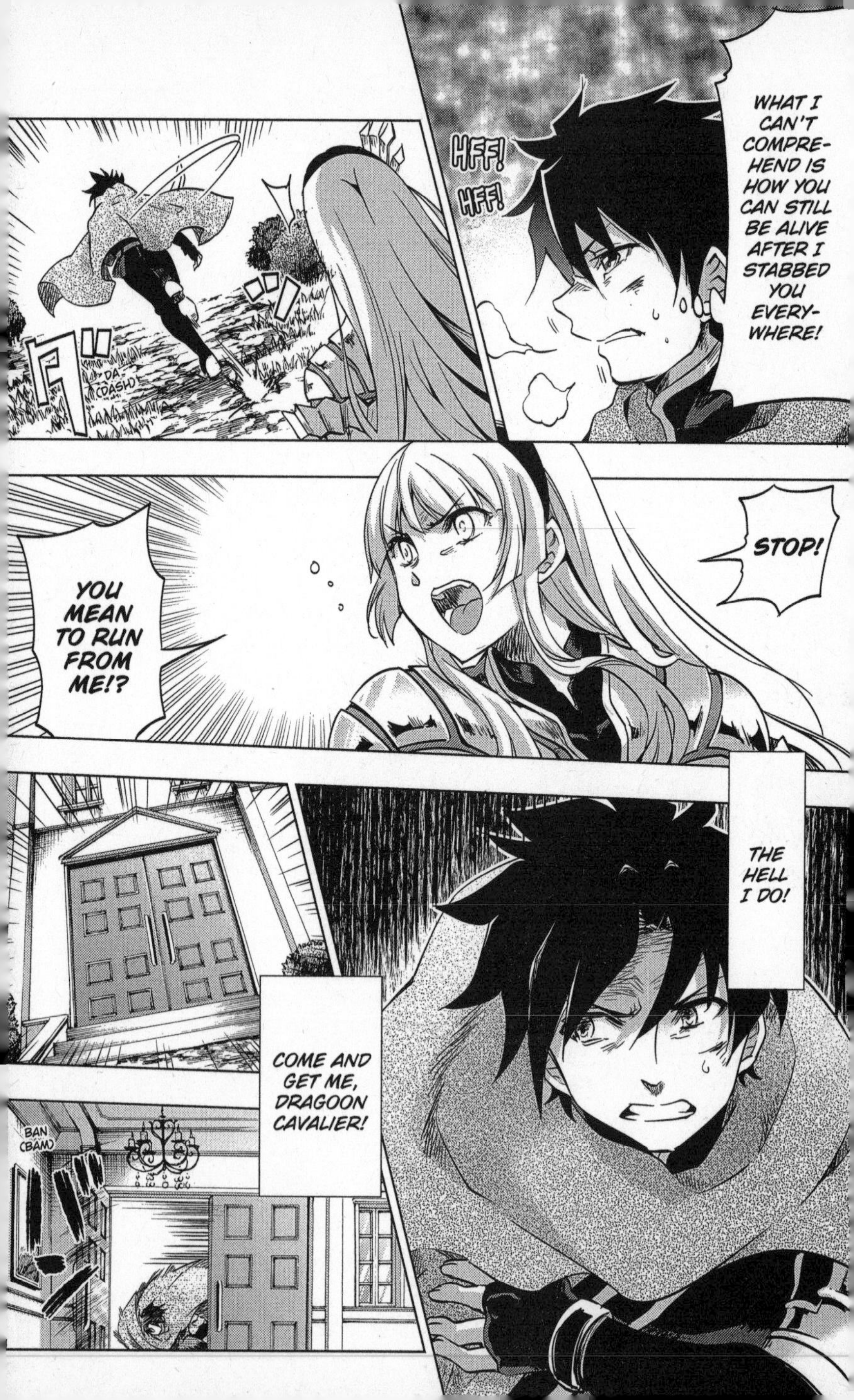
HFF!
HFF!
WHAT I CAN'T COMPREHEND IS HOW YOU CAN STILL BE ALIVE AFTER I STABBED YOU EVERYWHERE!
DA (DASH)
STOP!
YOU MEAN TO RUN FROM ME!?
THE HELL I DO!
COME AND GET ME, DRAGOON CAVALIER!
BAN (BAM)

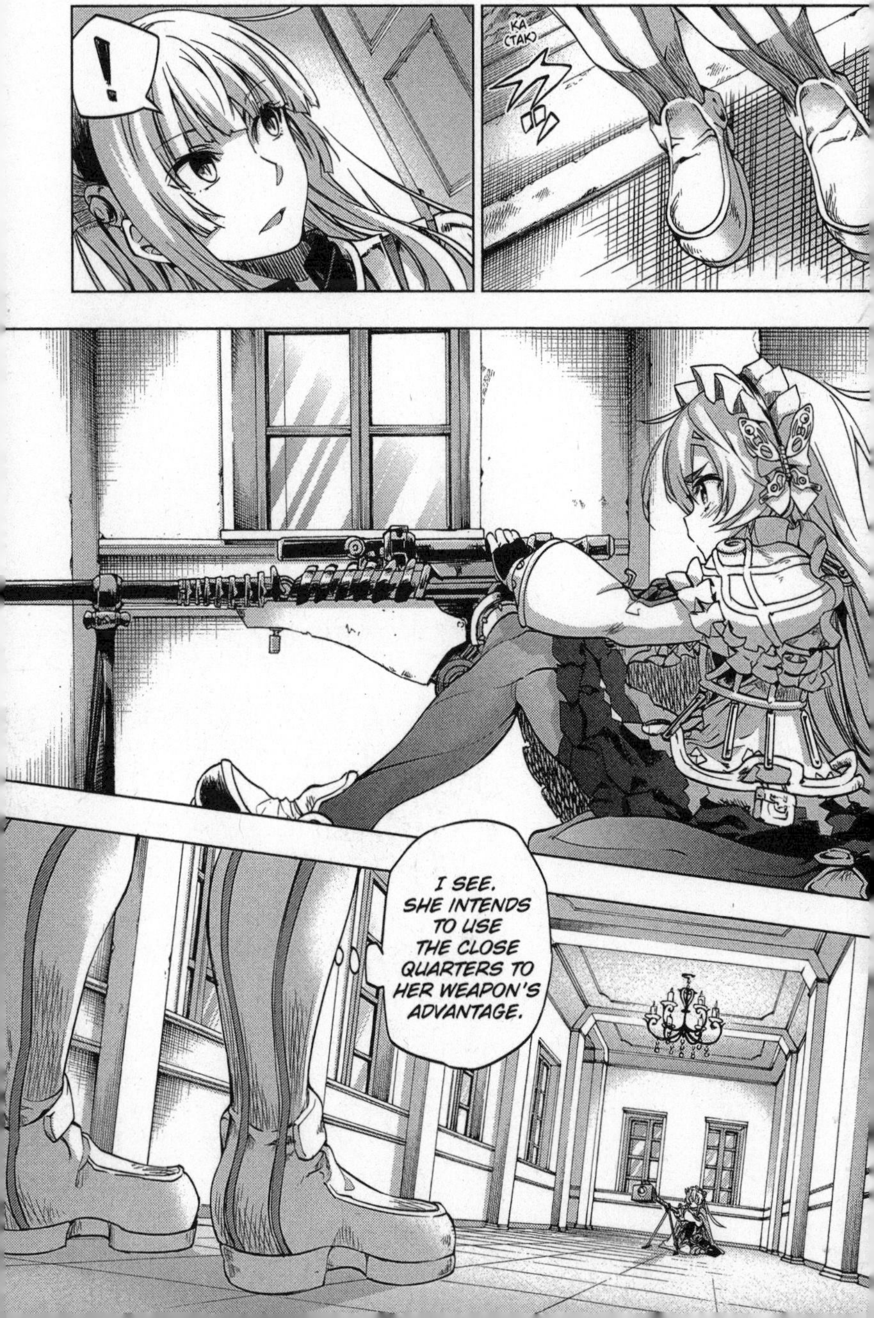
KA (TAK)
!
I SEE. SHE INTENDS TO USE THE CLOSE QUARTERS TO HER WEAPON'S ADVANTAGE.

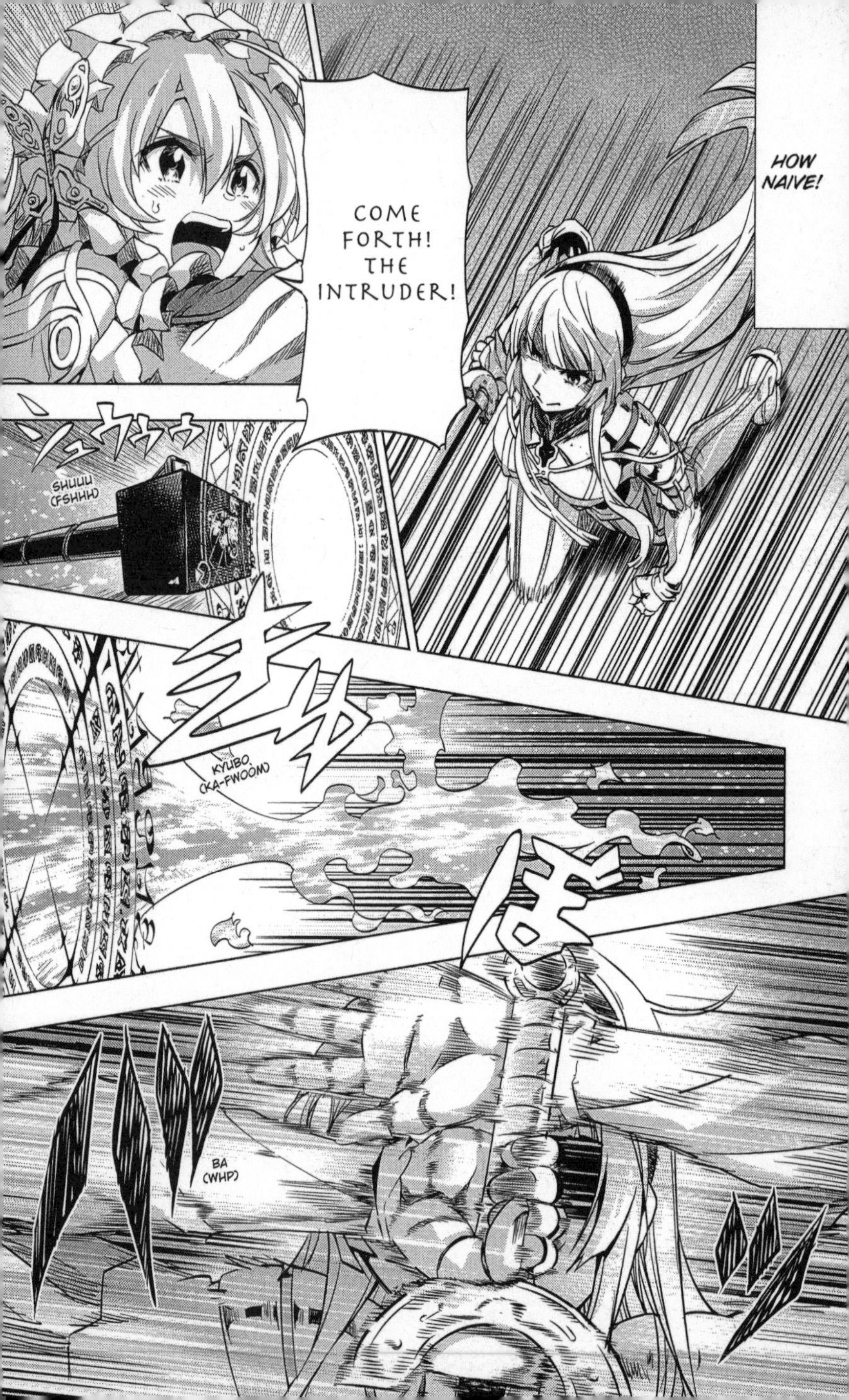
HOW NAIVE!
COME FORTH! THE INTRUDER!
SHUUU (FSHHH)
KYUBO (KA-FWOOM)
BA (WHP)

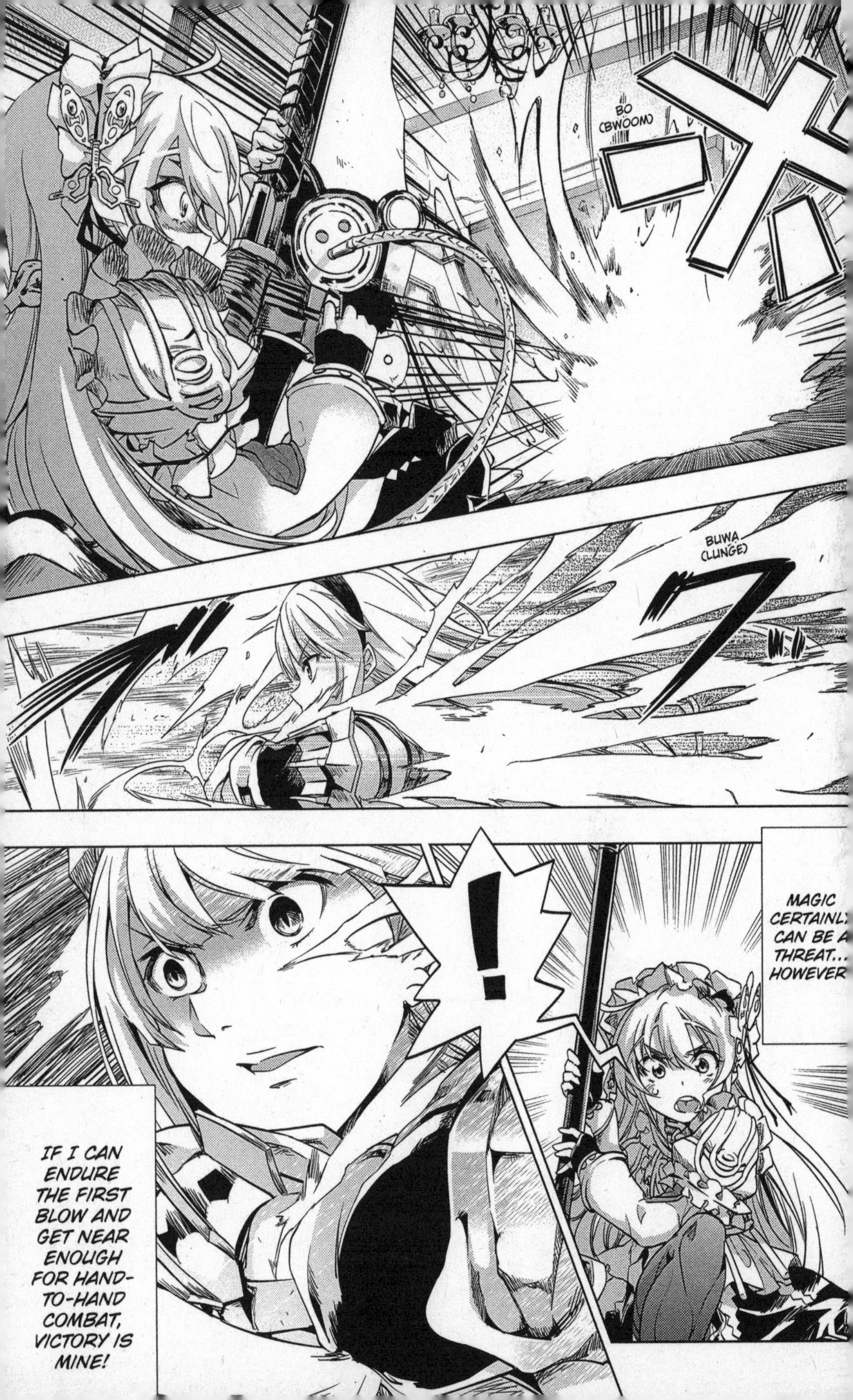
BO
(BWOOM)
BUWA
(LUNGE)
MAGIC CERTAINLY CAN BE A THREAT... HOWEVER
!
IF I CAN ENDURE THE FIRST BLOW AND GET NEAR ENOUGH FOR HAND-TO-HAND COMBAT, VICTORY IS MINE!

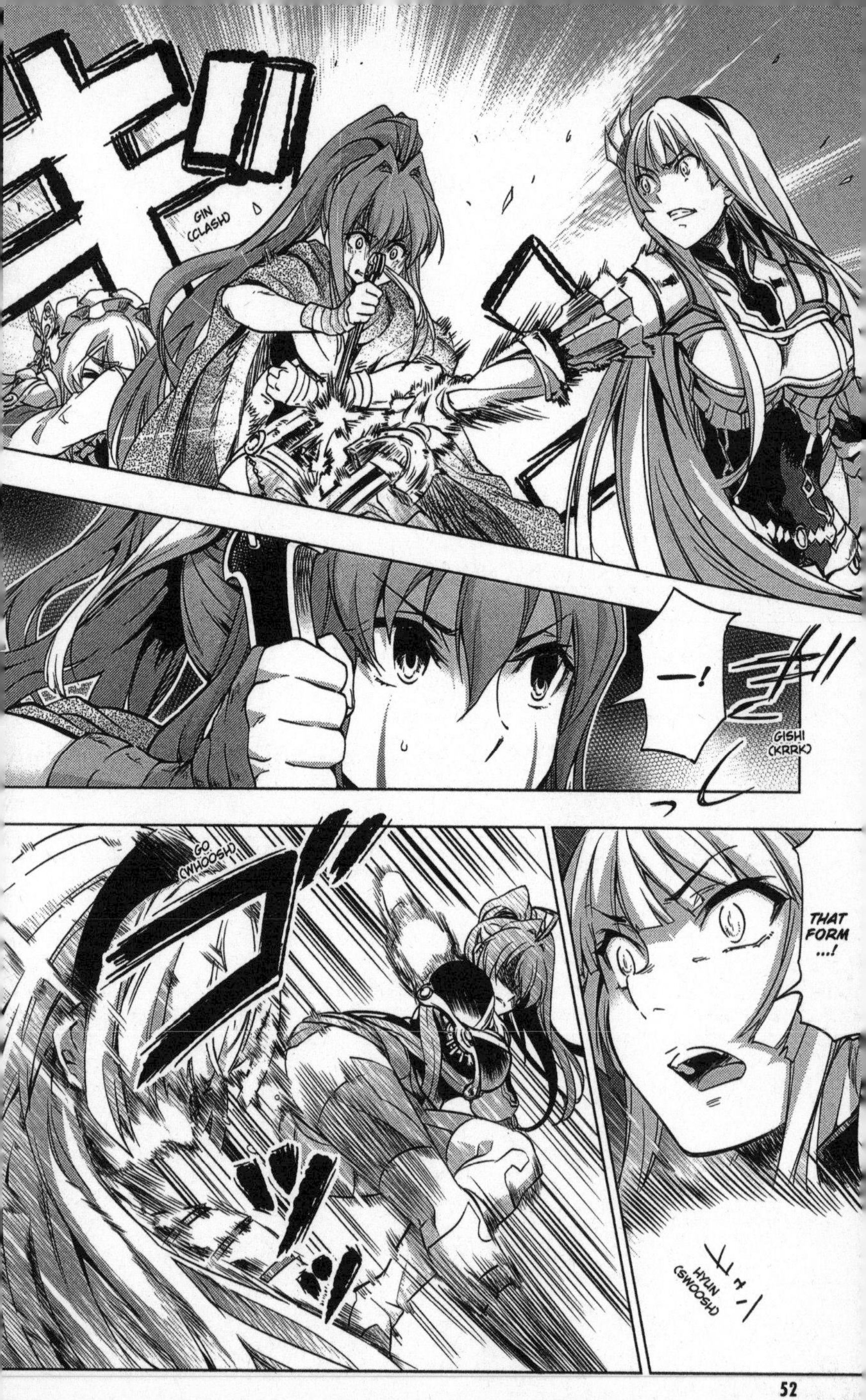
GIN (CLASH)
—!
GISHI (KRRK)
THAT FORM ...!
HYUN (SWOOSH)
GO (WHOOSH)

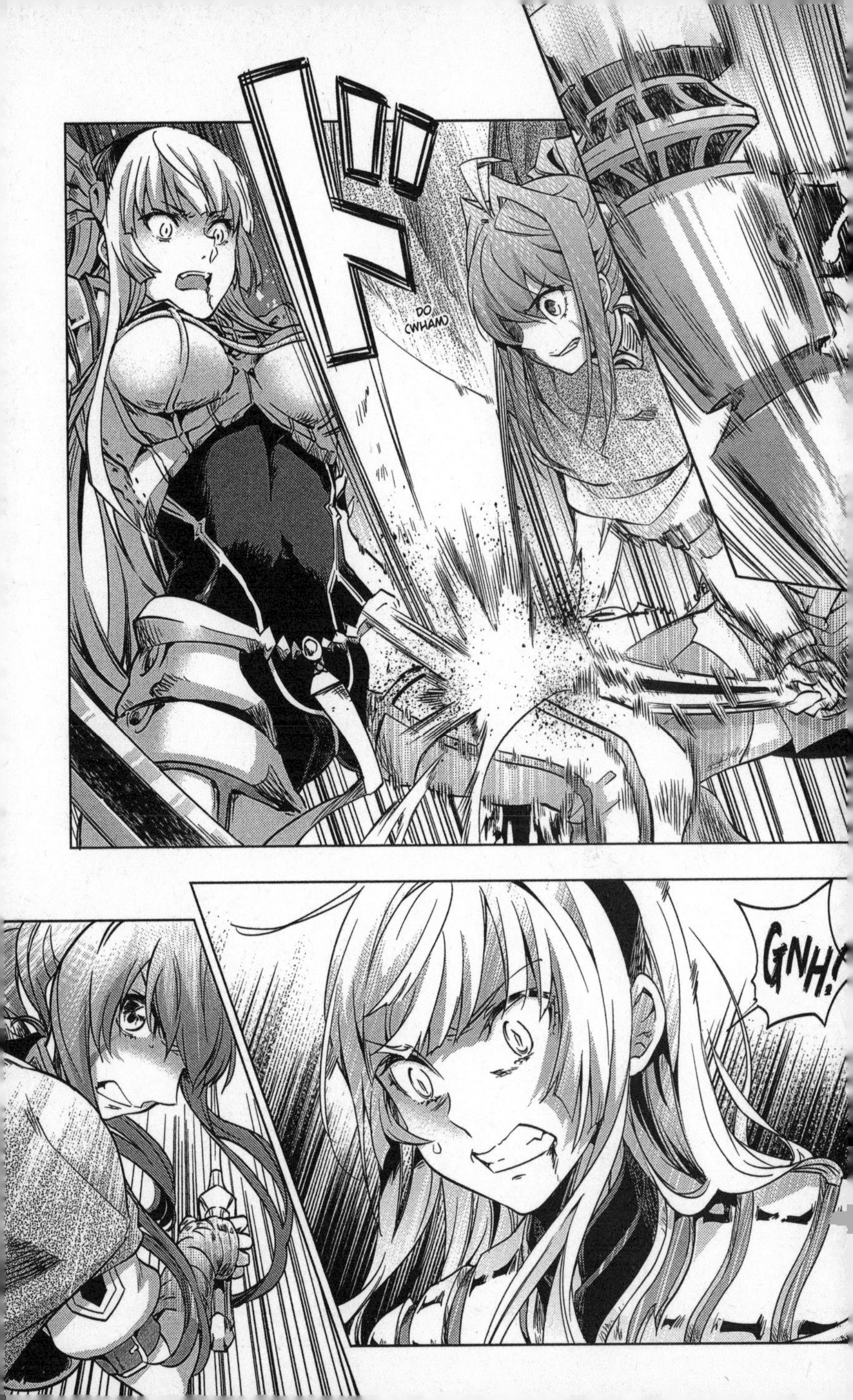
DO (WHAM)
GNH!

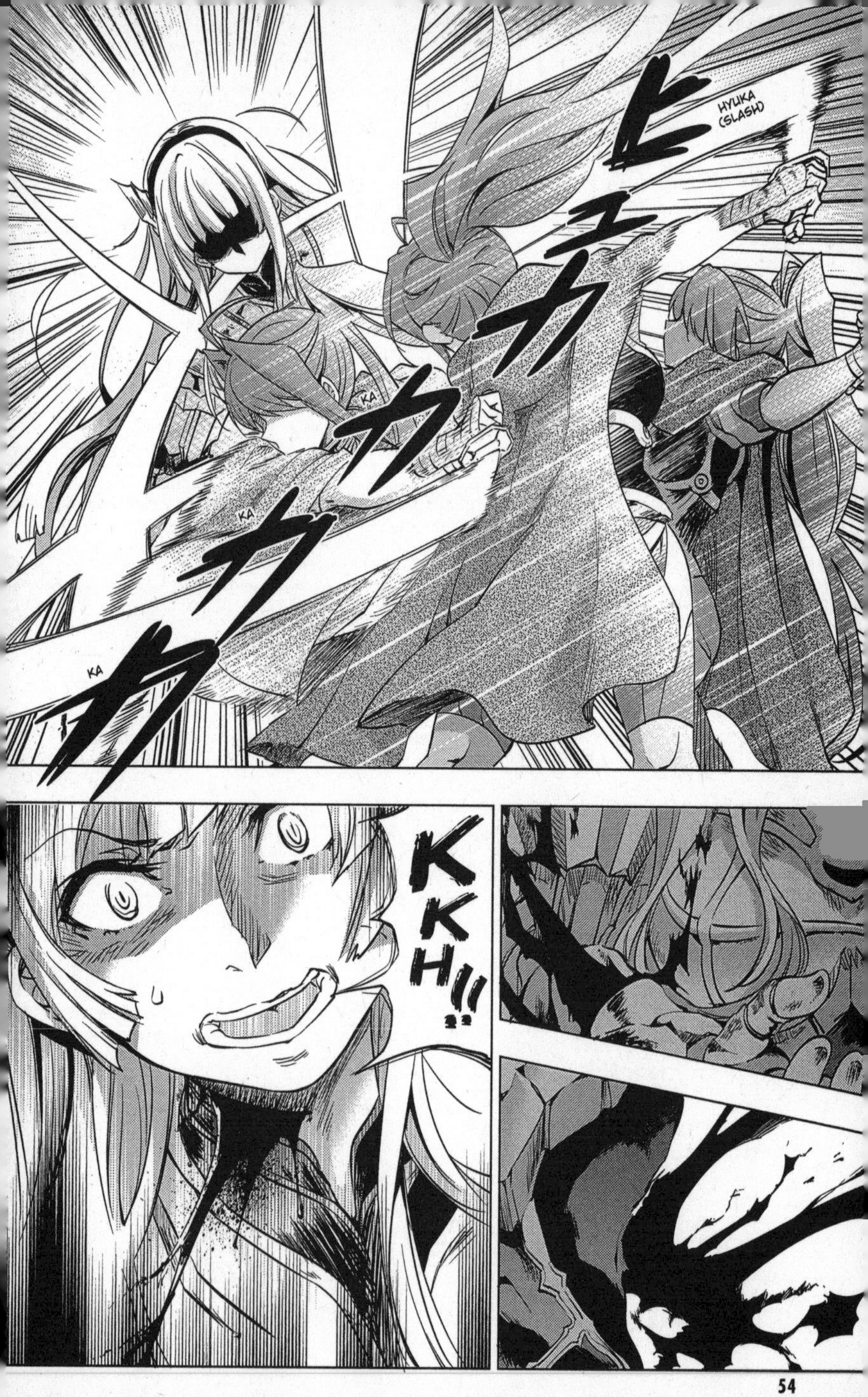
HYUKA
(SLASH)
KA
KA
KA
KKH!!

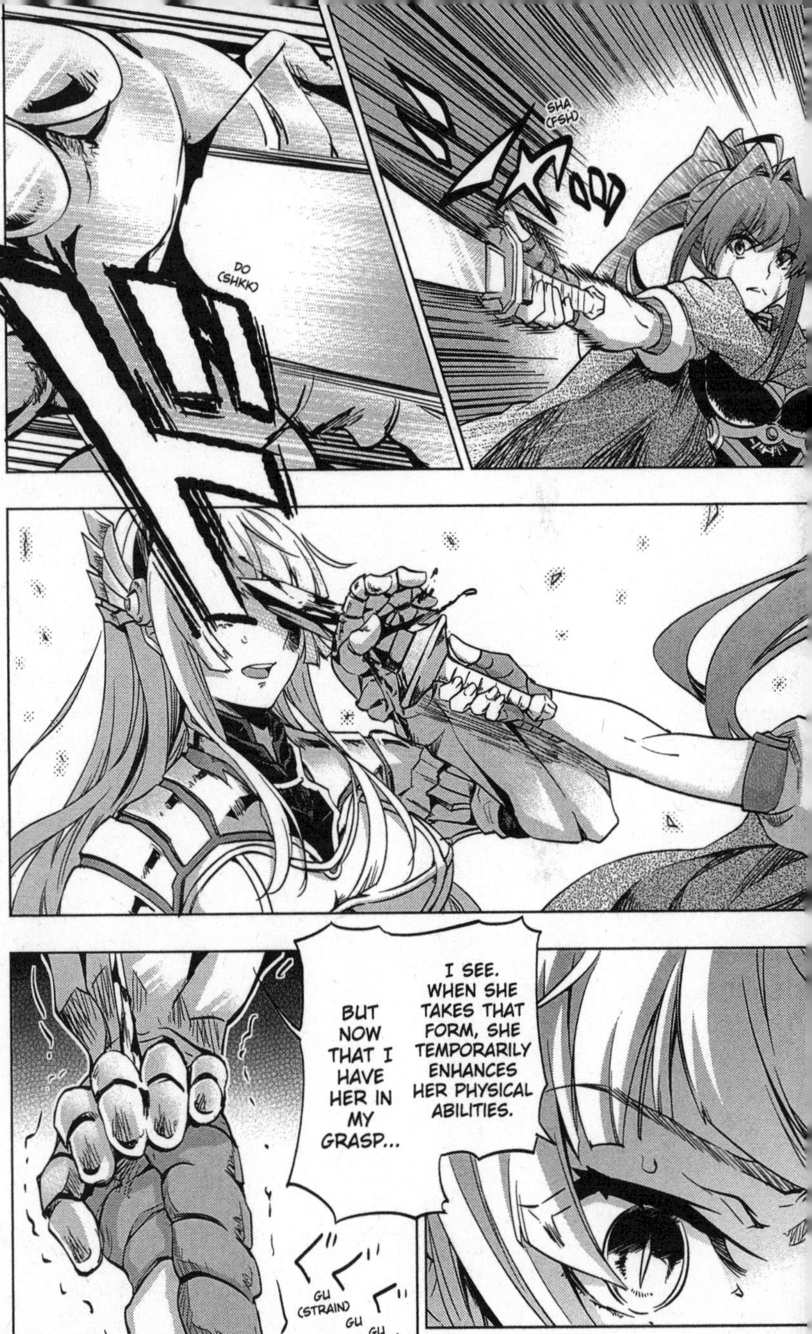
SHA (FSH)
DO (SHKK)
I SEE. WHEN SHE TAKES THAT FORM, SHE TEMPORARILY ENHANCES HER PHYSICAL ABILITIES.
BUT NOW THAT I HAVE HER IN MY GRASP...
GU (STRAIN) GU GU

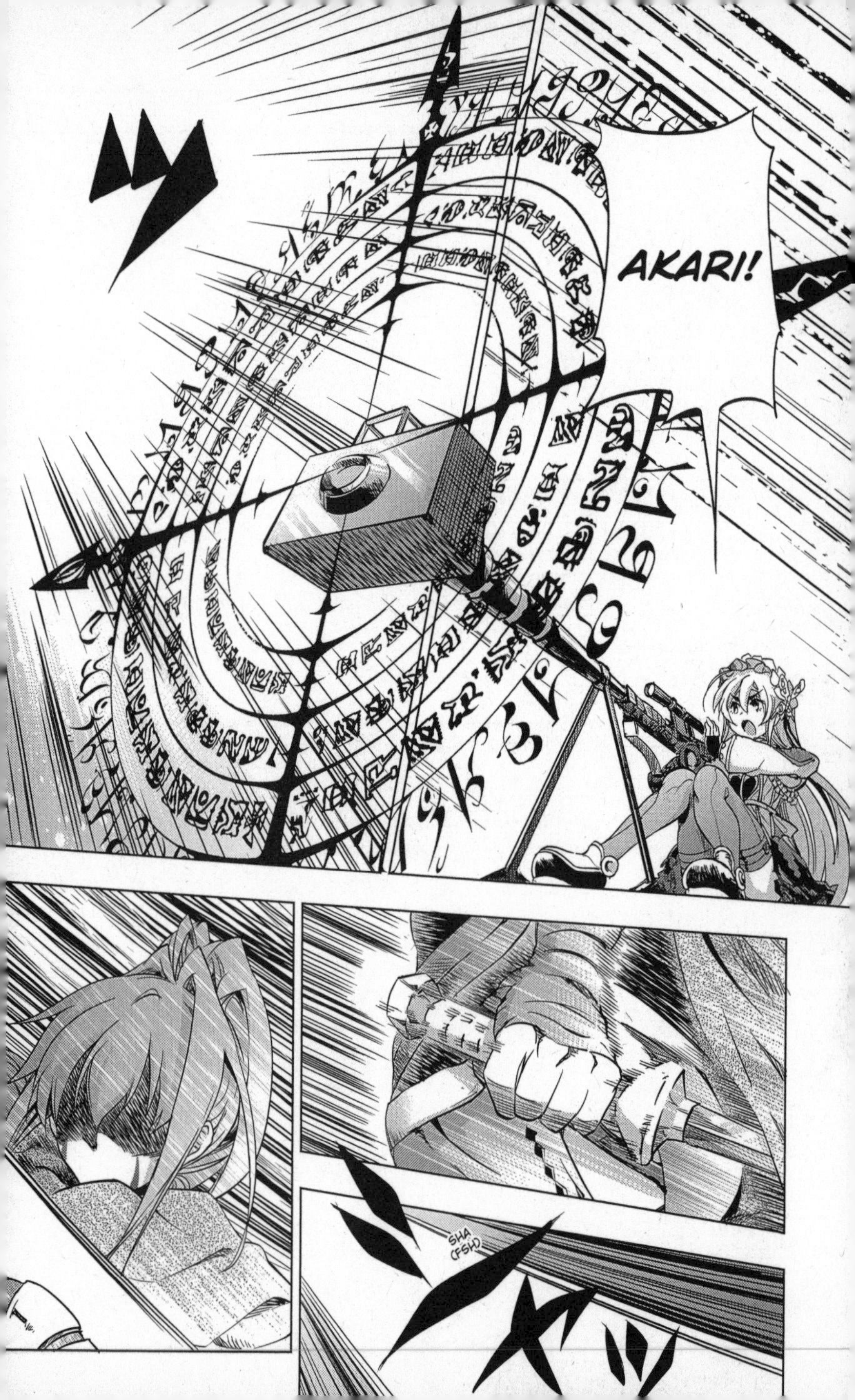
AKARI!
SHA (FSH)

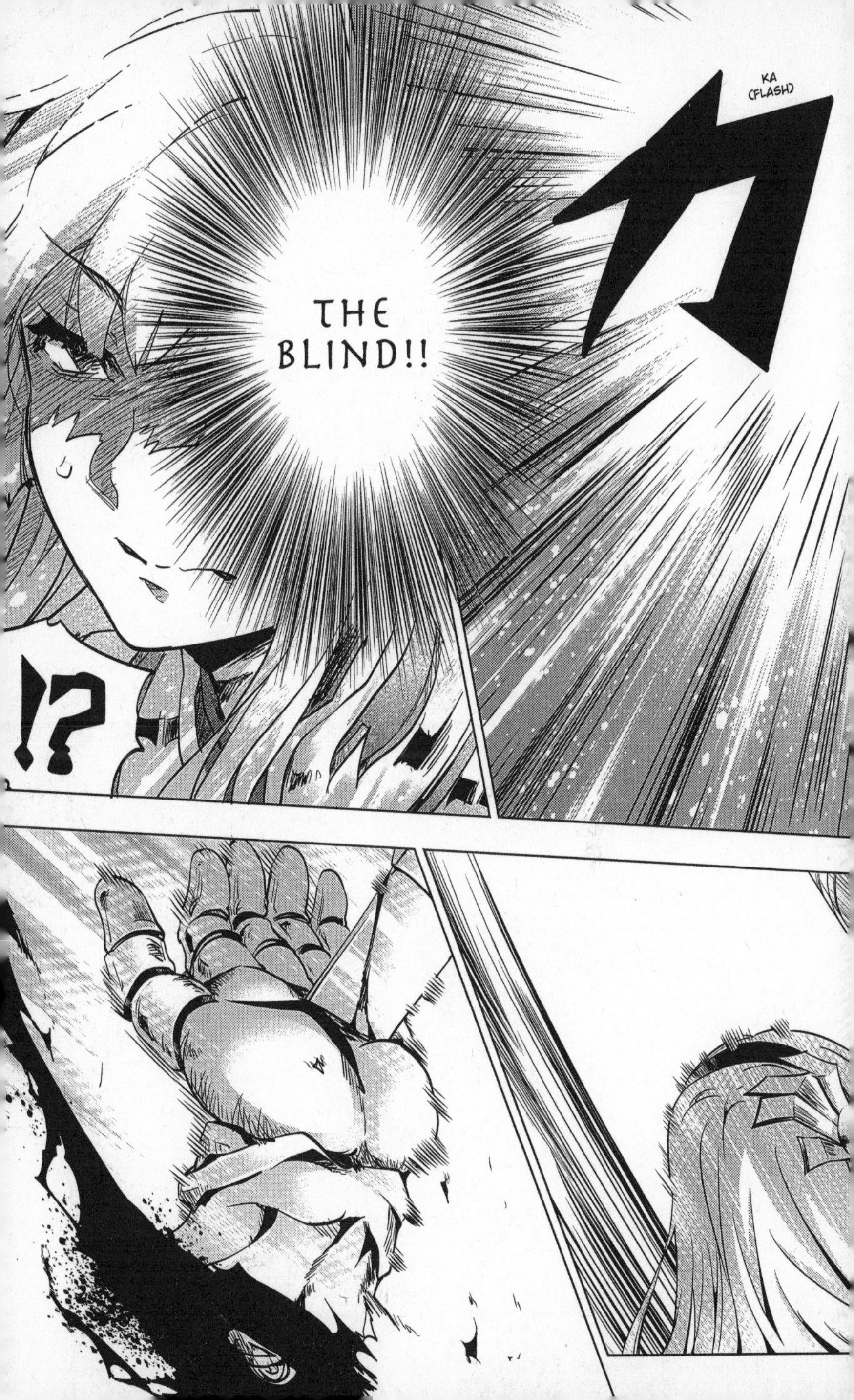
KA
(FLASH)
THE
BLIND!!
!?

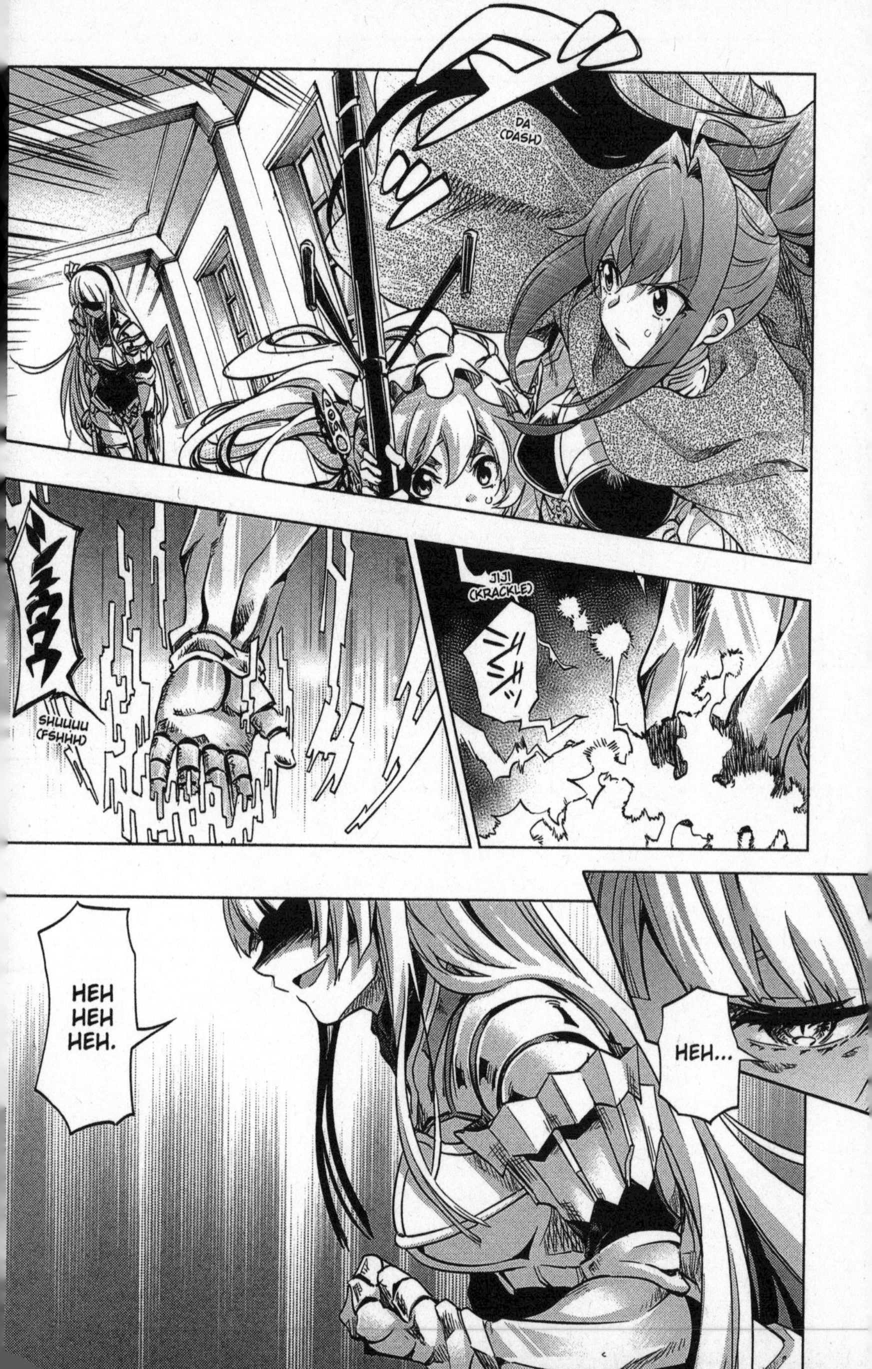
DA (DASH)
JIJI (KRACKLE)
SHUUUU (FSHHH)
HEH...
HEH HEH HEH.

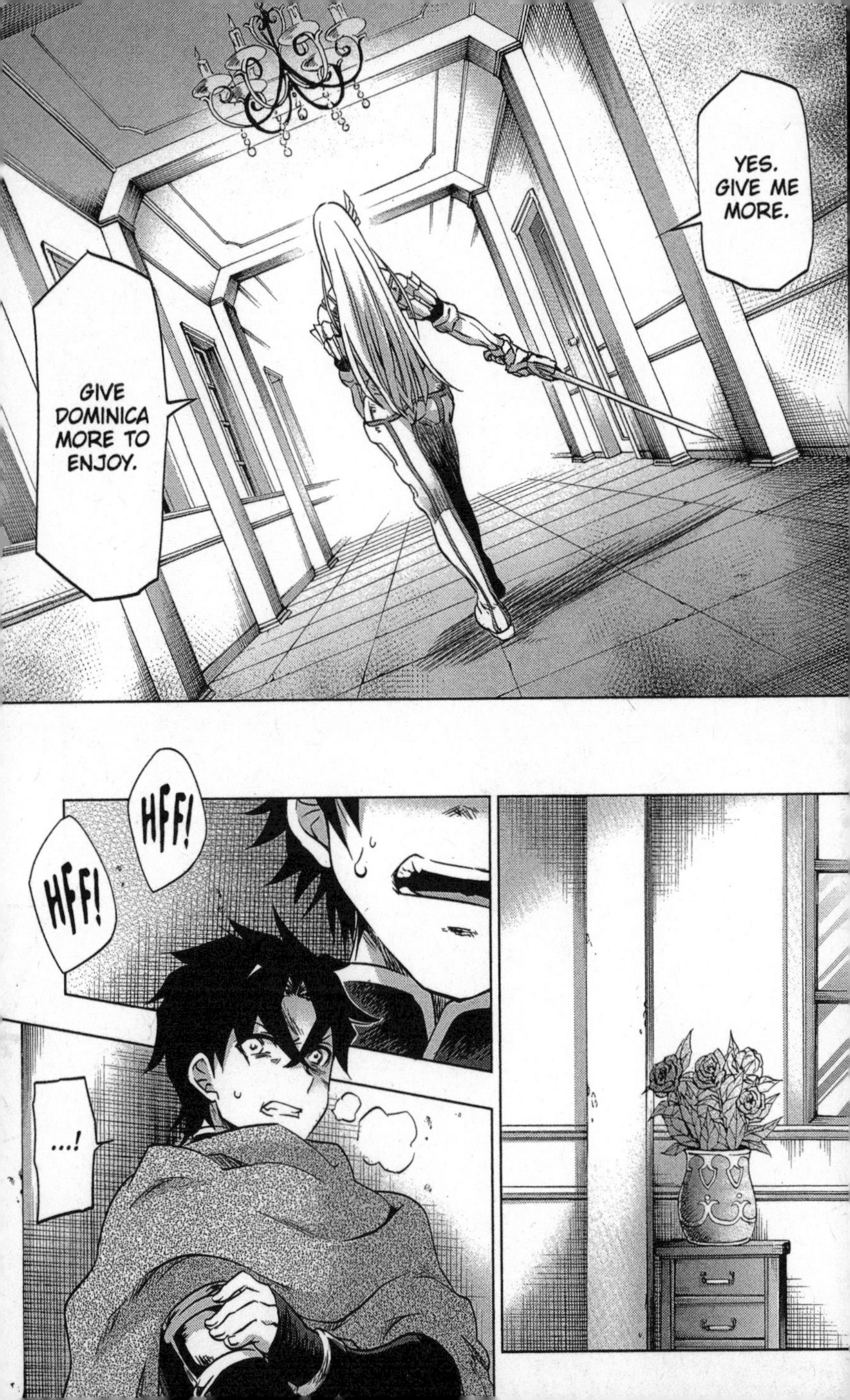
YES. GIVE ME MORE.
GIVE DOMINICA MORE TO ENJOY.
HFF!
HFF!
...!

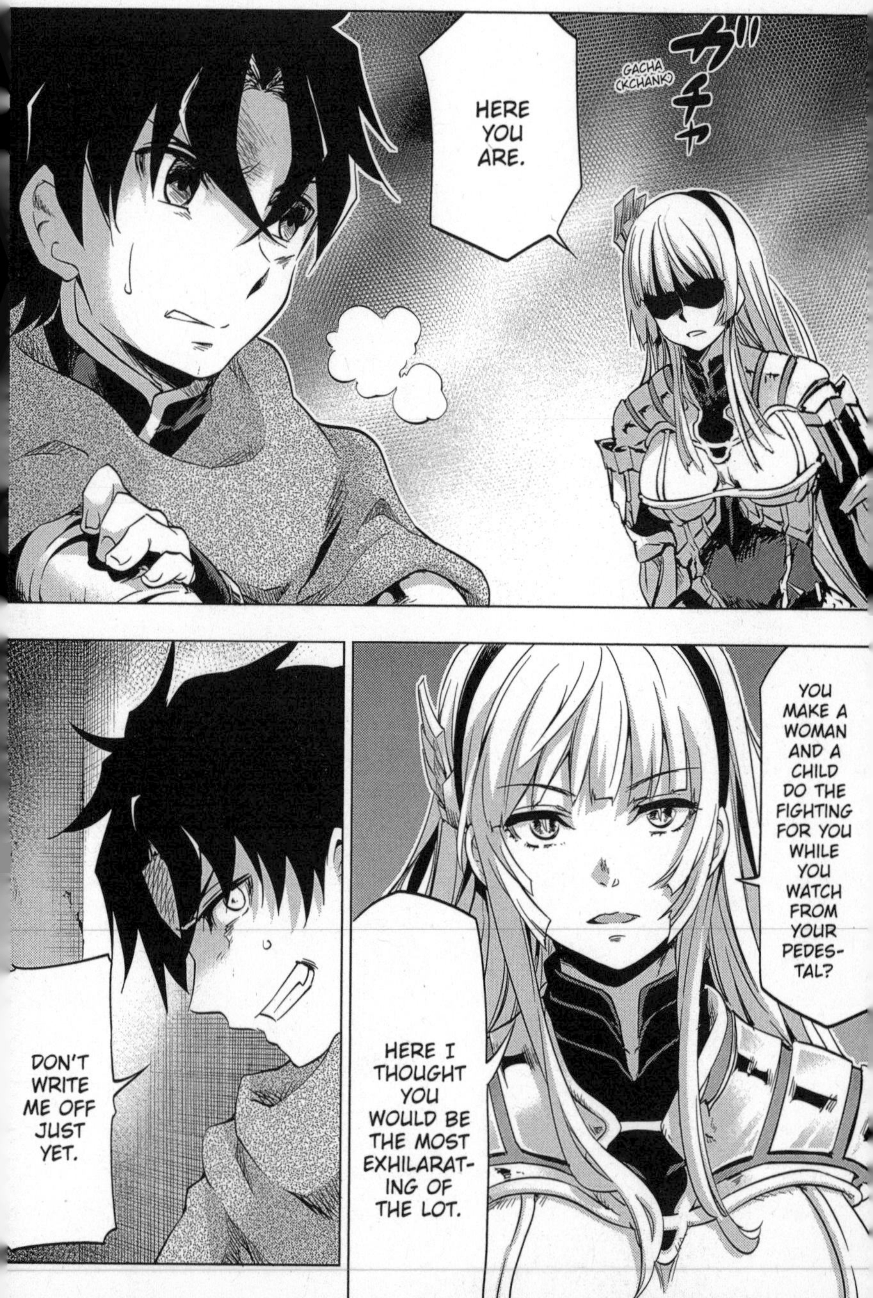
ガチャ
GACHA (KCHANK)
HERE YOU ARE.
YOU MAKE A WOMAN AND A CHILD DO THE FIGHTING FOR YOU WHILE YOU WATCH FROM YOUR PEDES-TAL?
HERE I THOUGHT YOU WOULD BE THE MOST EXHILARAT-ING OF THE LOT.
DON'T WRITE ME OFF JUST YET.

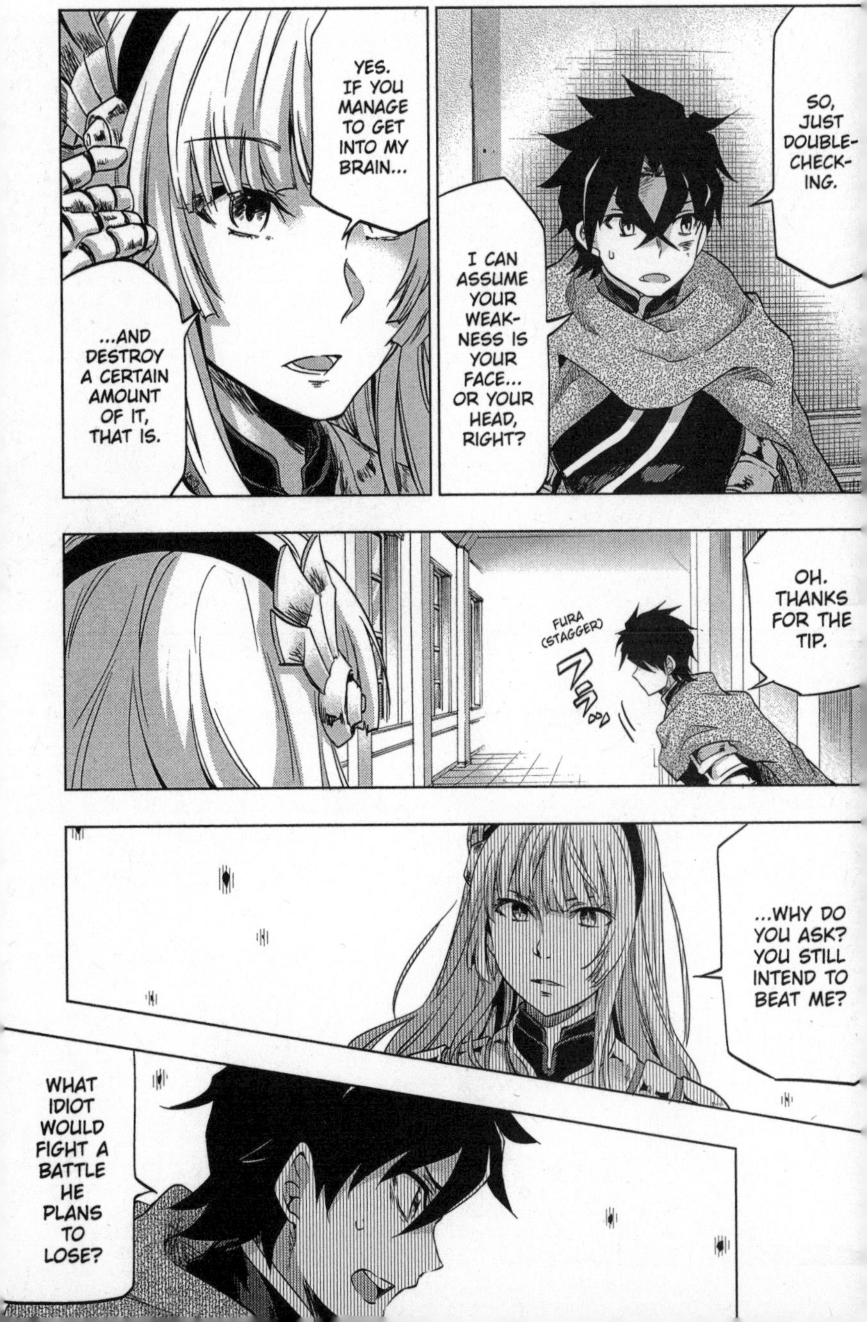
SO, JUST DOUBLE-CHECKING.
I CAN ASSUME YOUR WEAKNESS IS YOUR FACE... OR YOUR HEAD, RIGHT?
YES. IF YOU MANAGE TO GET INTO MY BRAIN...
...AND DESTROY A CERTAIN AMOUNT OF IT, THAT IS.
OH. THANKS FOR THE TIP.
FURA (STAGGER)
...WHY DO YOU ASK? YOU STILL INTEND TO BEAT ME?
WHAT IDIOT WOULD FIGHT A BATTLE HE PLANS TO LOSE?

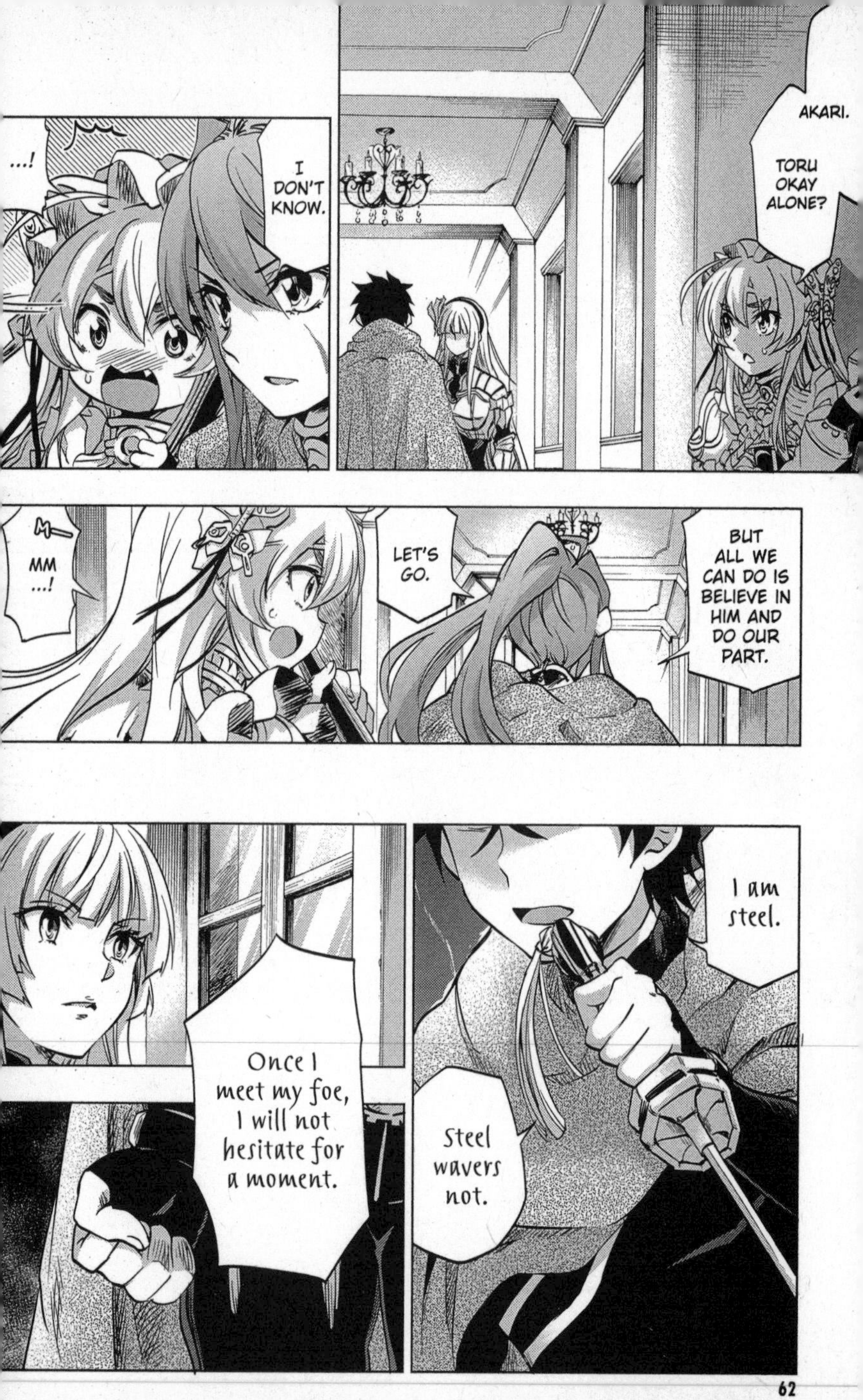
AKARI.
TORU OKAY ALONE?
I DON'T KNOW.
...!
BUT ALL WE CAN DO IS BELIEVE IN HIM AND DO OUR PART.
LET'S GO.
MM ...!
I am steel.
Steel wavers not.
Once I meet my foe, I will not hesitate for a moment.

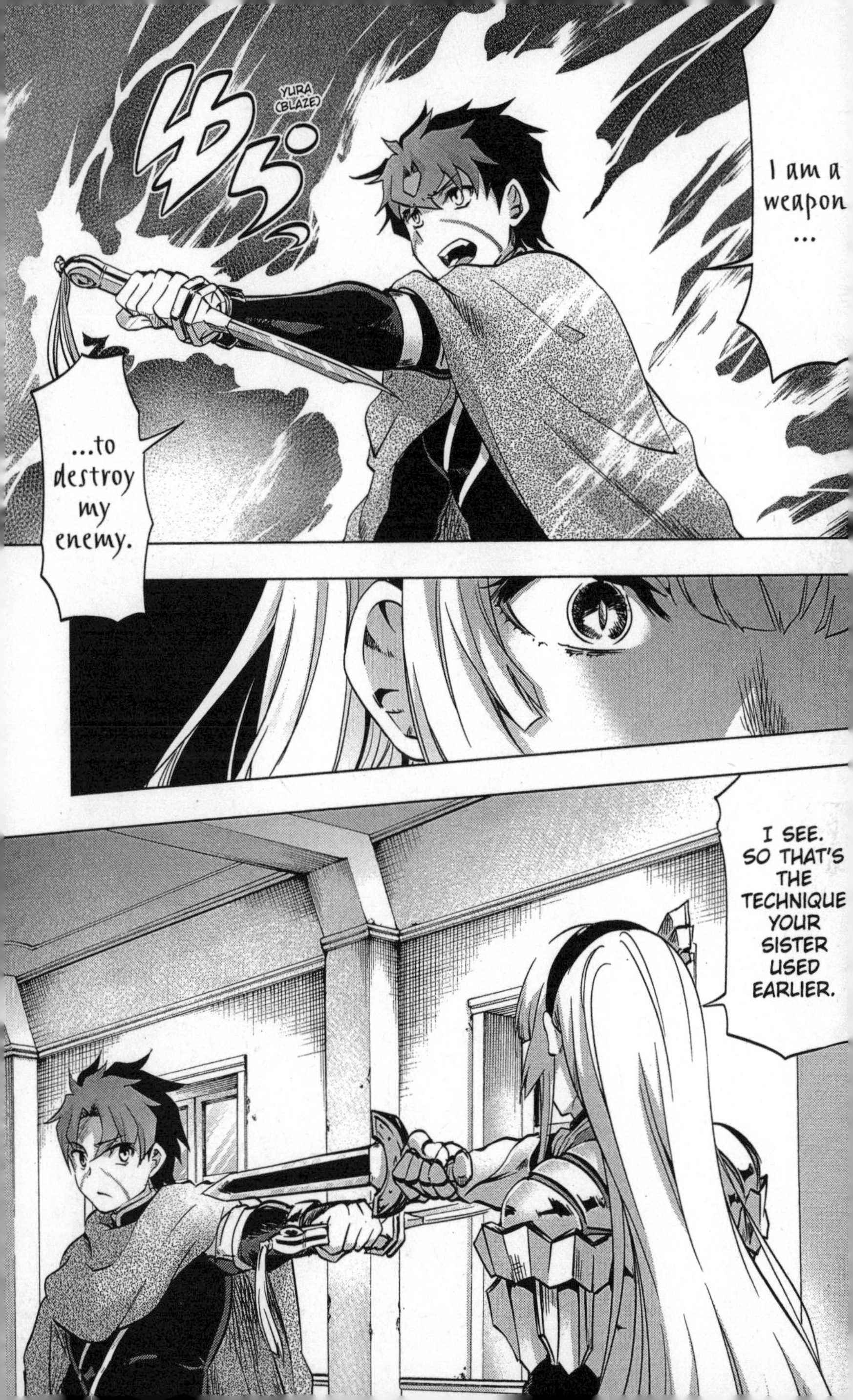
I am a weapon ...
YURA (BLAZE)
...to destroy my enemy.
I SEE. SO THAT'S THE TECHNIQUE YOUR SISTER USED EARLIER.

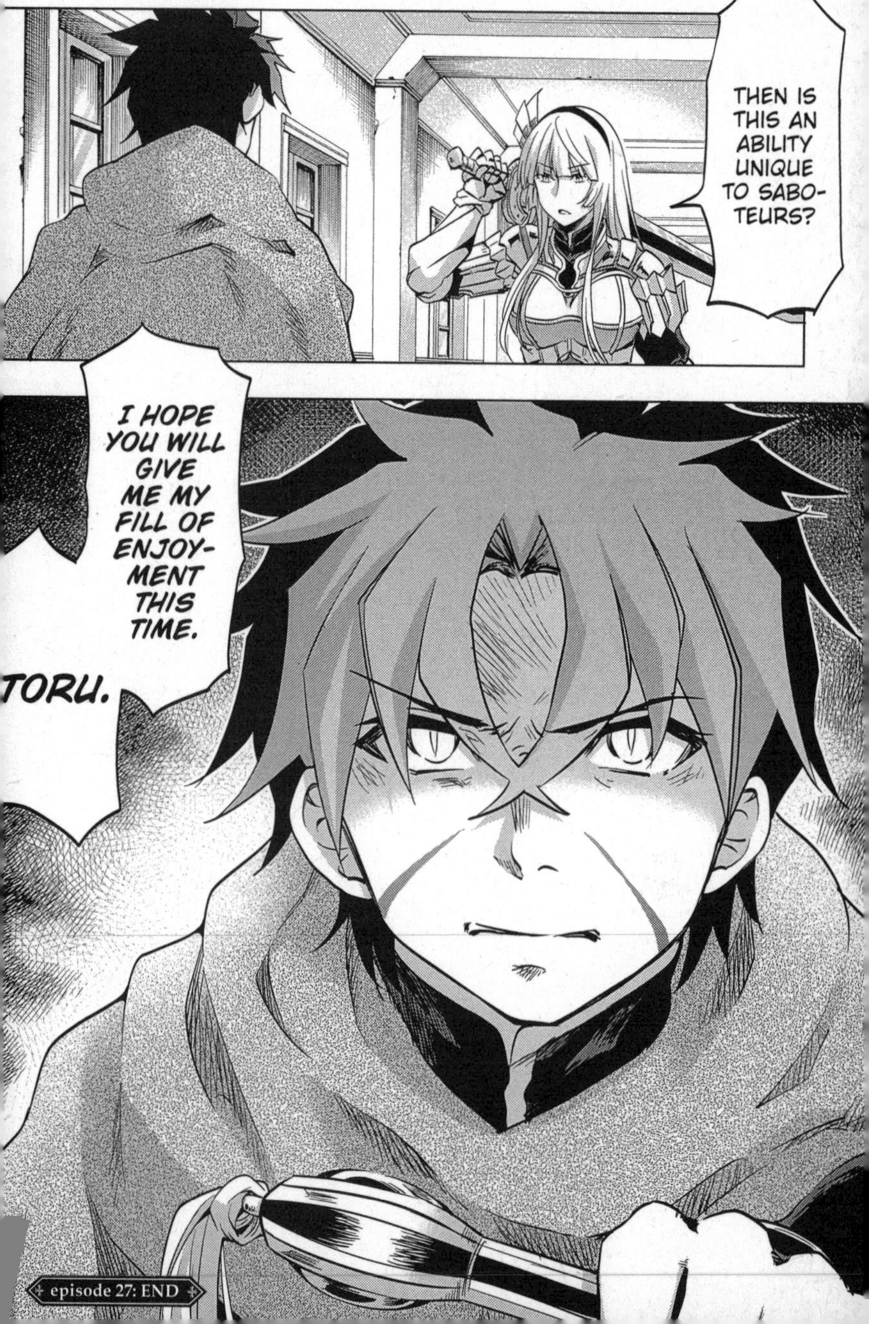
THEN IS THIS AN ABILITY UNIQUE TO SABOTEURS?
I HOPE YOU WILL GIVE ME MY FILL OF ENJOYMENT THIS TIME.
TORU.
episode 27: END

CHAIKA: THE COFFIN PRINCESS

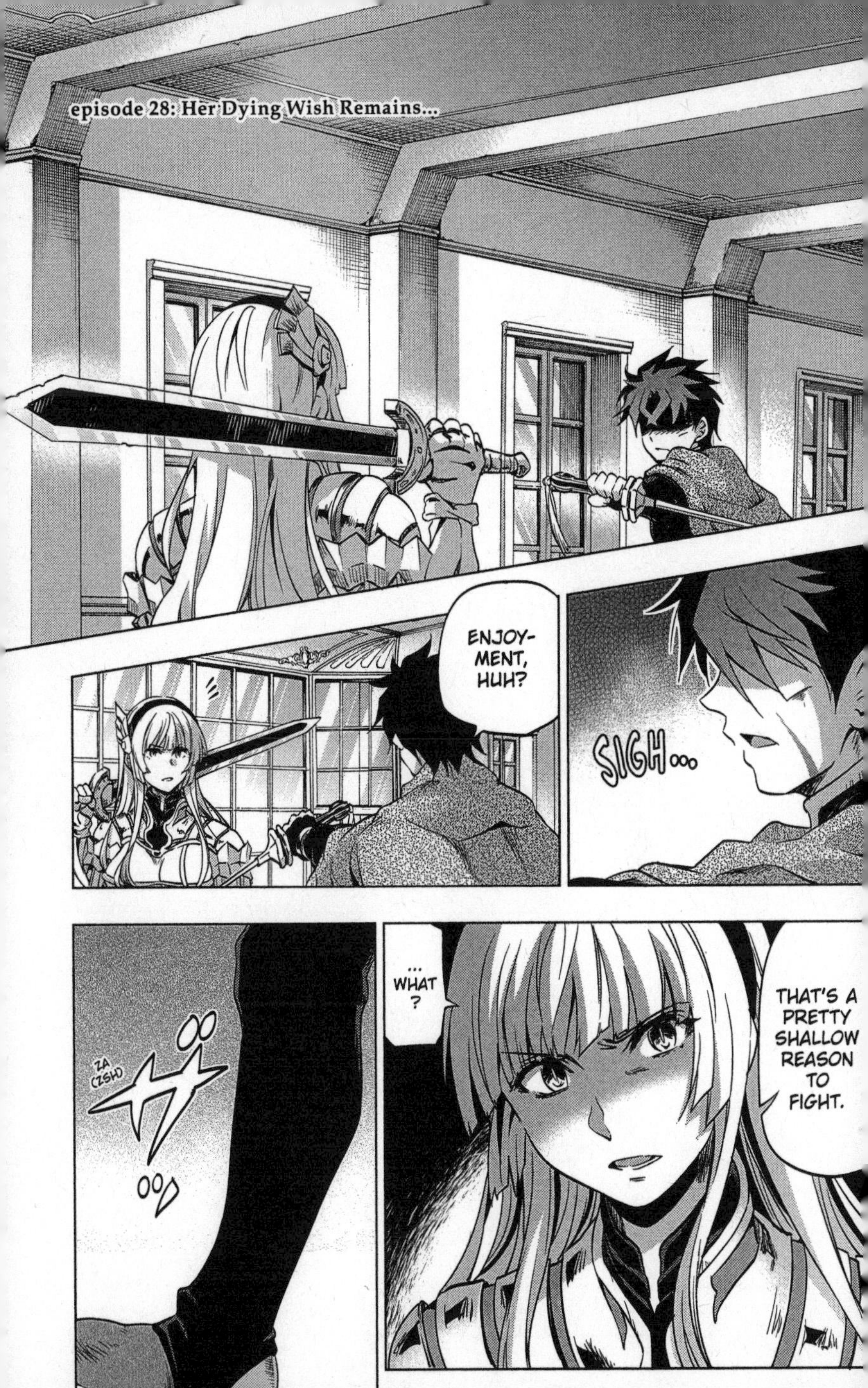
episode 28: Her Dying Wish Remains...
SIGH...
ENJOYMENT, HUH?
THAT'S A PRETTY SHALLOW REASON TO FIGHT.
...WHAT?
ZA (ZSH)

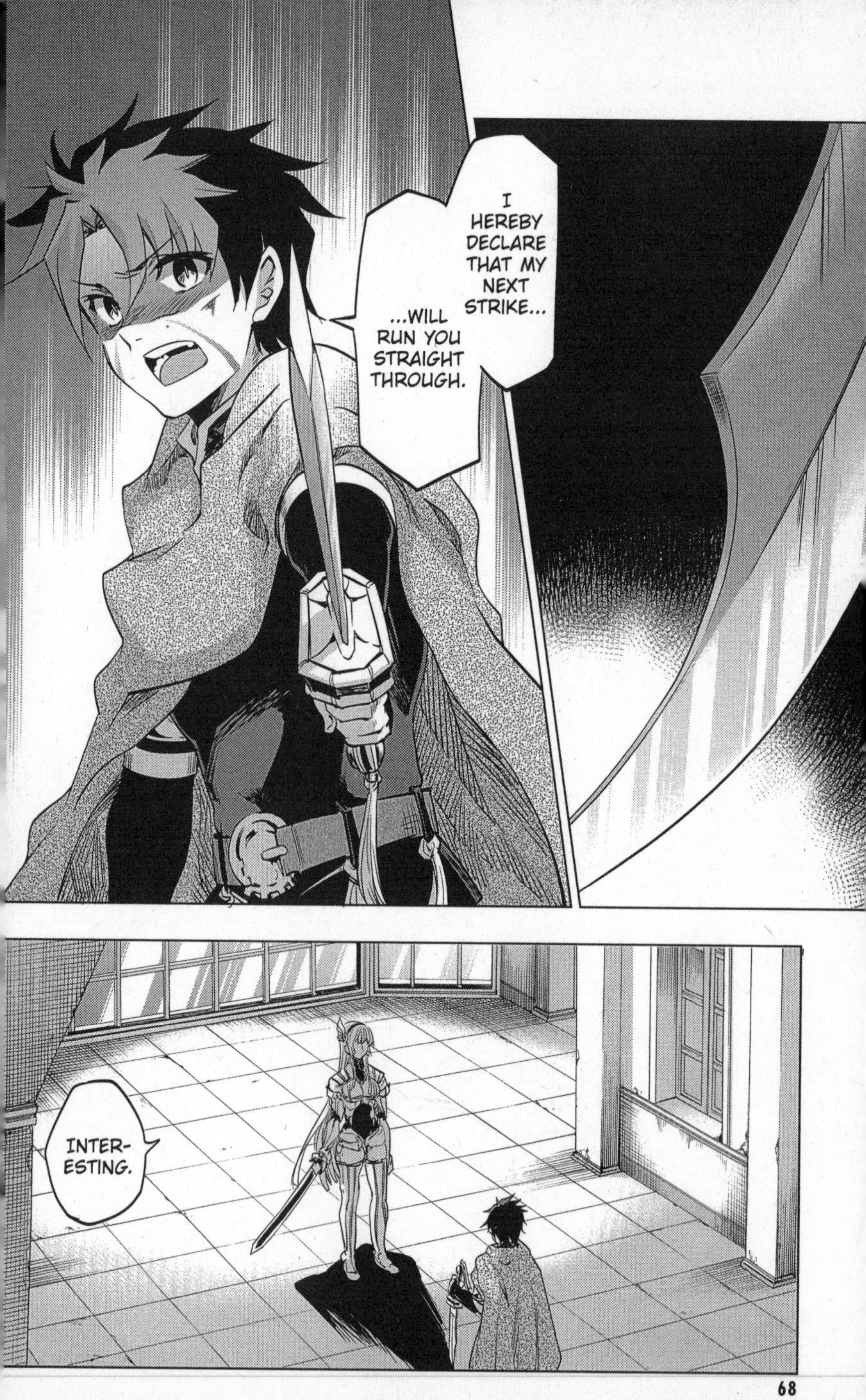
I HEREBY DECLARE THAT MY NEXT STRIKE...
...WILL RUN YOU STRAIGHT THROUGH.
INTER-ESTING.

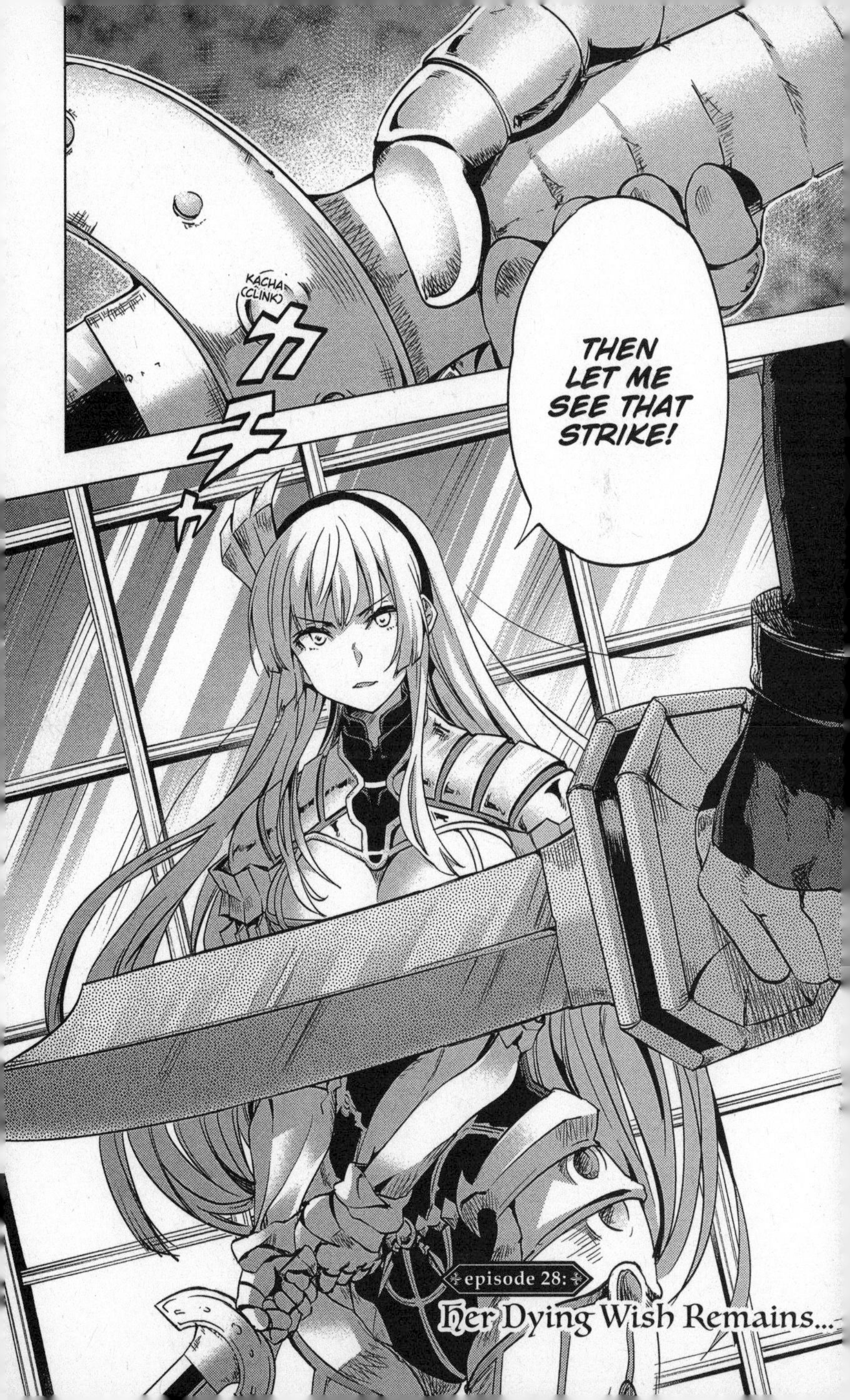
THEN LET ME SEE THAT STRIKE!
KACHA (CLINK)
カチャ
episode 28:
Her Dying Wish Remains...

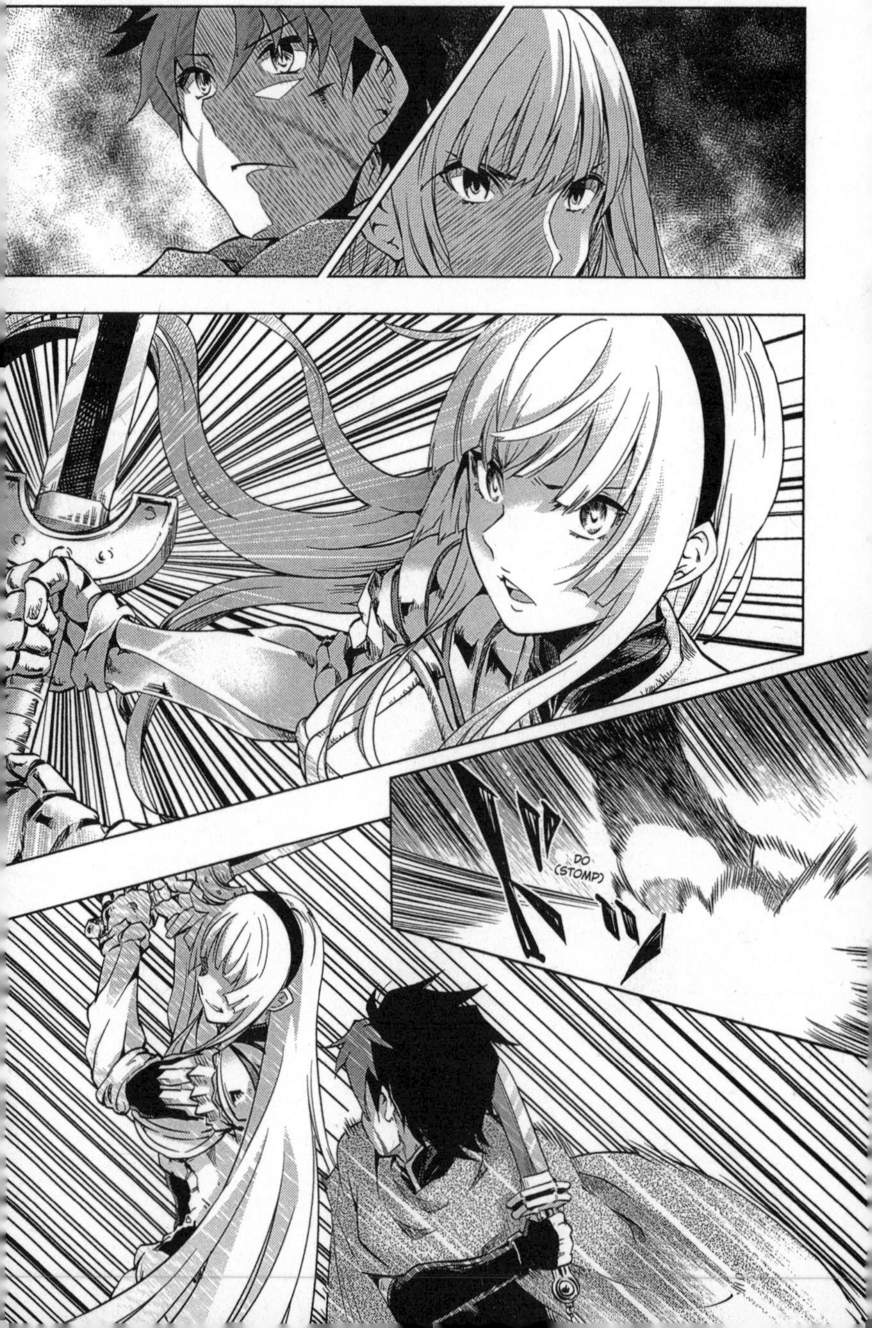
DO
(STOMP)

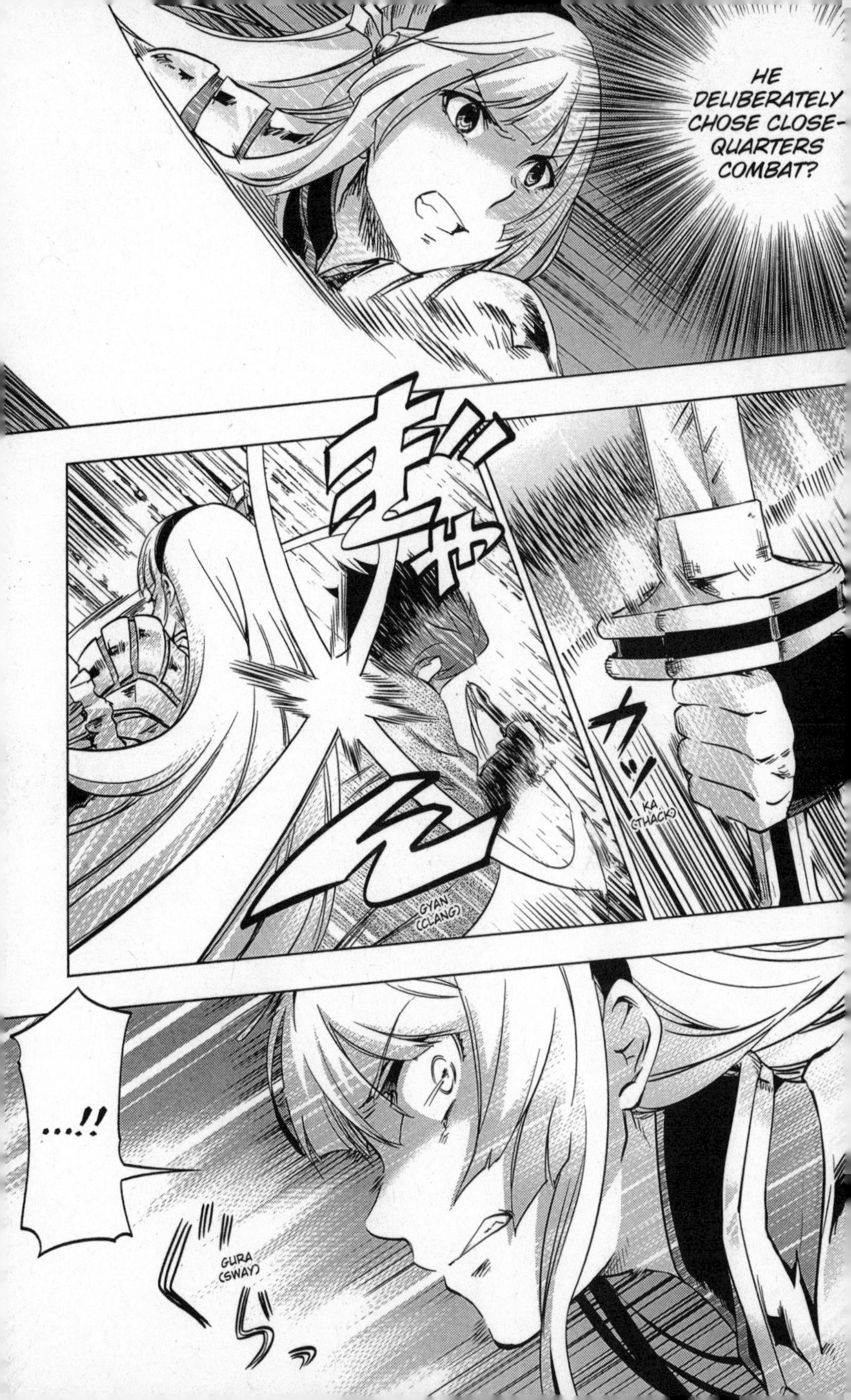
HE DELIBERATELY CHOSE CLOSE-QUARTERS COMBAT?
KA (THACK)
GYAN (CLANG)
...!!
GURA (SWAY)

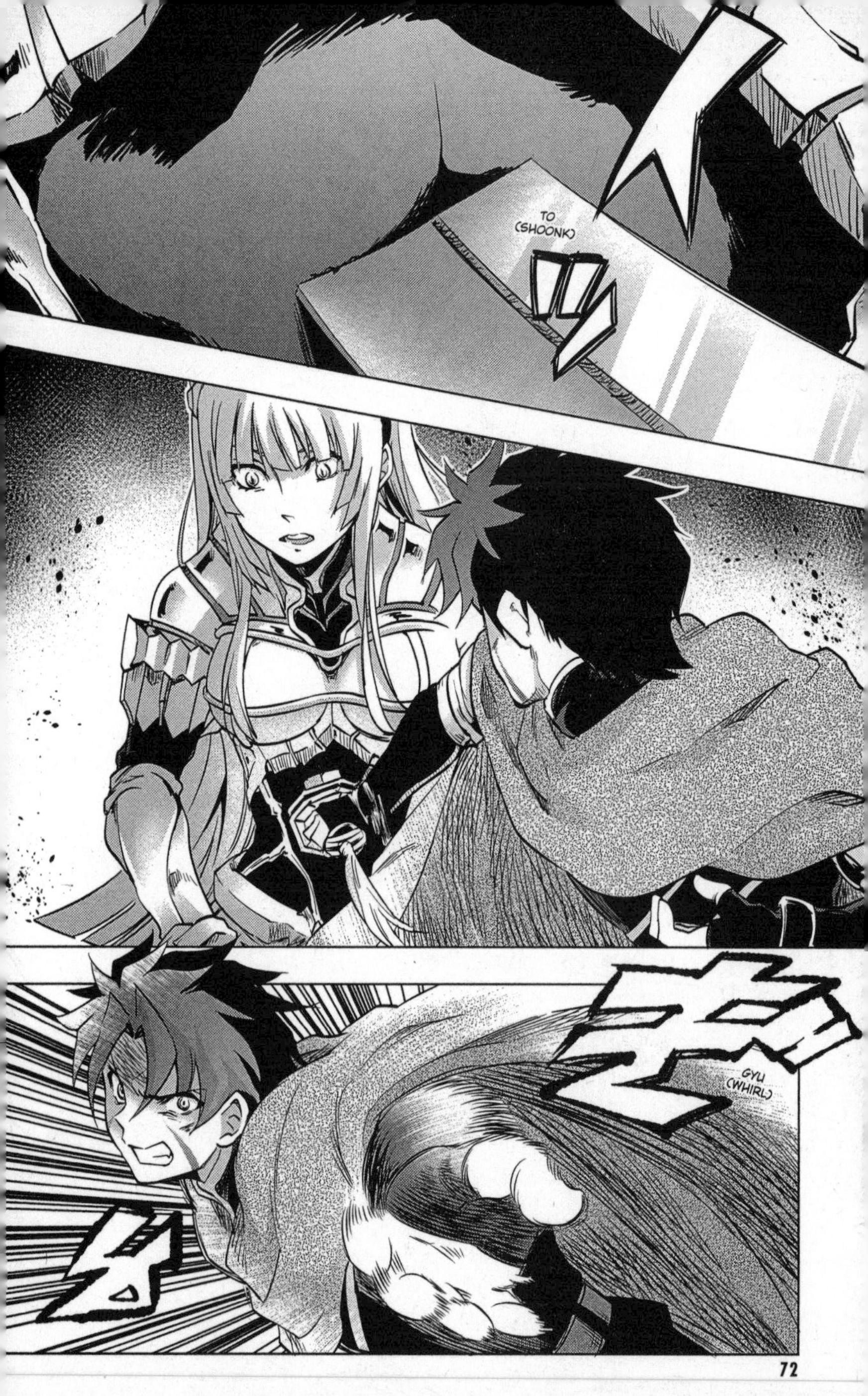
TO
(SHOONK)
GYU
(WHIRL)

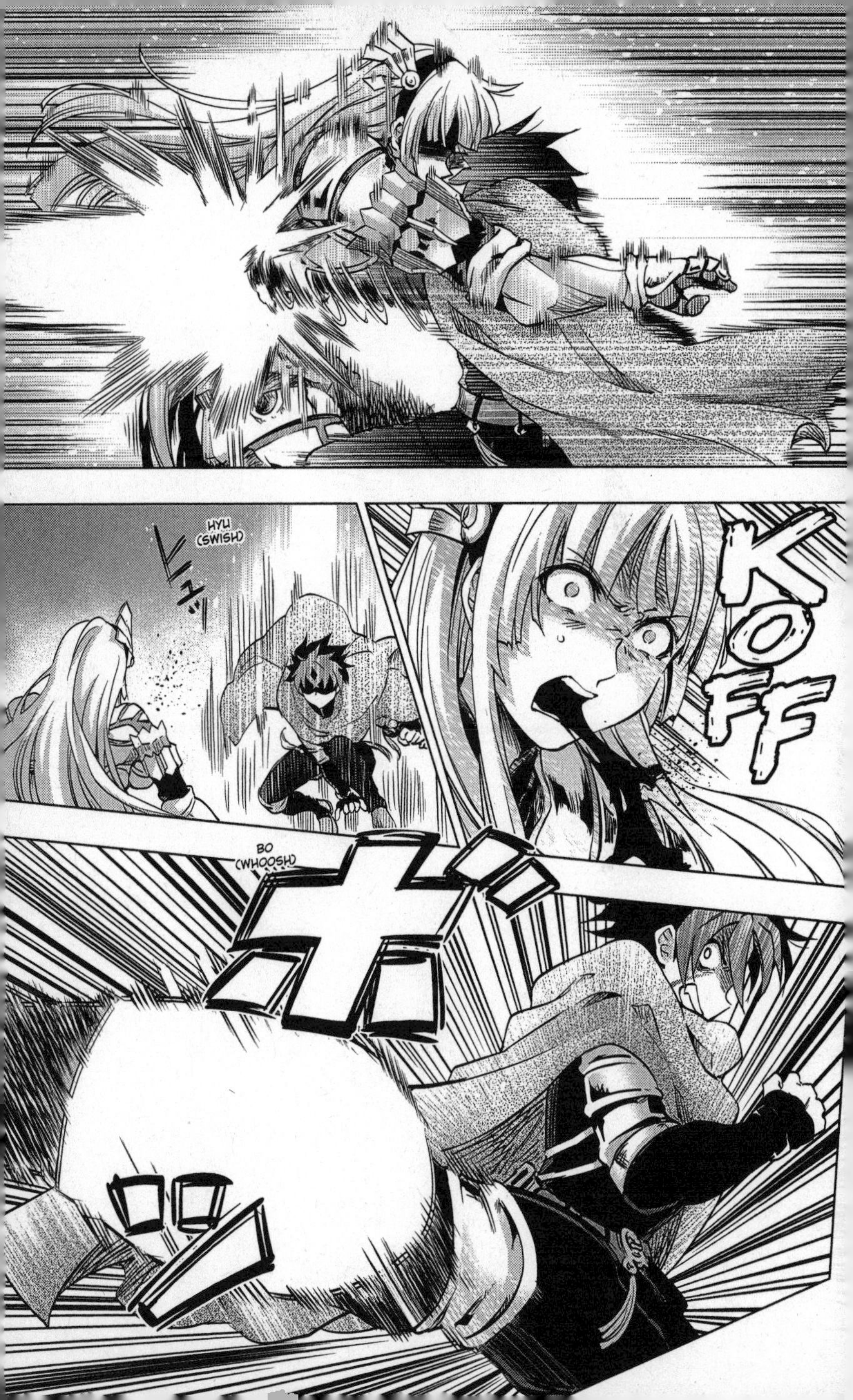
KOFF
HYU (SWISH)
BO (WHOOSH)

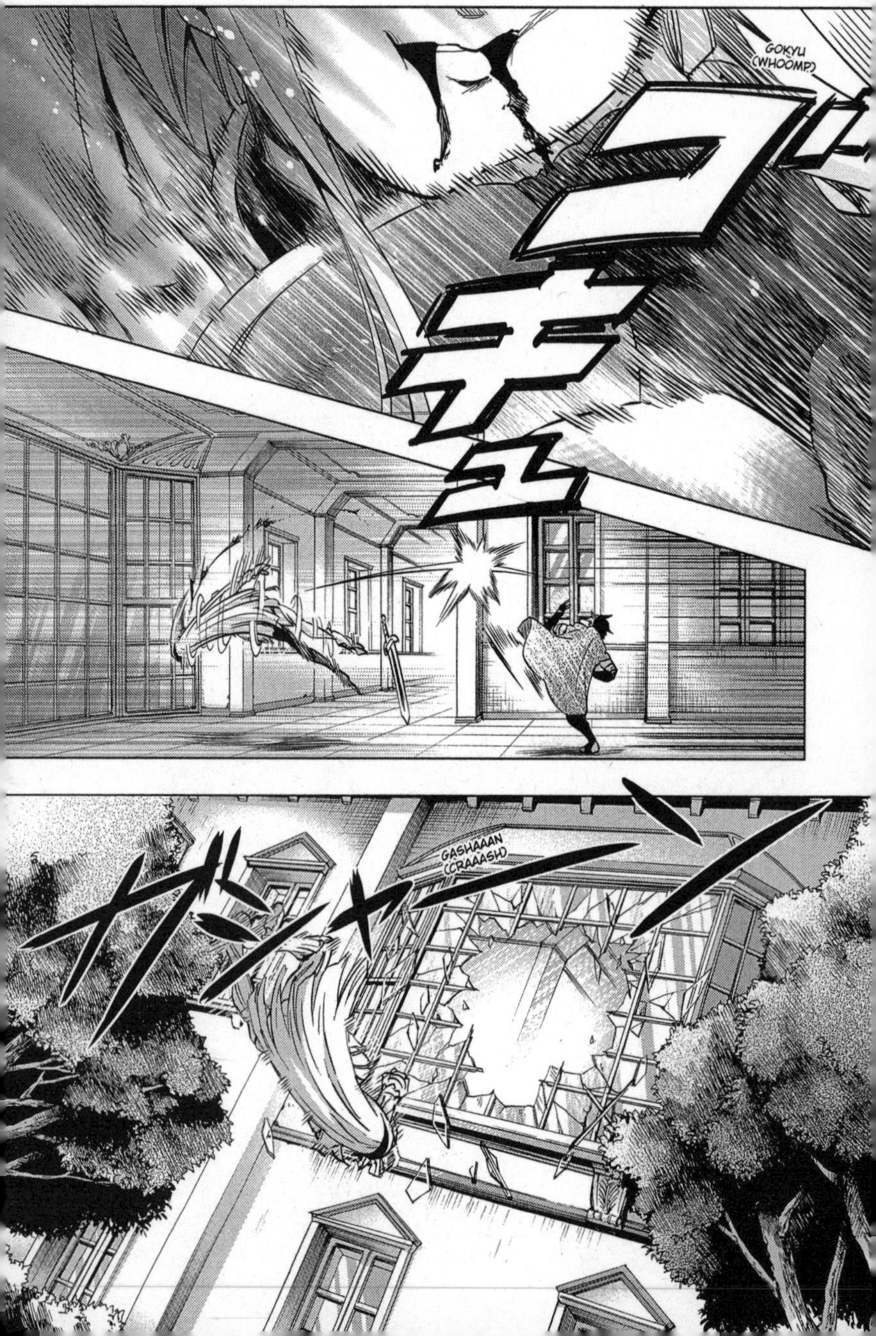
GOKYU (WHOOMP)
GASHAAAN (CRAAASH)

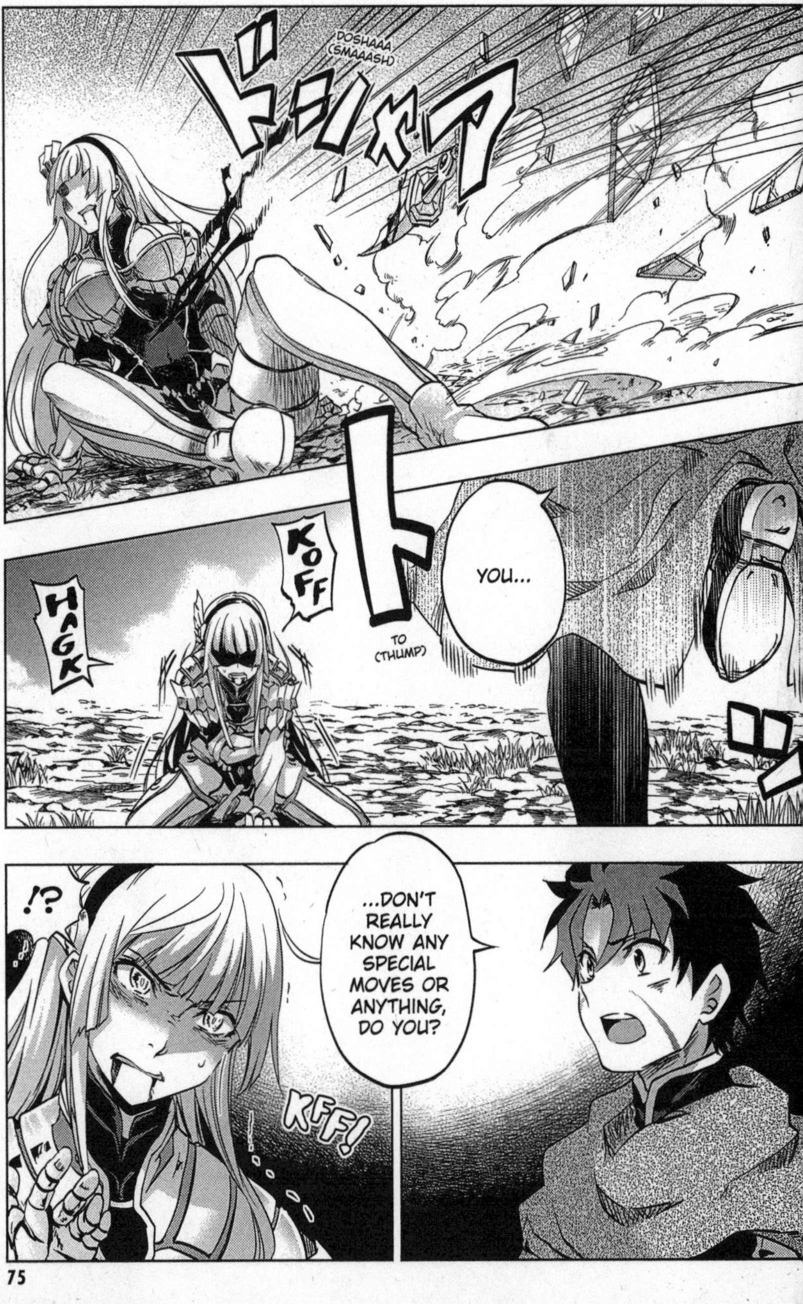

ドシャア
DOSHAAA (SMAAASH)
ト
TO (THUMP)
YOU...
KOFF
HAGK
...DON'T REALLY KNOW ANY SPECIAL MOVES OR ANYTHING, DO YOU?
!?
KFF!

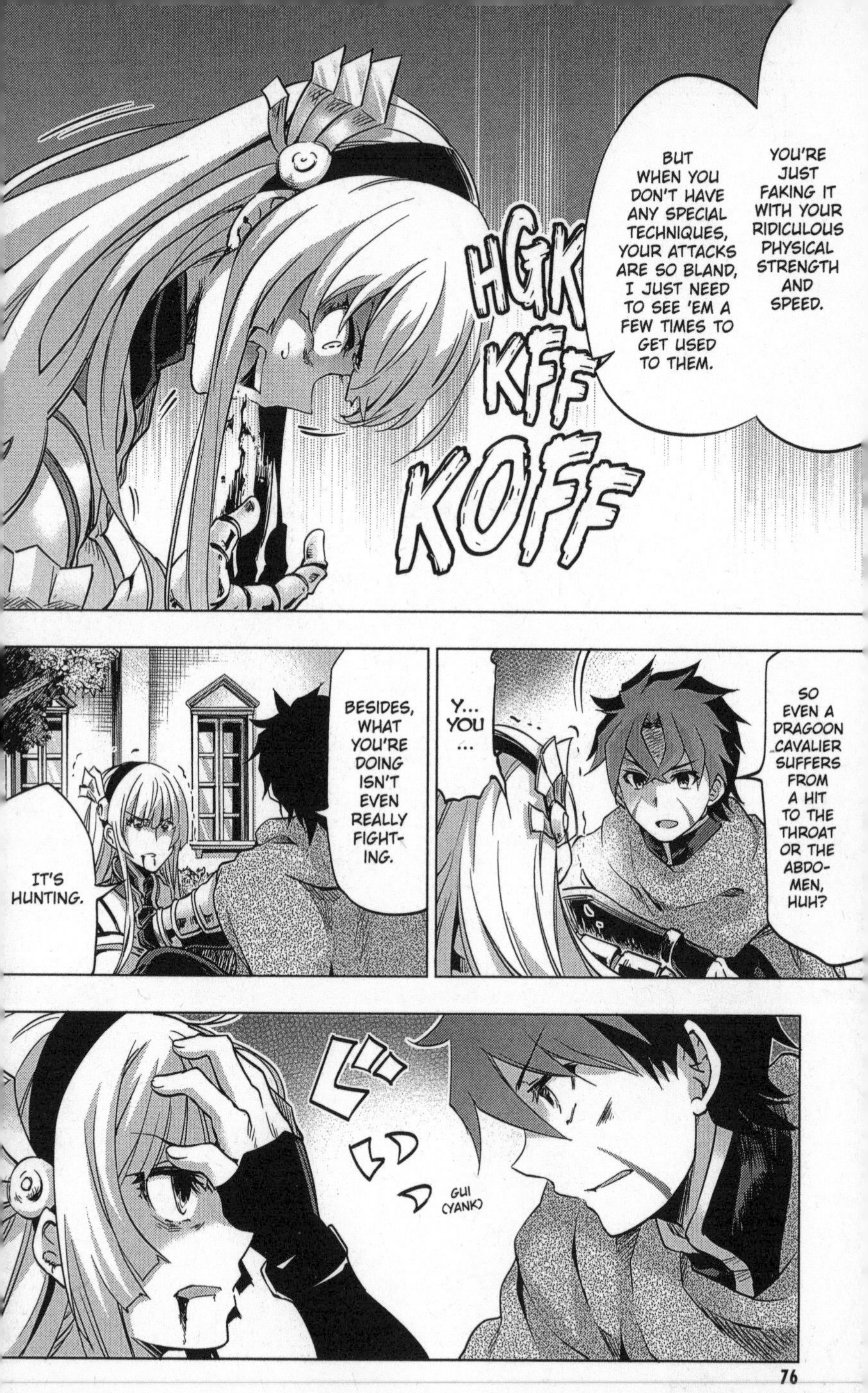
YOU'RE JUST FAKING IT WITH YOUR RIDICULOUS PHYSICAL STRENGTH AND SPEED.
BUT WHEN YOU DON'T HAVE ANY SPECIAL TECHNIQUES, YOUR ATTACKS ARE SO BLAND, I JUST NEED TO SEE 'EM A FEW TIMES TO GET USED TO THEM.
HGK KFF KOFF
SO EVEN A DRAGOON CAVALIER SUFFERS FROM A HIT TO THE THROAT OR THE ABDO-MEN, HUH?
Y... YOU ...
BESIDES, WHAT YOU'RE DOING ISN'T EVEN REALLY FIGHT-ING.
IT'S HUNTING.
GUI (YANK)

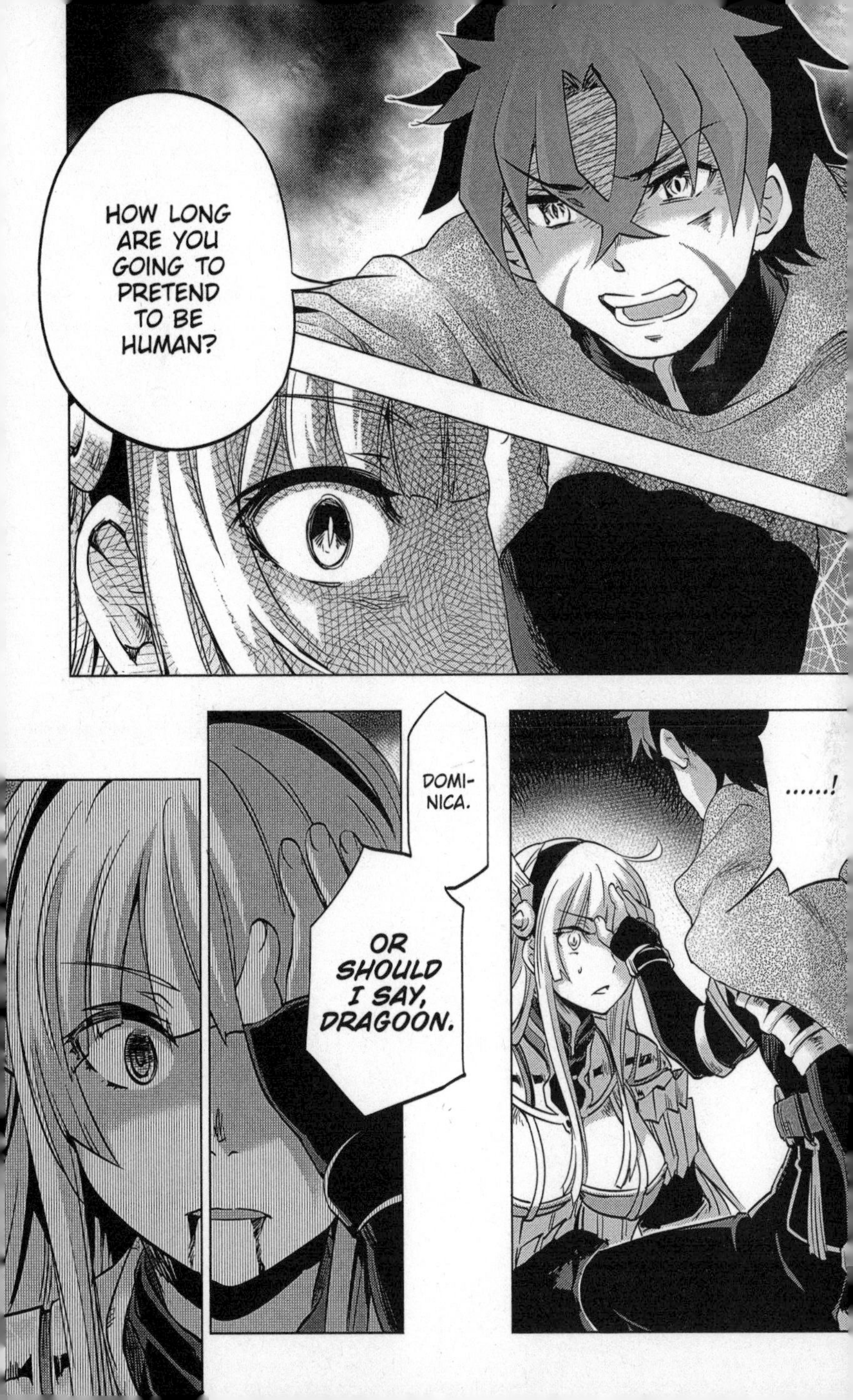
HOW LONG ARE YOU GOING TO PRETEND TO BE HUMAN?
......!
DOMINICA.
OR SHOULD I SAY, DRAGOON.

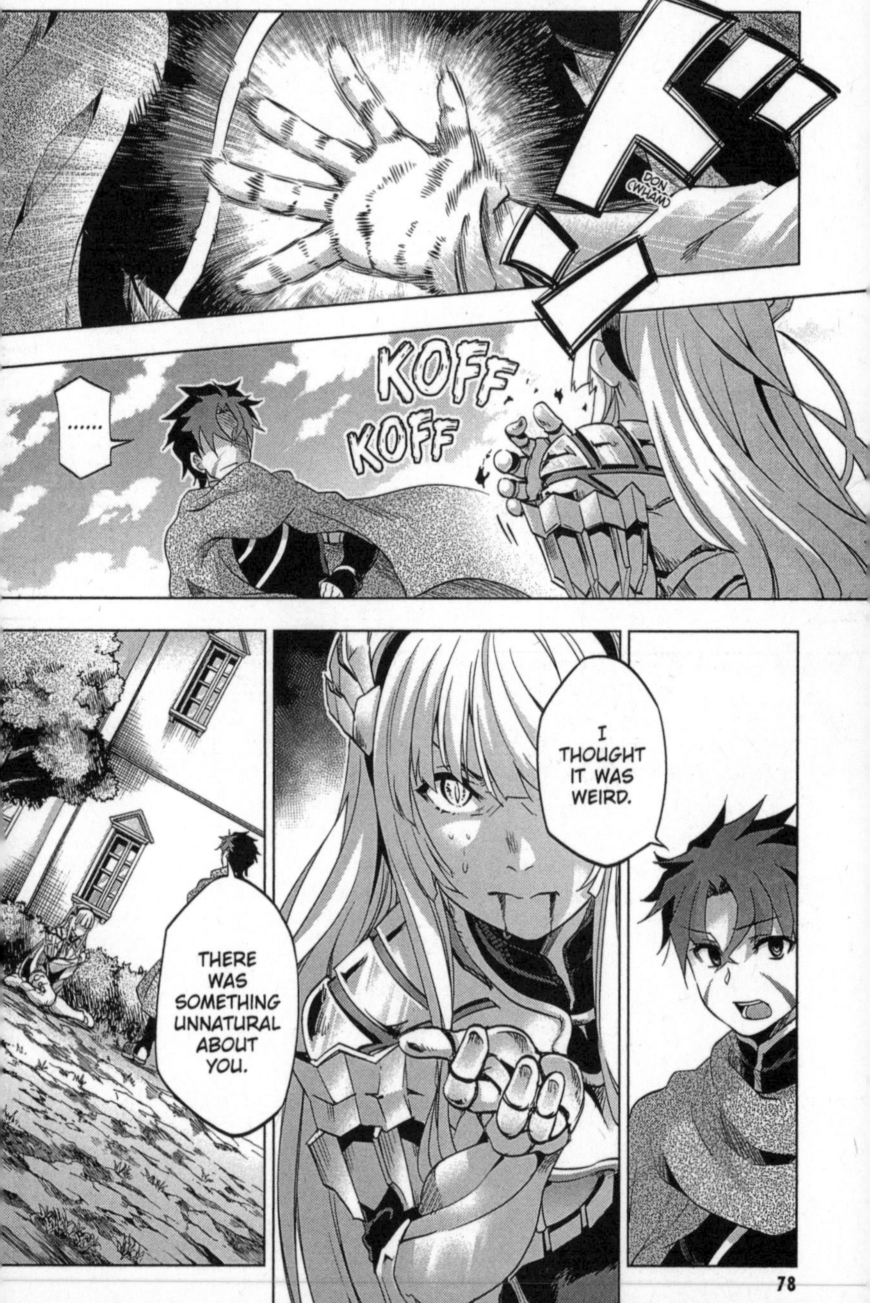
DON (WHAM)
KOFF KOFF
......
I THOUGHT IT WAS WEIRD.
THERE WAS SOMETHING UNNATURAL ABOUT YOU.

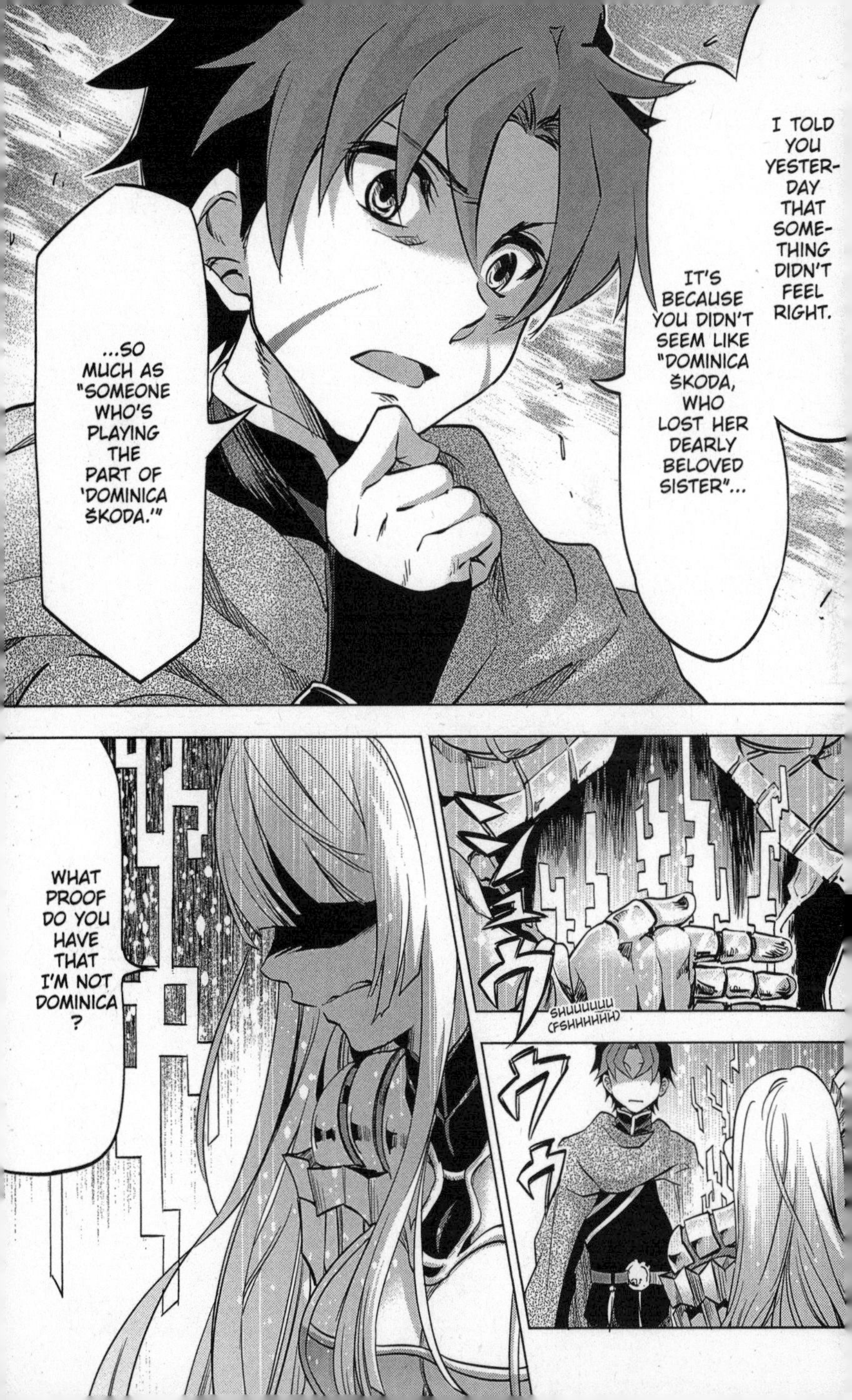
I TOLD YOU YESTER-DAY THAT SOME-THING DIDN'T FEEL RIGHT.
IT'S BECAUSE YOU DIDN'T SEEM LIKE "DOMINICA ŠKODA, WHO LOST HER DEARLY BELOVED SISTER"...
...SO MUCH AS "SOMEONE WHO'S PLAYING THE PART OF 'DOMINICA ŠKODA.'"
SHUUUUUU (FSHHHHHH)
WHAT PROOF DO YOU HAVE THAT I'M NOT DOMINICA?

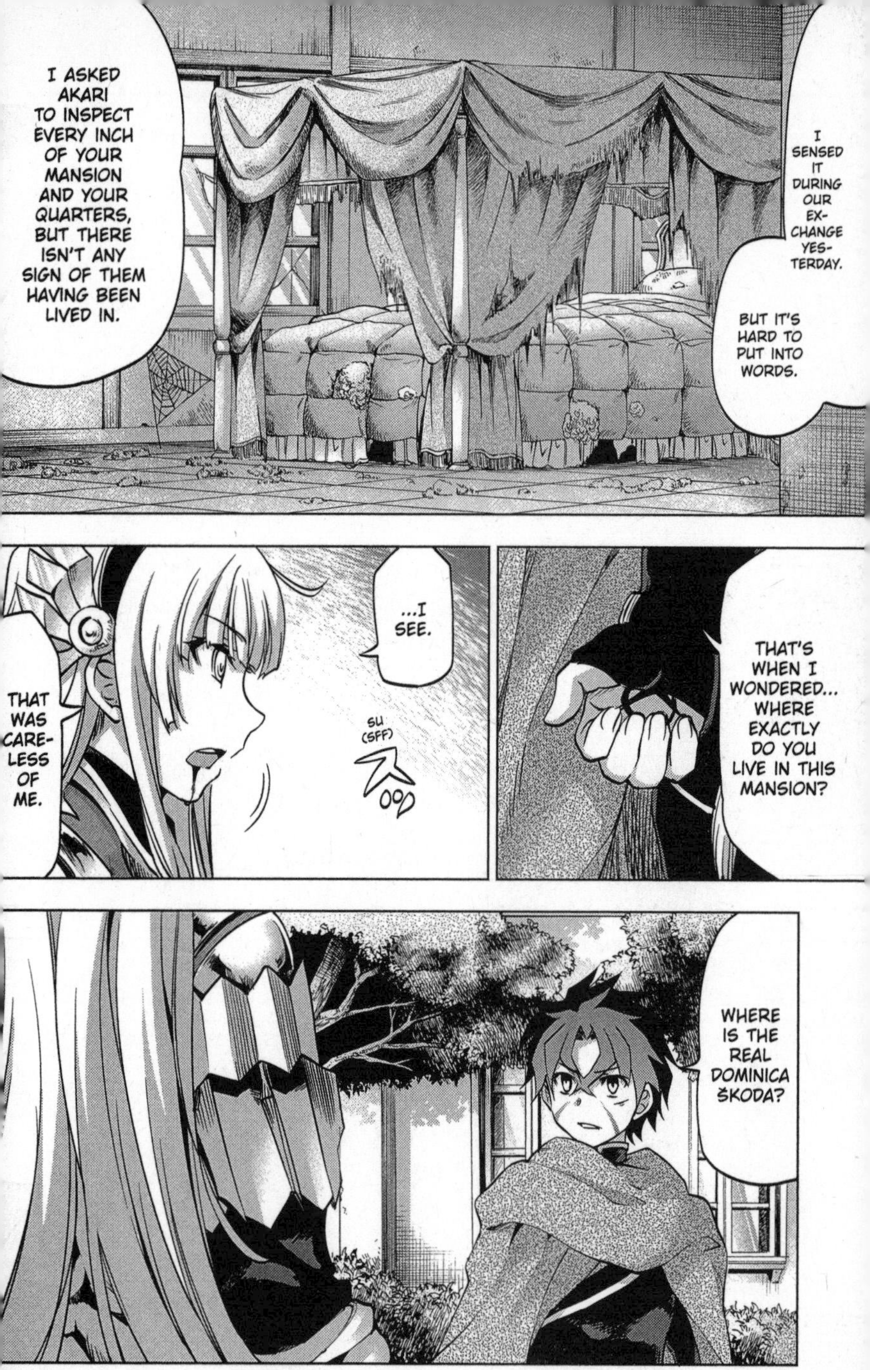
I SENSED IT DURING OUR EX-CHANGE YES-TERDAY.
BUT IT'S HARD TO PUT INTO WORDS.
I ASKED AKARI TO INSPECT EVERY INCH OF YOUR MANSION AND YOUR QUARTERS, BUT THERE ISN'T ANY SIGN OF THEM HAVING BEEN LIVED IN.
THAT'S WHEN I WONDERED... WHERE EXACTLY DO YOU LIVE IN THIS MANSION?
...I SEE.
SU (SFF)
THAT WAS CARE-LESS OF ME.
WHERE IS THE REAL DOMINICA ŠKODA?

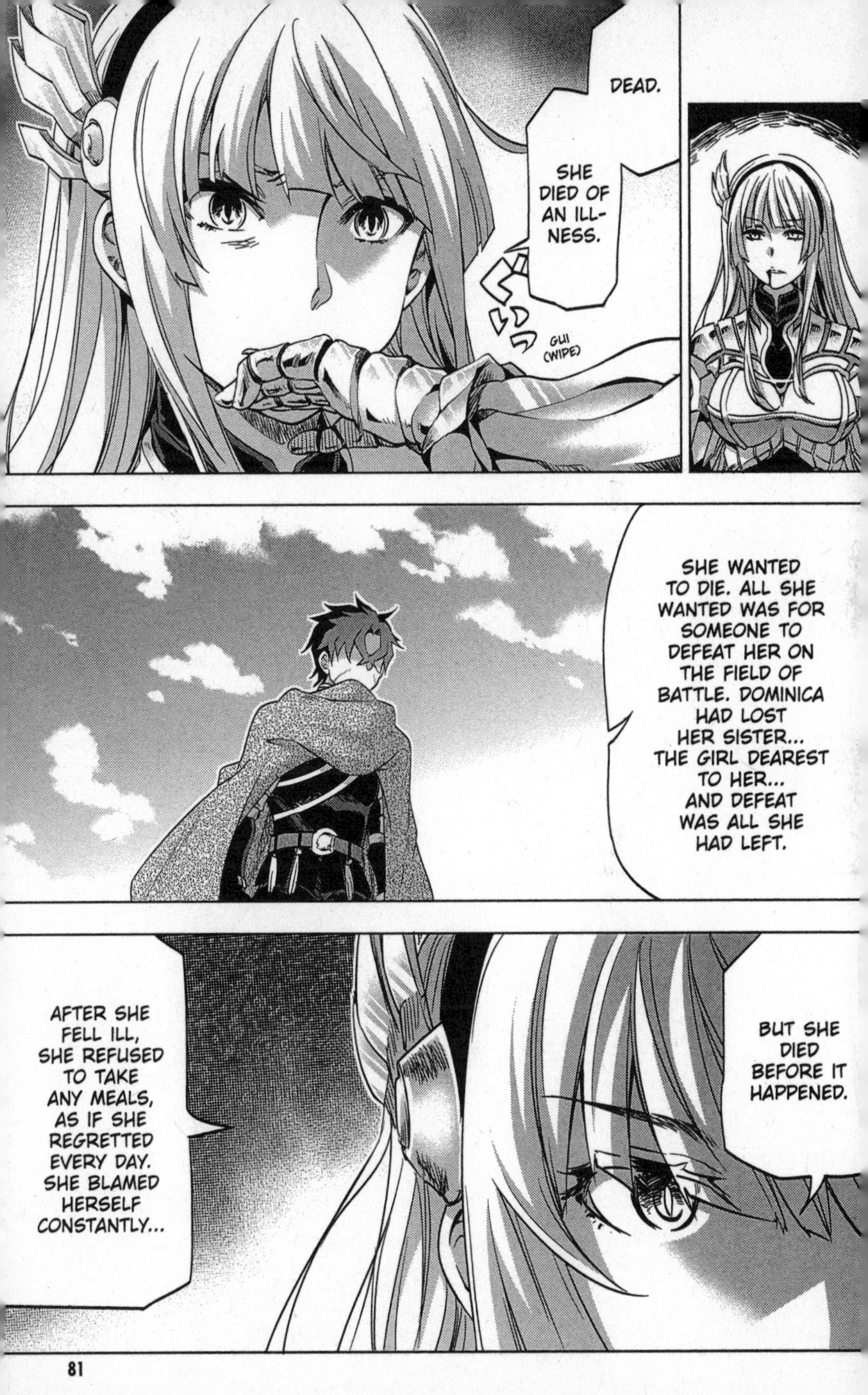
DEAD.
SHE DIED OF AN ILLNESS.
GUI (WIPE)
SHE WANTED TO DIE. ALL SHE WANTED WAS FOR SOMEONE TO DEFEAT HER ON THE FIELD OF BATTLE. DOMINICA HAD LOST HER SISTER... THE GIRL DEAREST TO HER... AND DEFEAT WAS ALL SHE HAD LEFT.
BUT SHE DIED BEFORE IT HAPPENED.
AFTER SHE FELL ILL, SHE REFUSED TO TAKE ANY MEALS, AS IF SHE REGRETTED EVERY DAY. SHE BLAMED HERSELF CONSTANTLY...

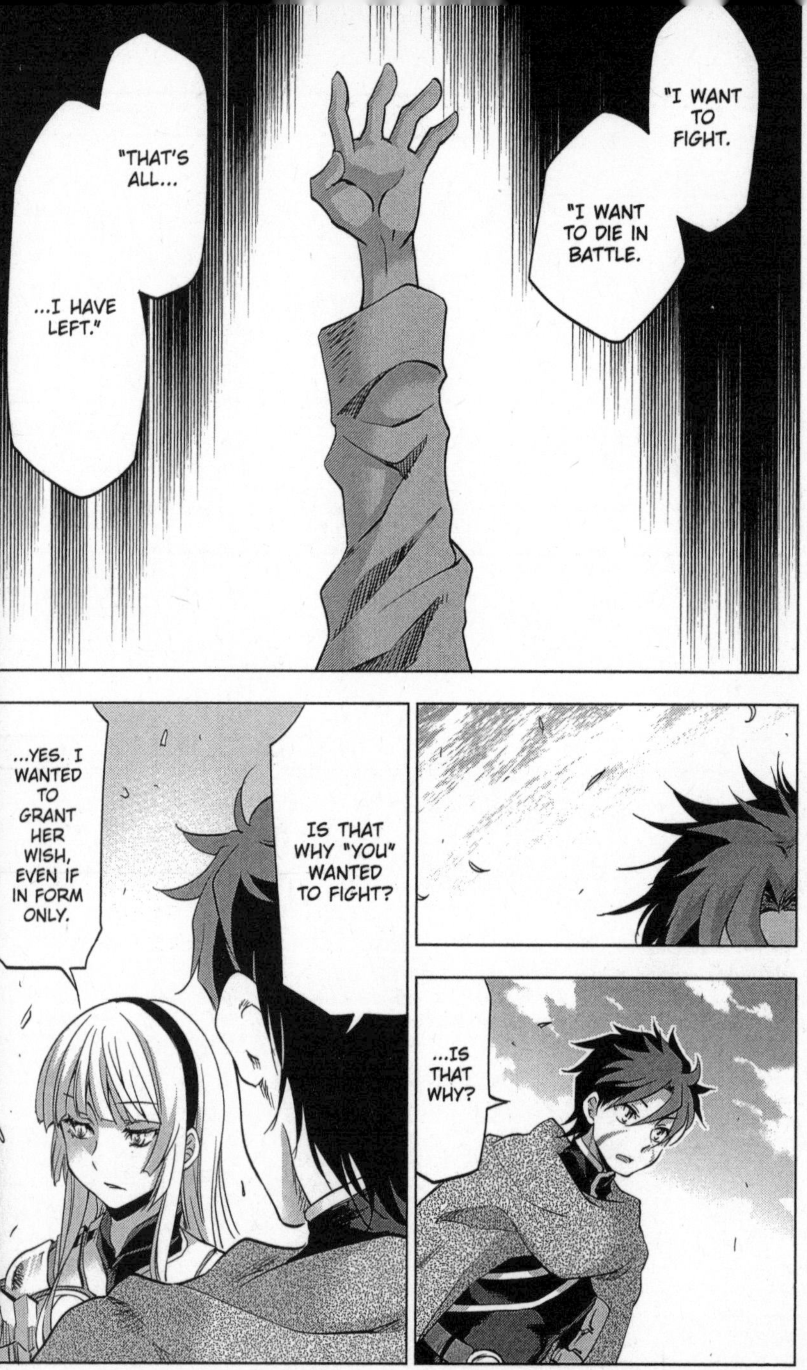
"I WANT TO FIGHT.
"I WANT TO DIE IN BATTLE.
"THAT'S ALL...
...I HAVE LEFT."
...IS THAT WHY?
IS THAT WHY "YOU" WANTED TO FIGHT?
...YES. I WANTED TO GRANT HER WISH, EVEN IF IN FORM ONLY.

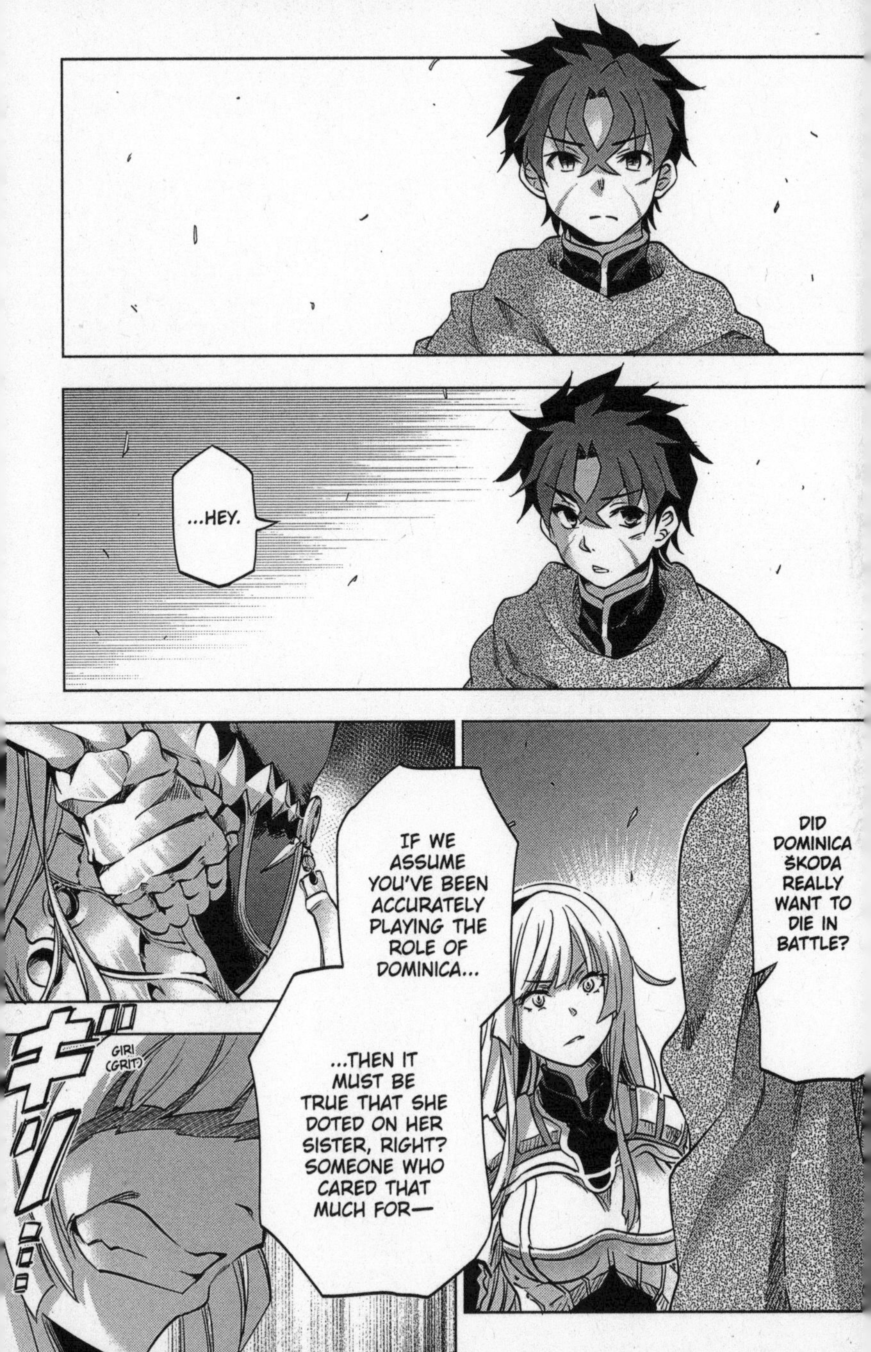
...HEY.
DID DOMINICA ŠKODA REALLY WANT TO DIE IN BATTLE?
IF WE ASSUME YOU'VE BEEN ACCURATELY PLAYING THE ROLE OF DOMINICA...
...THEN IT MUST BE TRUE THAT SHE DOTED ON HER SISTER, RIGHT? SOMEONE WHO CARED THAT MUCH FOR—
GIRI (GRIT)

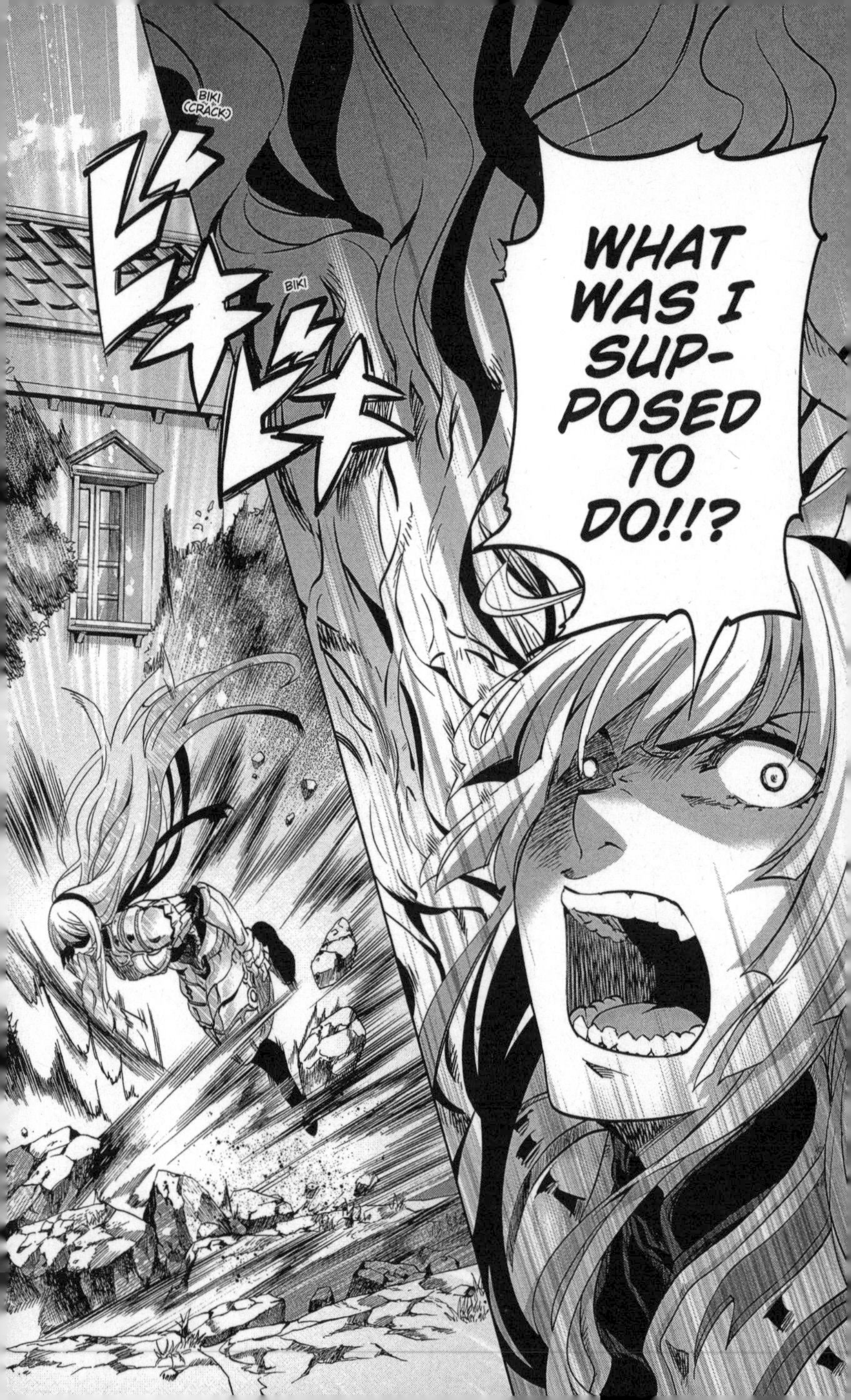
WHAT WAS I SUP-POSED TO DO!!?
BIKI (CRACK)
BIKI

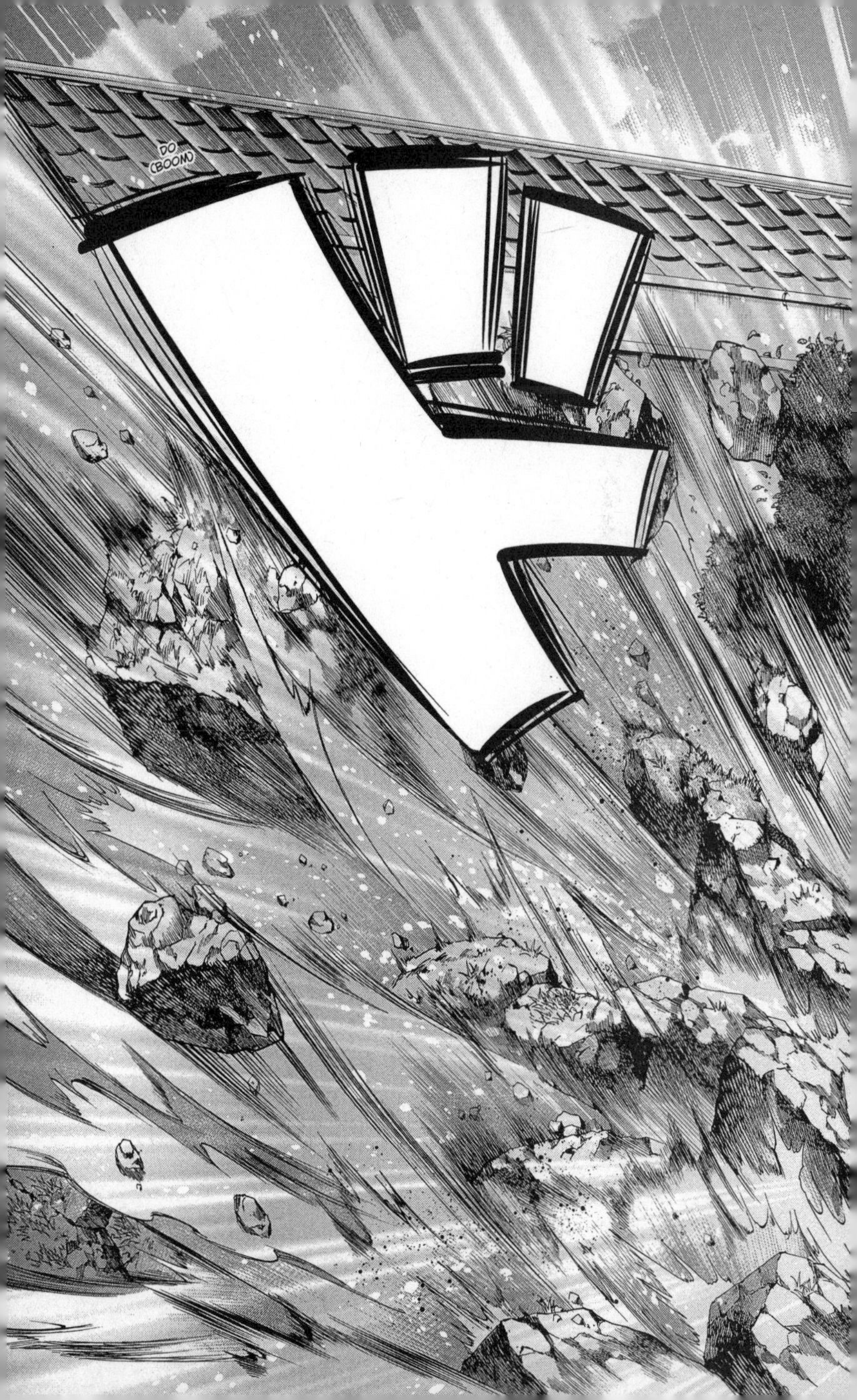
DO
(BOOM)

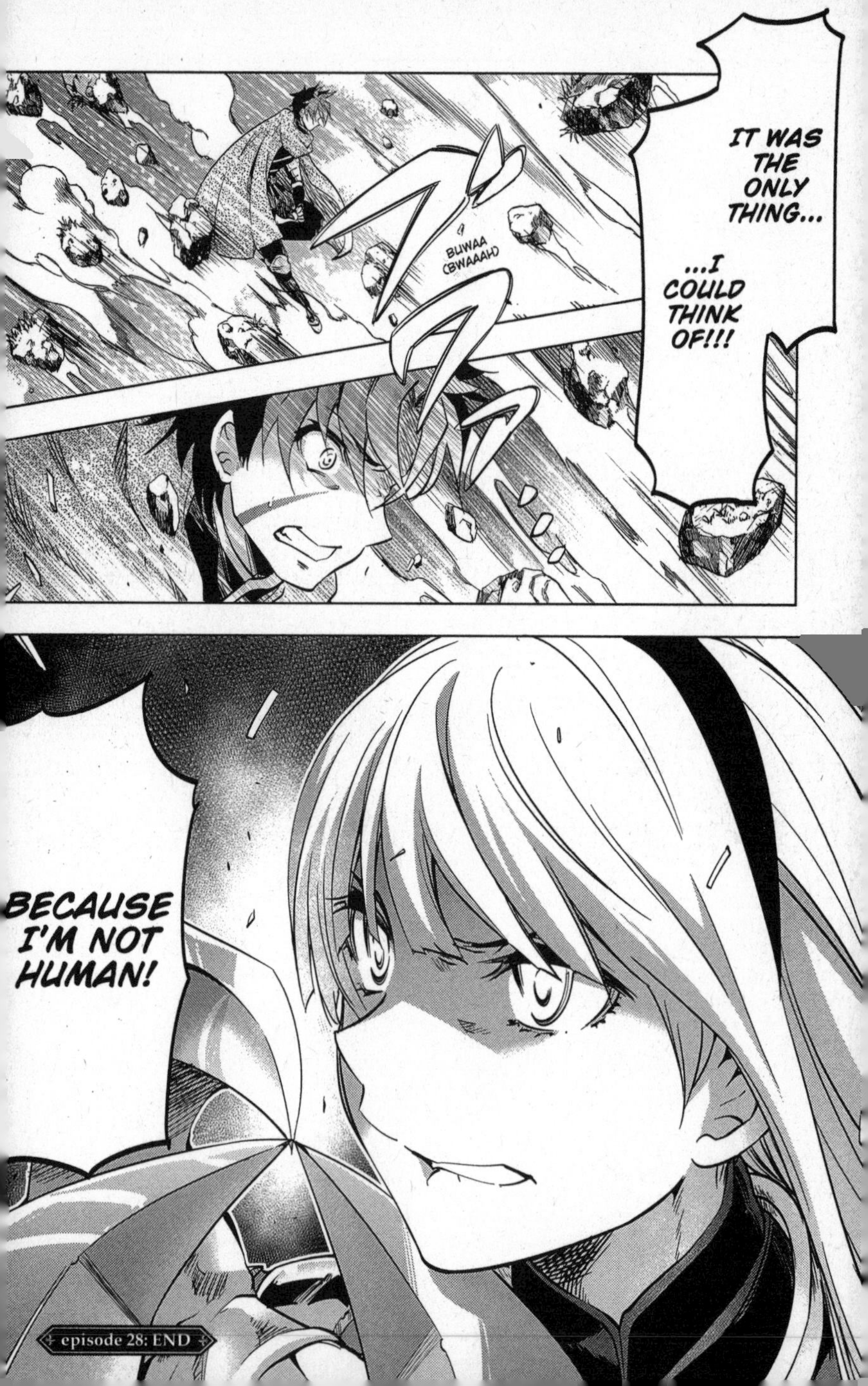
IT WAS THE ONLY THING...
...I COULD THINK OF!!!
BUWAA (BWAAAH)
BECAUSE I'M NOT HUMAN!
episode 28: END

CHAIKA: THE COFFiN PRINCESS

episode 29: The Battle Ends

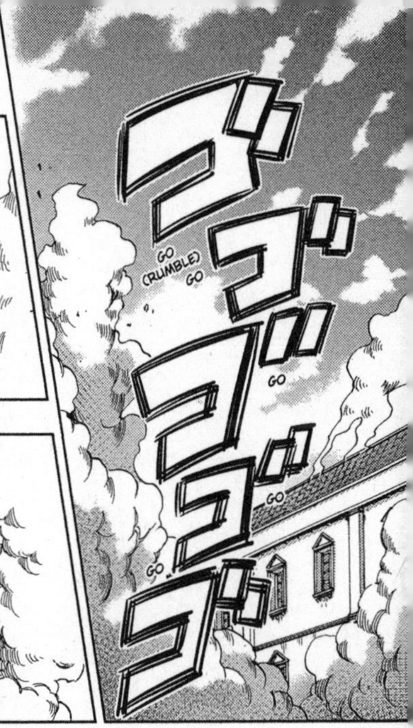
GO (RUMBLE) GO
GO
GO
GO

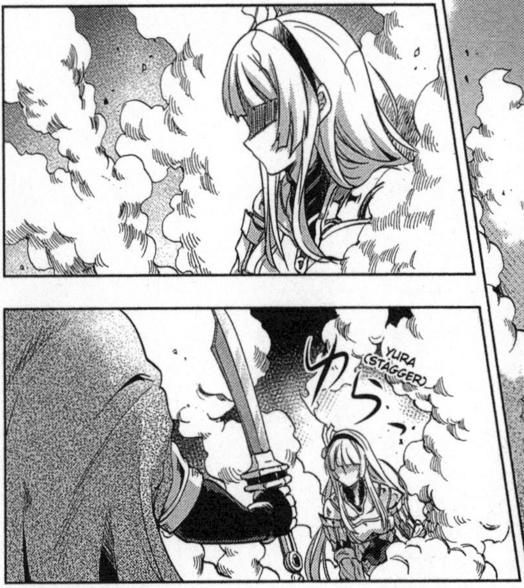
YURA (STAGGER)

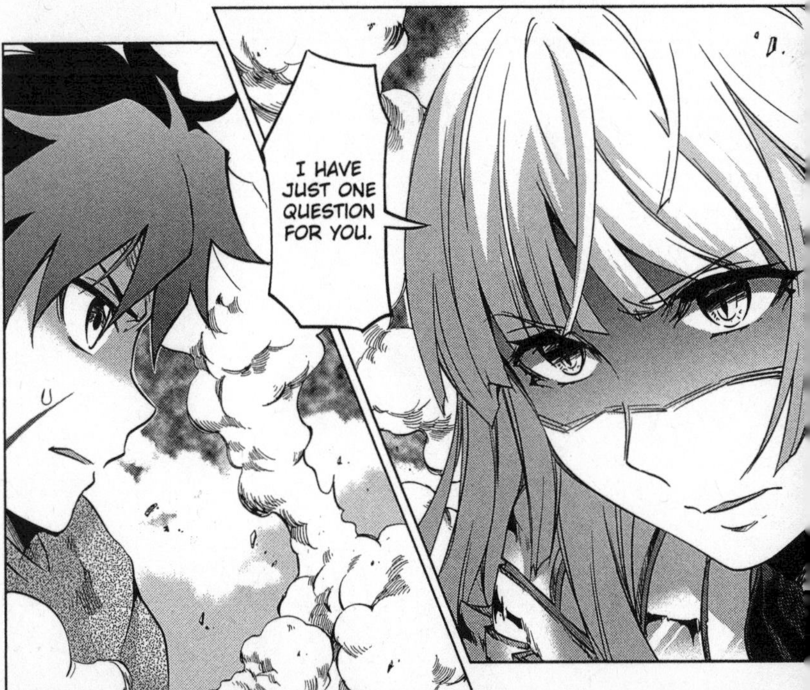
I HAVE JUST ONE QUESTION FOR YOU.

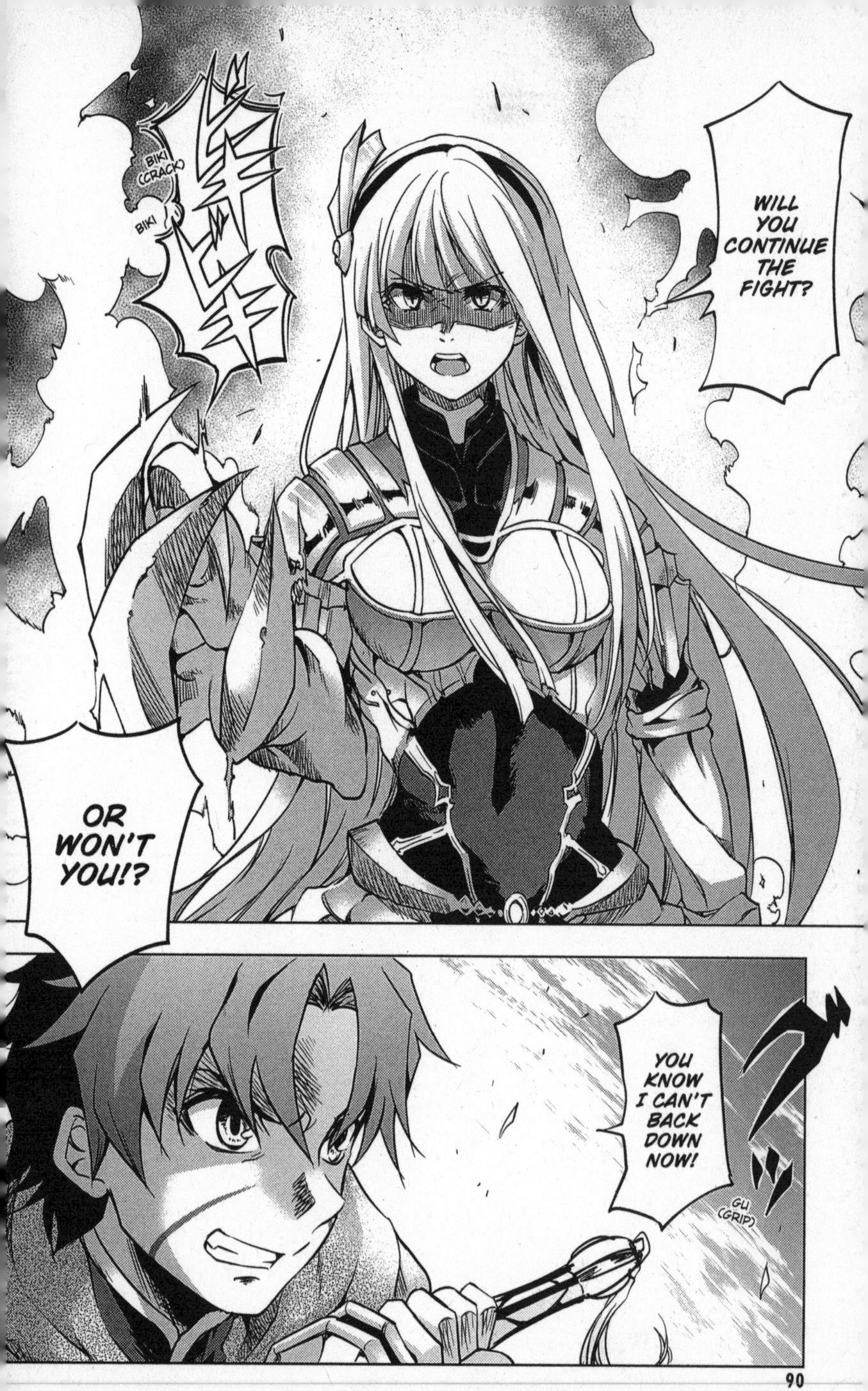
WILL YOU CONTINUE THE FIGHT?
BIKI (CRACK)
BIKI
OR WON'T YOU!?
GU (GRIP)
YOU KNOW I CAN'T BACK DOWN NOW!

episode 29:

The Battle Ends

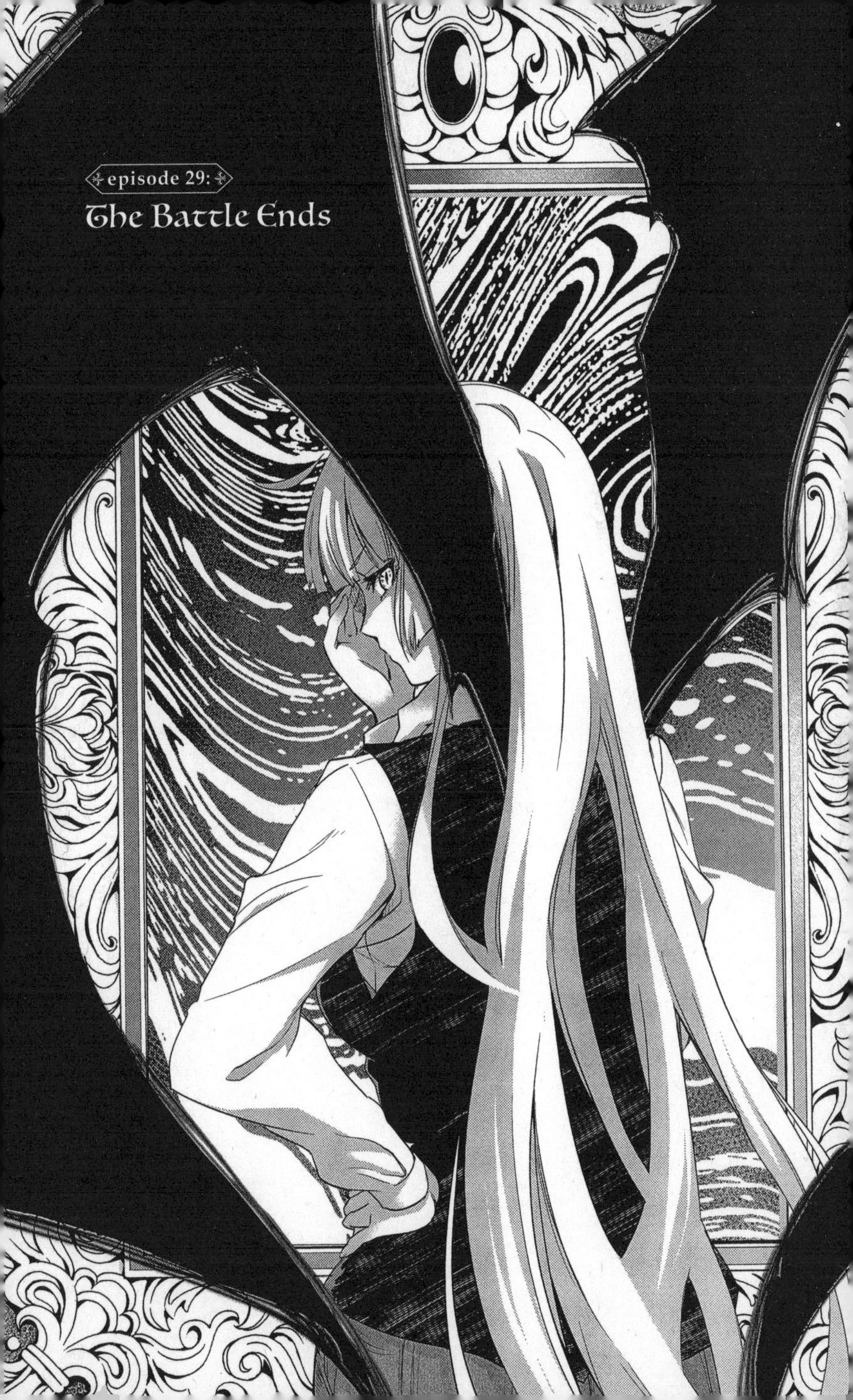

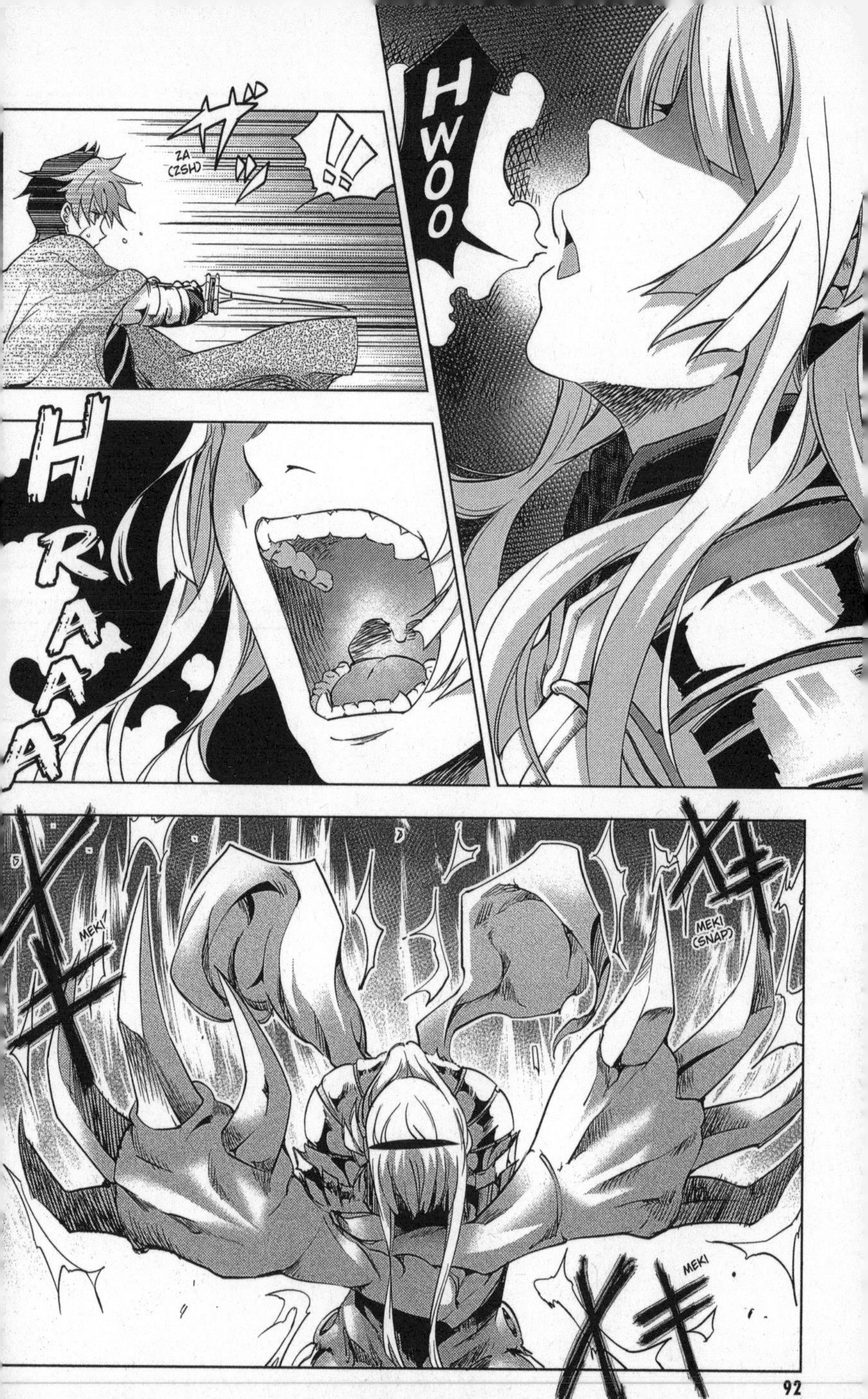
HWOO
ZA (ZSH)
!!
HRAAAA
MEKI (SNAP)
MEKI
MEKI

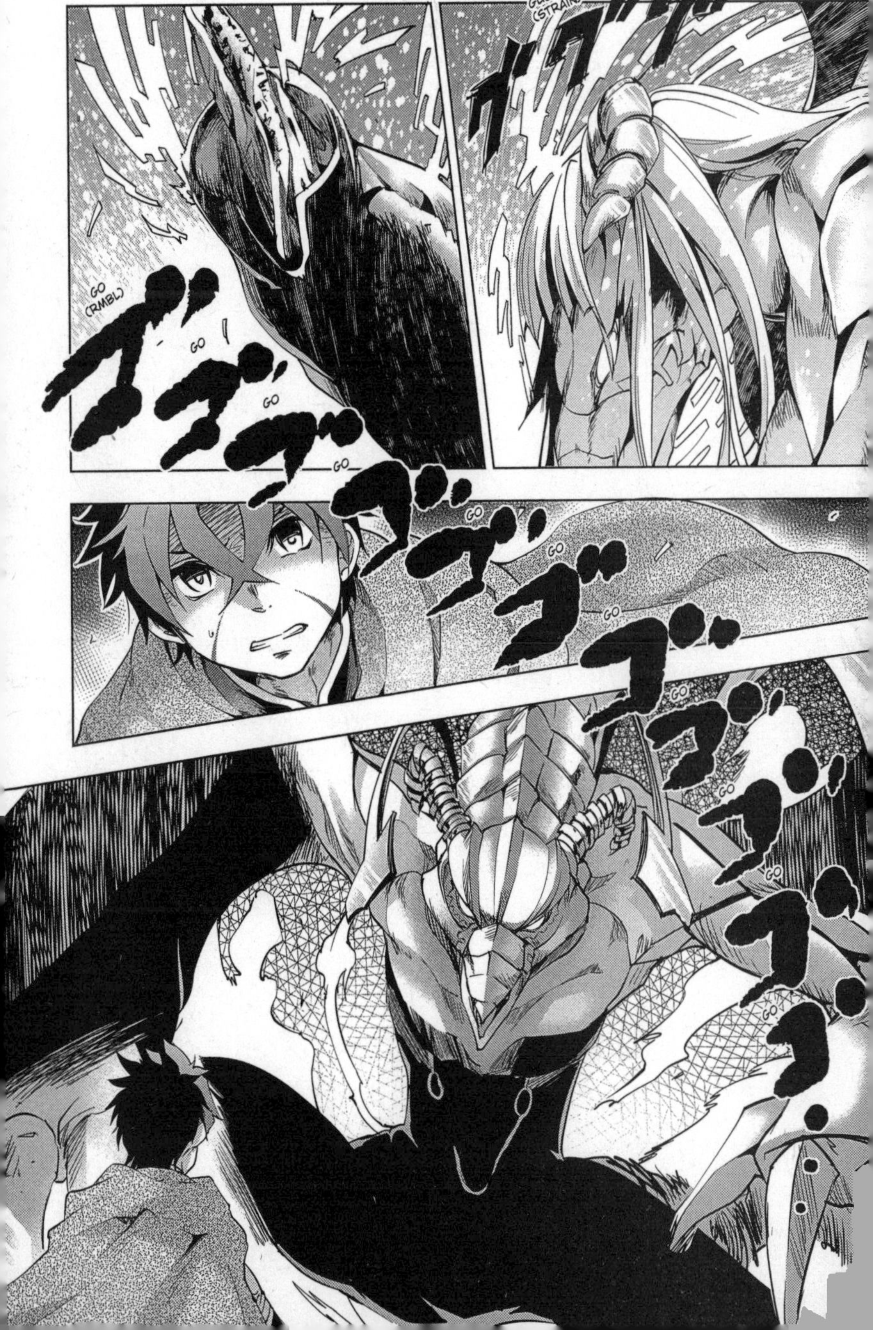
GUGUGU (STRAIN)
GO (RMBL)
GO
GO
GO
GO
GO
GO
GO
GO
GO
GO

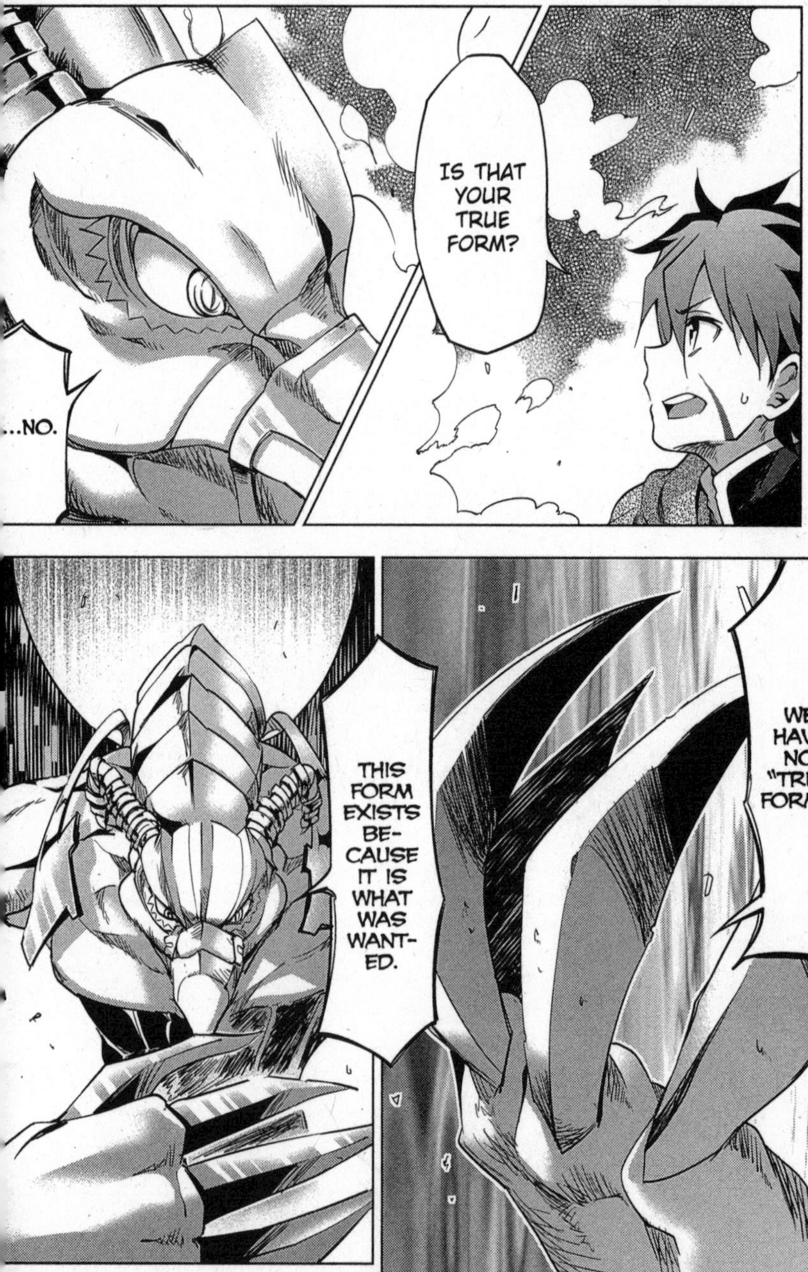
IS THAT YOUR TRUE FORM?
...NO.
WE HAVE NO "TRUE FORM."
THIS FORM EXISTS BE-CAUSE IT IS WHAT WAS WANT-ED.

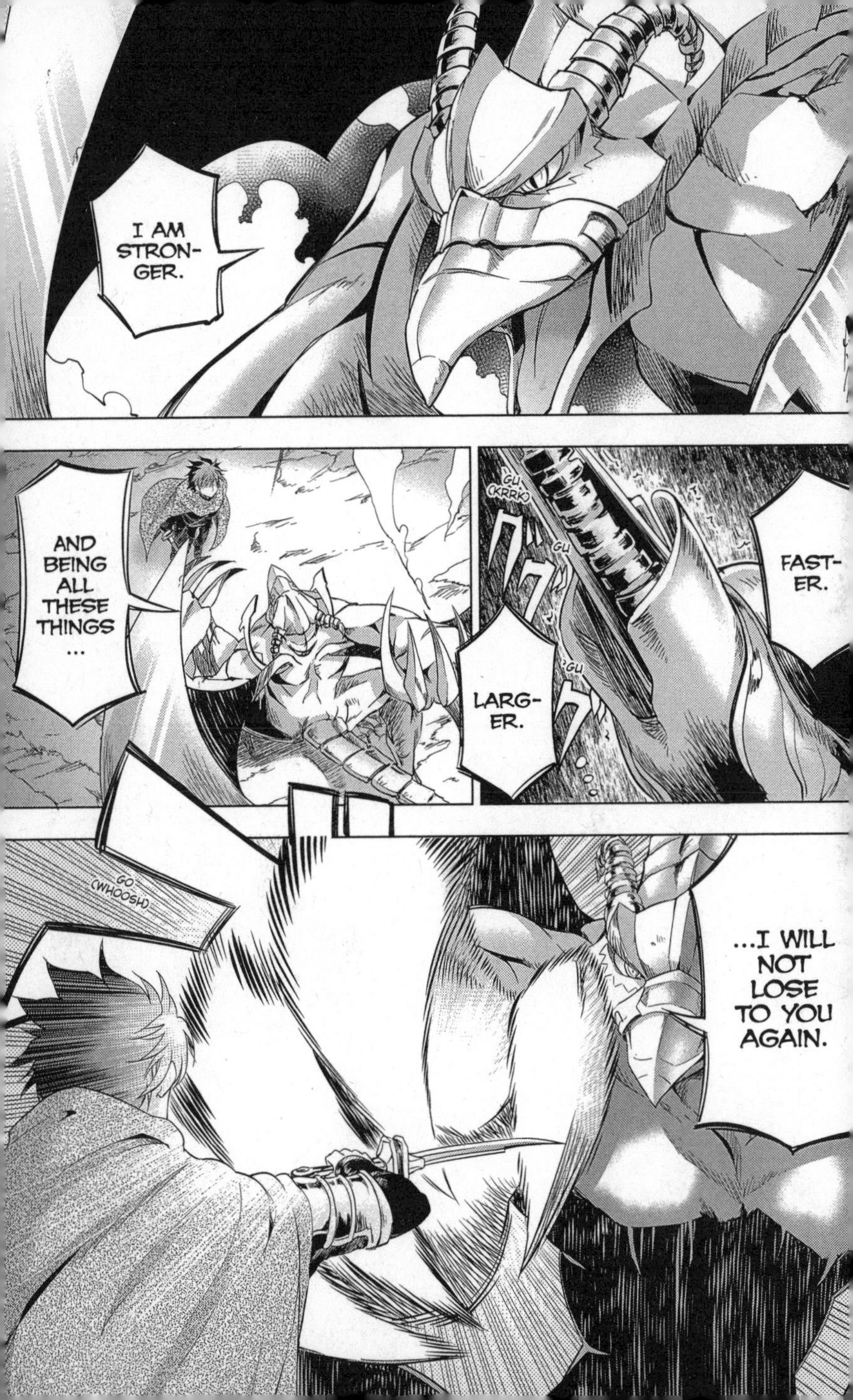
I AM STRONG-ER.
GU (KRRK)
GU
GU
FAST-ER.
LARG-ER.
AND BEING ALL THESE THINGS...
...I WILL NOT LOSE TO YOU AGAIN.
GO (WHOOSH)

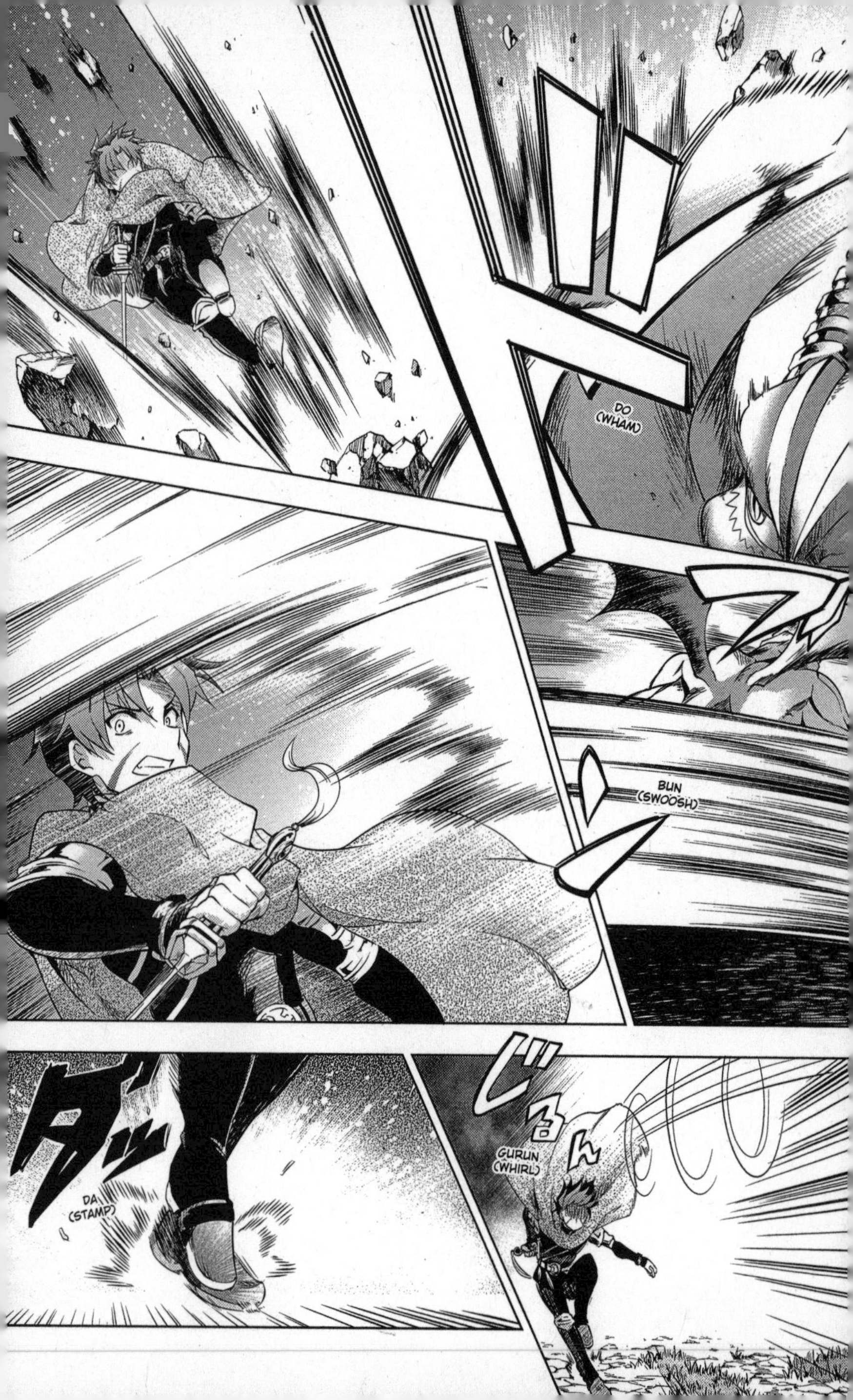
DO
(WHAM)
BUN
(SWOOSH)
GURUN
(WHIRL)
DA
(STAMP)

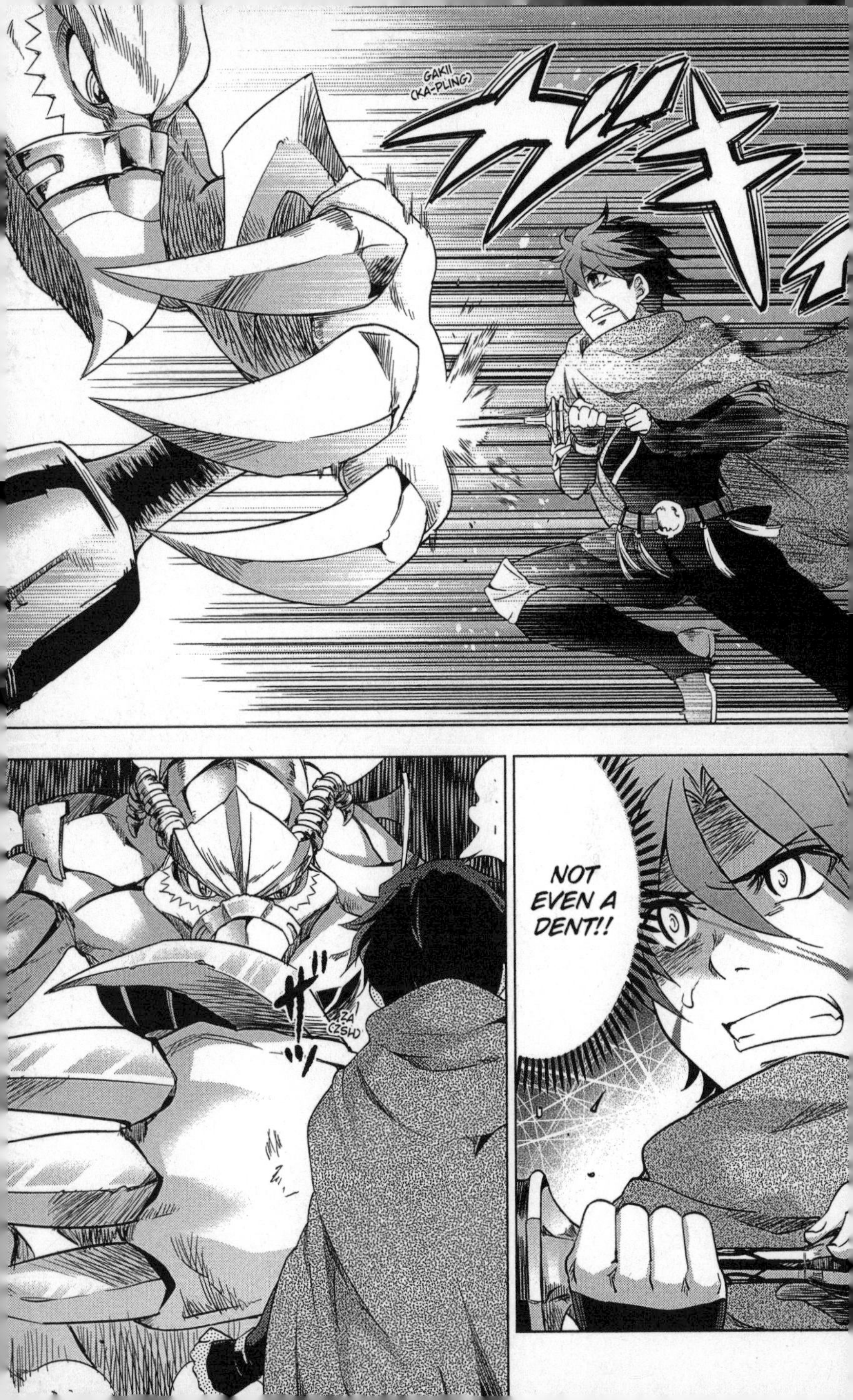
GAKII (KA-PLING)
NOT EVEN A DENT!!
ZA (ZSH)

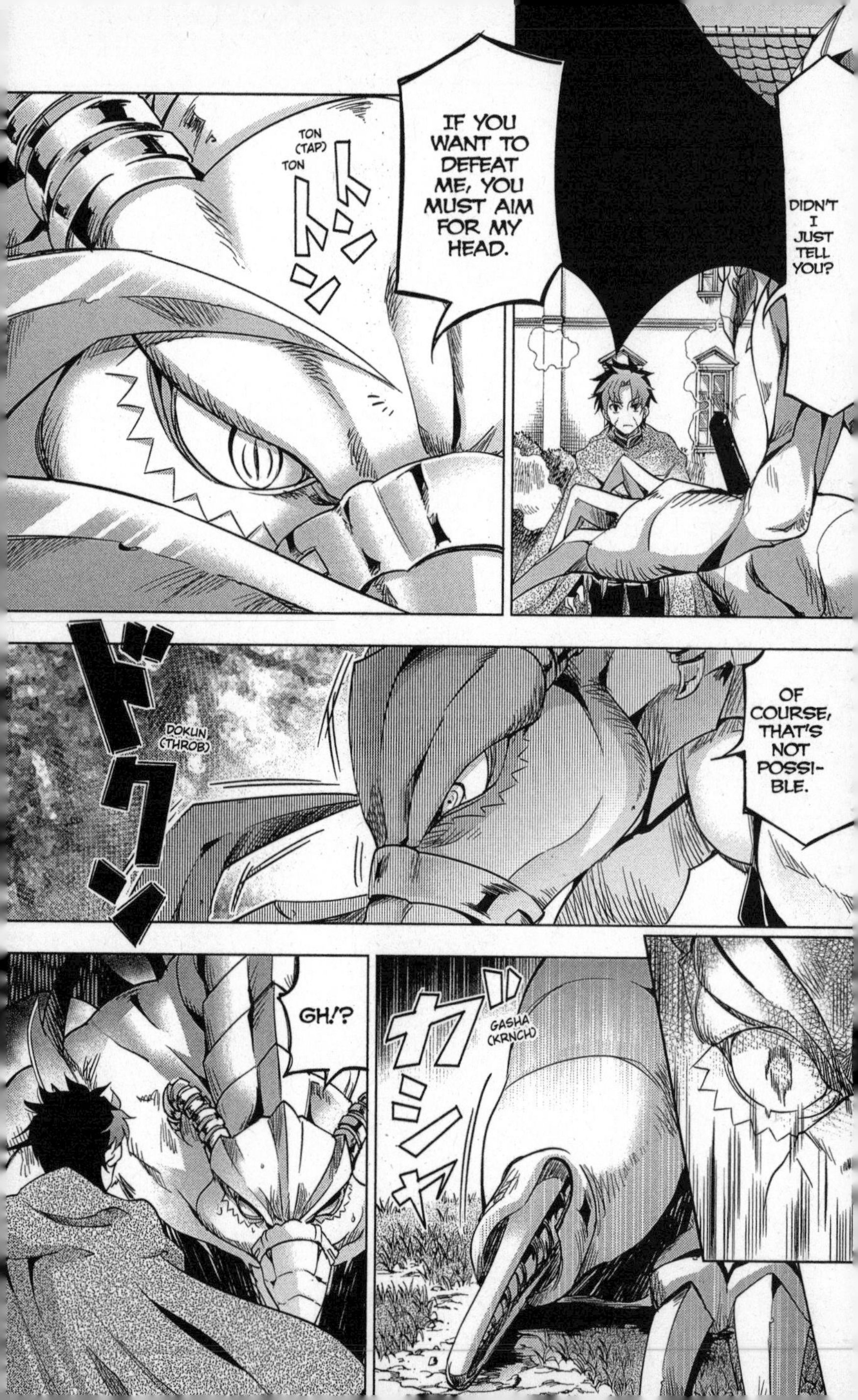
DIDN'T I JUST TELL YOU?
IF YOU WANT TO DEFEAT ME, YOU MUST AIM FOR MY HEAD.
TON (TAP) TON
OF COURSE, THAT'S NOT POSSI-BLE.
DOKUN (THROB)
GASHA (KRNCH)
GH!?

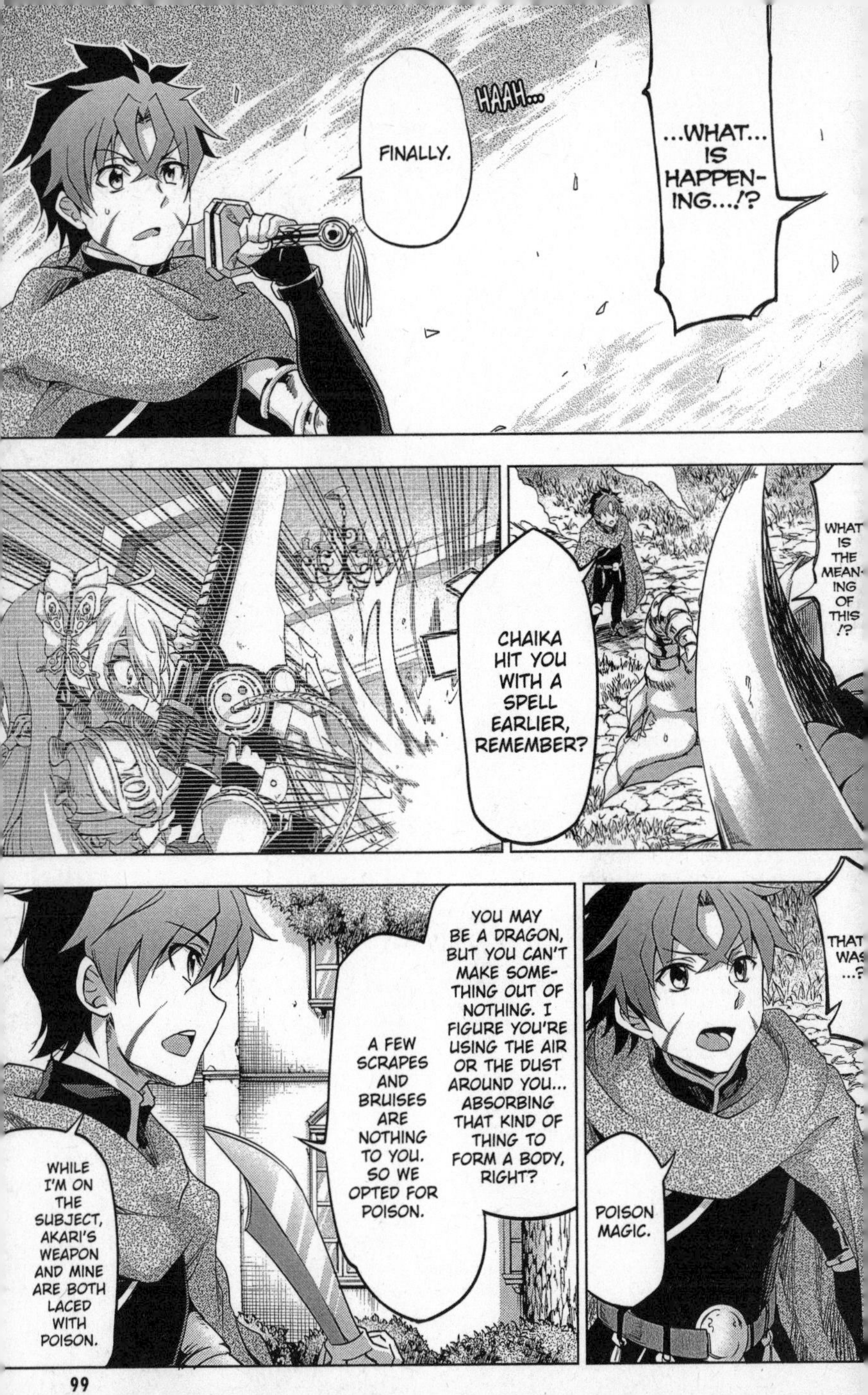

...WHAT... IS HAPPEN-ING...!?
HAAH...
FINALLY.
WHAT IS THE MEAN-ING OF THIS!?
CHAIKA HIT YOU WITH A SPELL EARLIER, REMEMBER?
THAT WAS ...?
POISON MAGIC.
YOU MAY BE A DRAGON, BUT YOU CAN'T MAKE SOME-THING OUT OF NOTHING. I FIGURE YOU'RE USING THE AIR OR THE DUST AROUND YOU... ABSORBING THAT KIND OF THING TO FORM A BODY, RIGHT?
A FEW SCRAPES AND BRUISES ARE NOTHING TO YOU. SO WE OPTED FOR POISON.
WHILE I'M ON THE SUBJECT, AKARI'S WEAPON AND MINE ARE BOTH LACED WITH POISON.

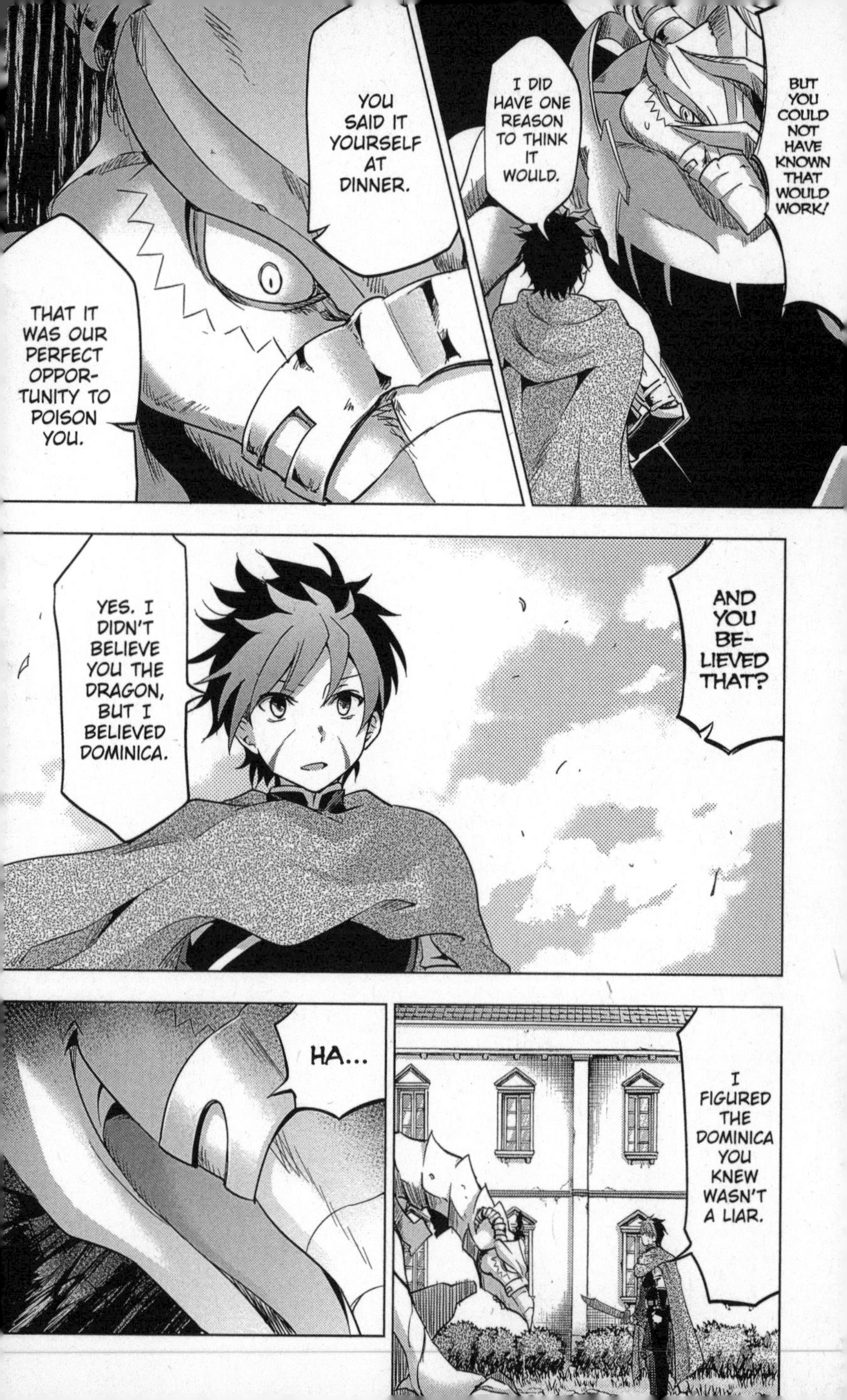

BUT YOU COULD NOT HAVE KNOWN THAT WOULD WORK!
I DID HAVE ONE REASON TO THINK IT WOULD.
YOU SAID IT YOURSELF AT DINNER.
THAT IT WAS OUR PERFECT OPPOR-TUNITY TO POISON YOU.
AND YOU BE-LIEVED THAT?
YES. I DIDN'T BELIEVE YOU THE DRAGON, BUT I BELIEVED DOMINICA.
I FIGURED THE DOMINICA YOU KNEW WASN'T A LIAR.
HA...

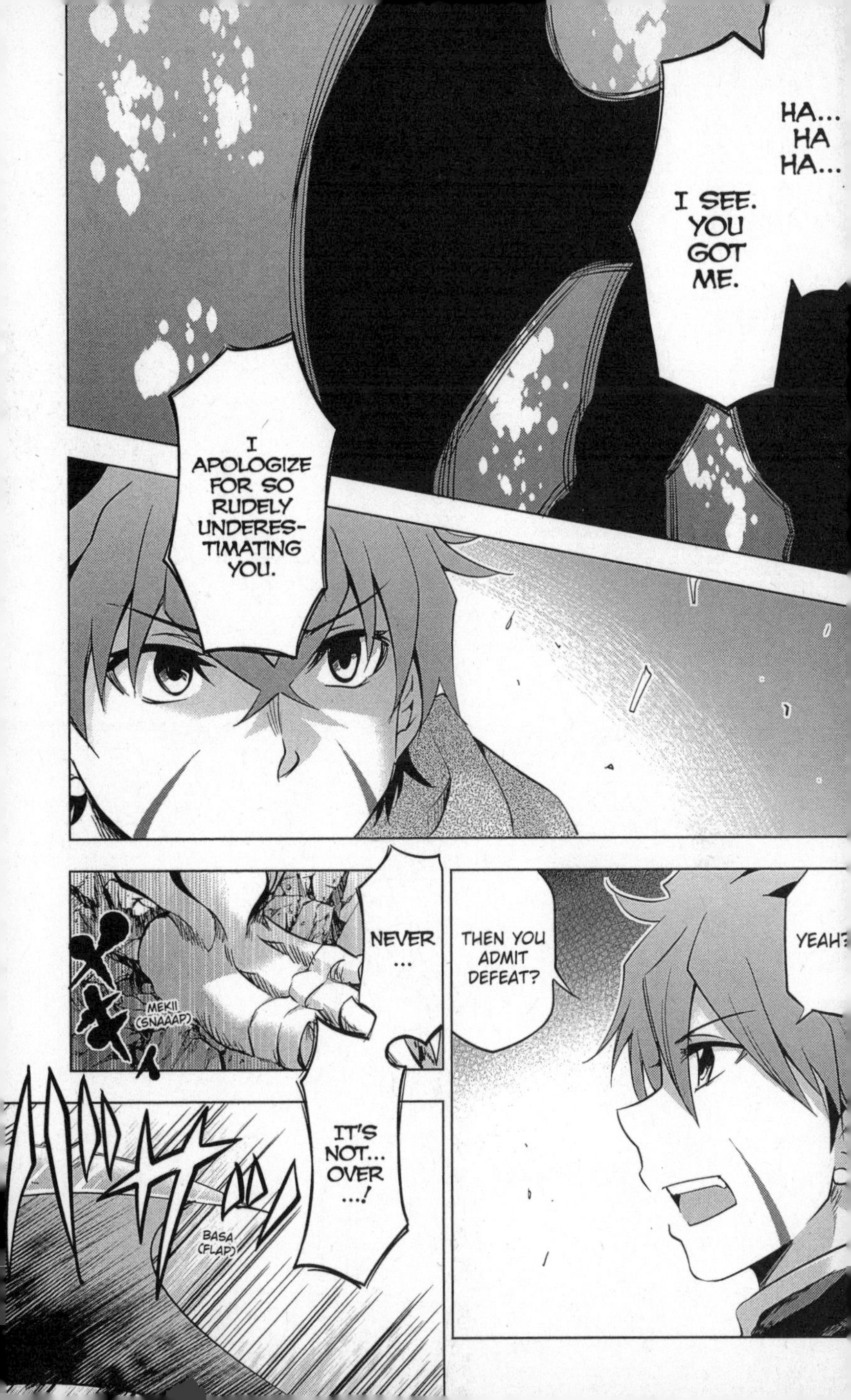
HA... HA HA...
I SEE. YOU GOT ME.
I APOLOGIZE FOR SO RUDELY UNDERES-TIMATING YOU.
YEAH?
THEN YOU ADMIT DEFEAT?
NEVER ...
MEKII (SNAAAP)
IT'S NOT... OVER ...!
BASA (FLAP)

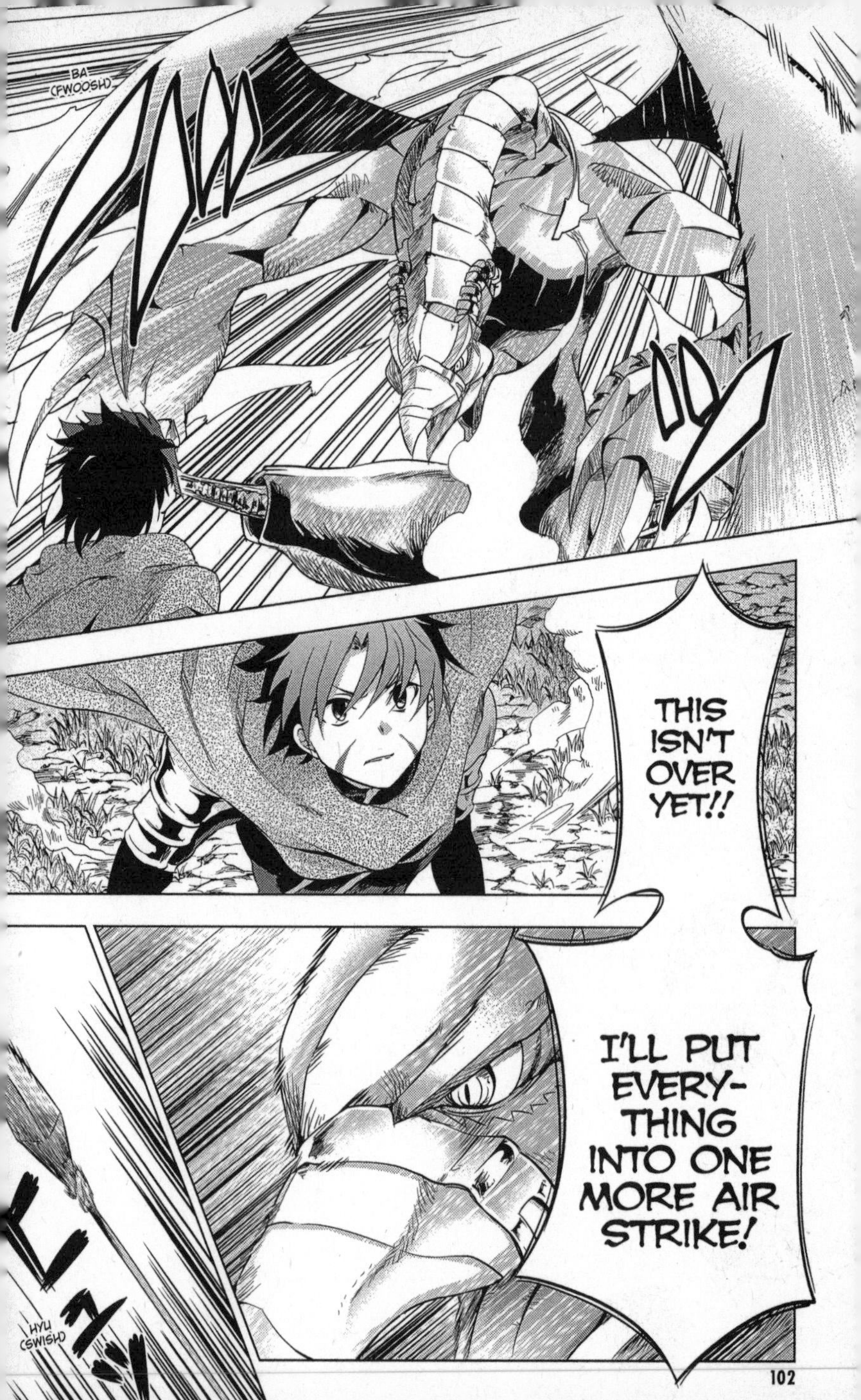
BA (FWOOSH)
THIS ISN'T OVER YET!!
I'LL PUT EVERYTHING INTO ONE MORE AIR STRIKE!
HYU (SWISH)

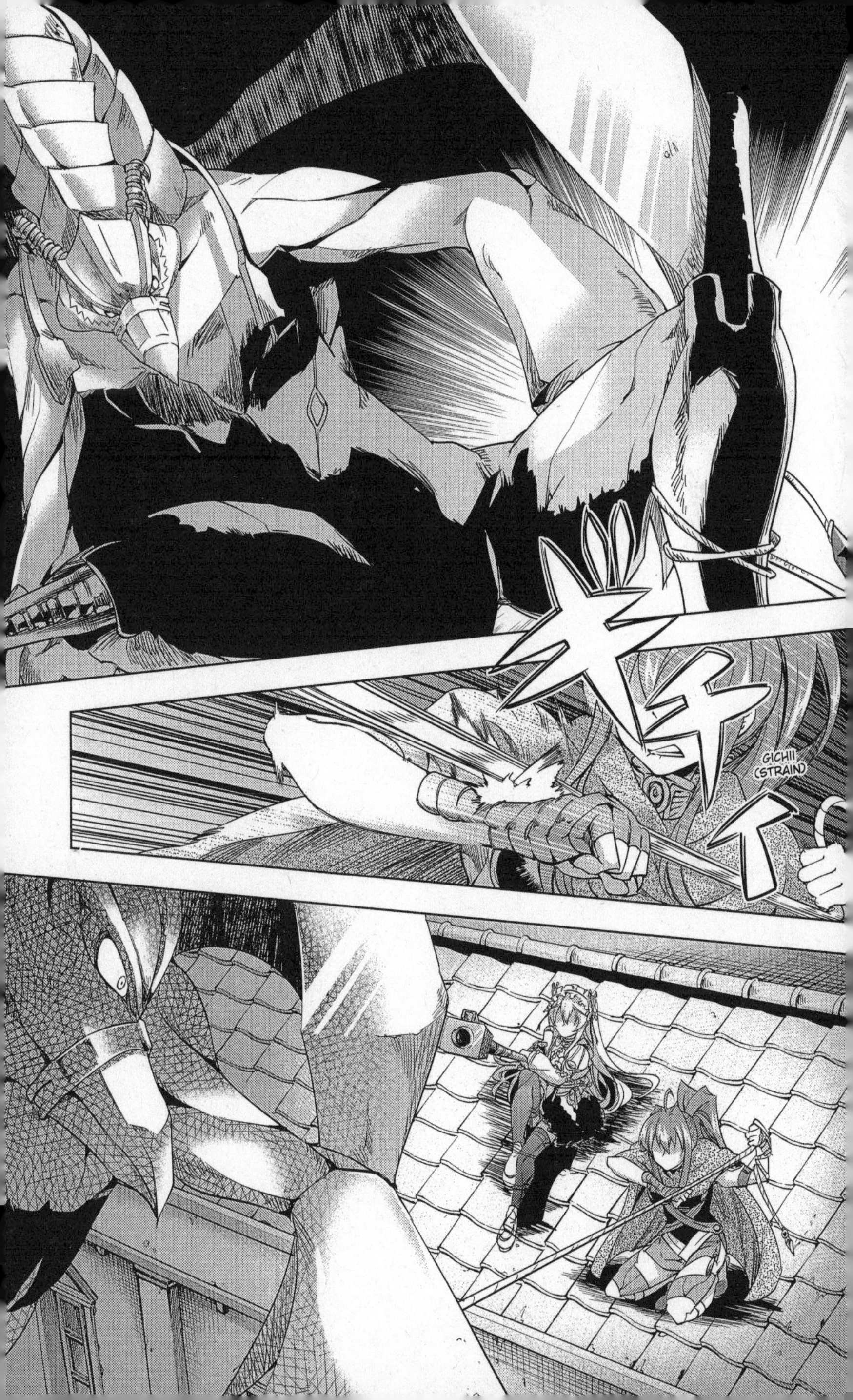
GICHII (STRAIN)

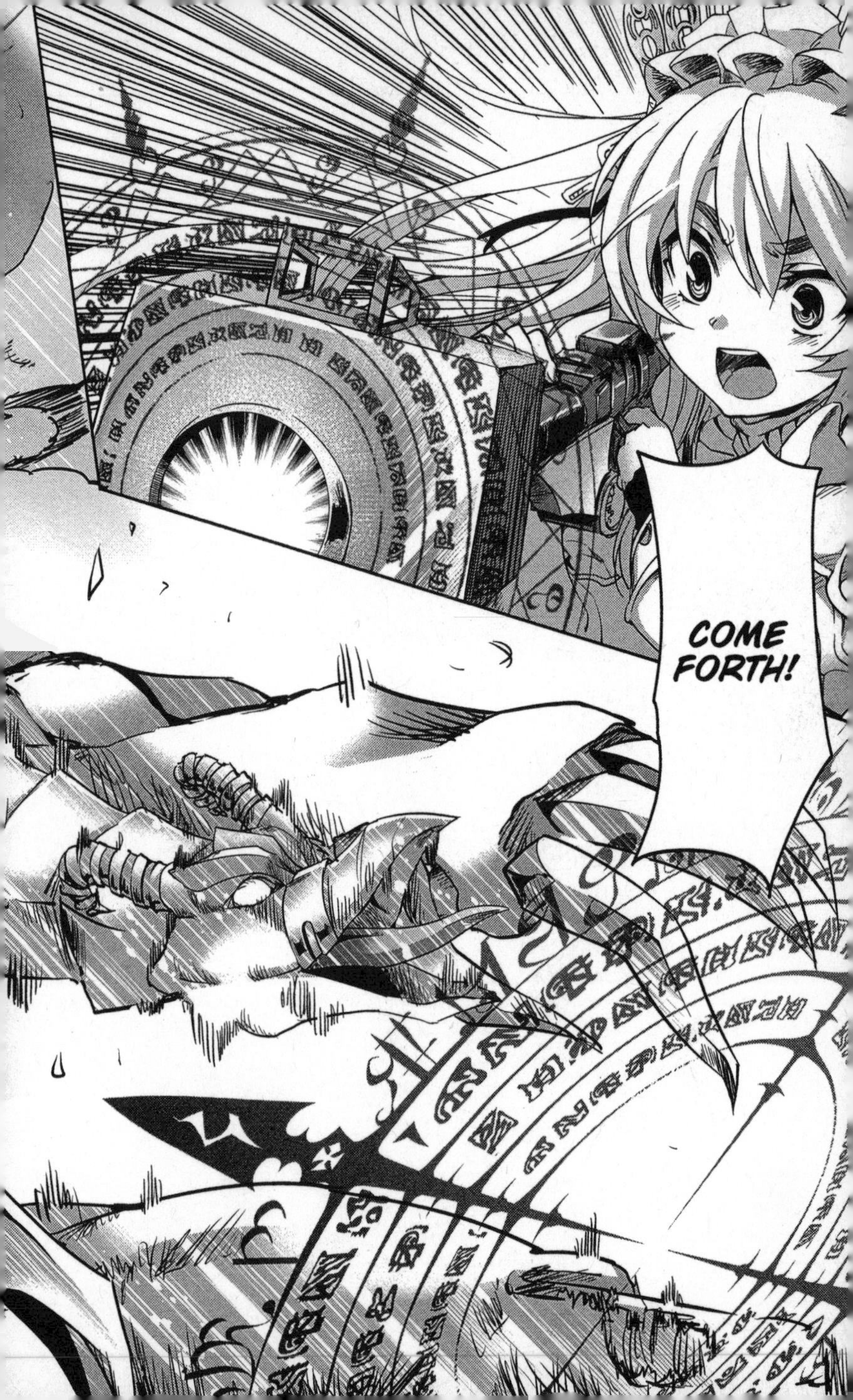
COME FORTH!

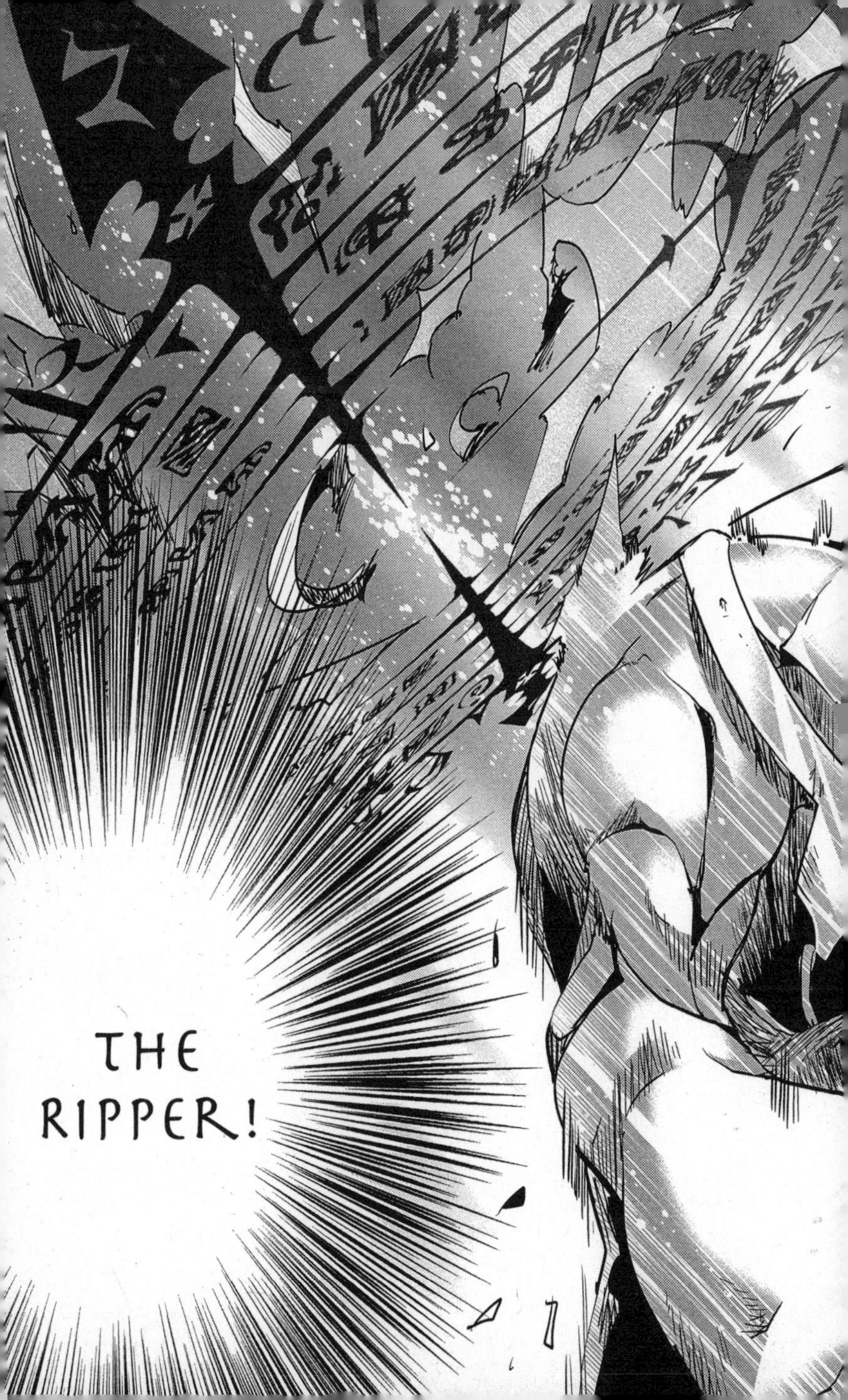
THE RIPPER!

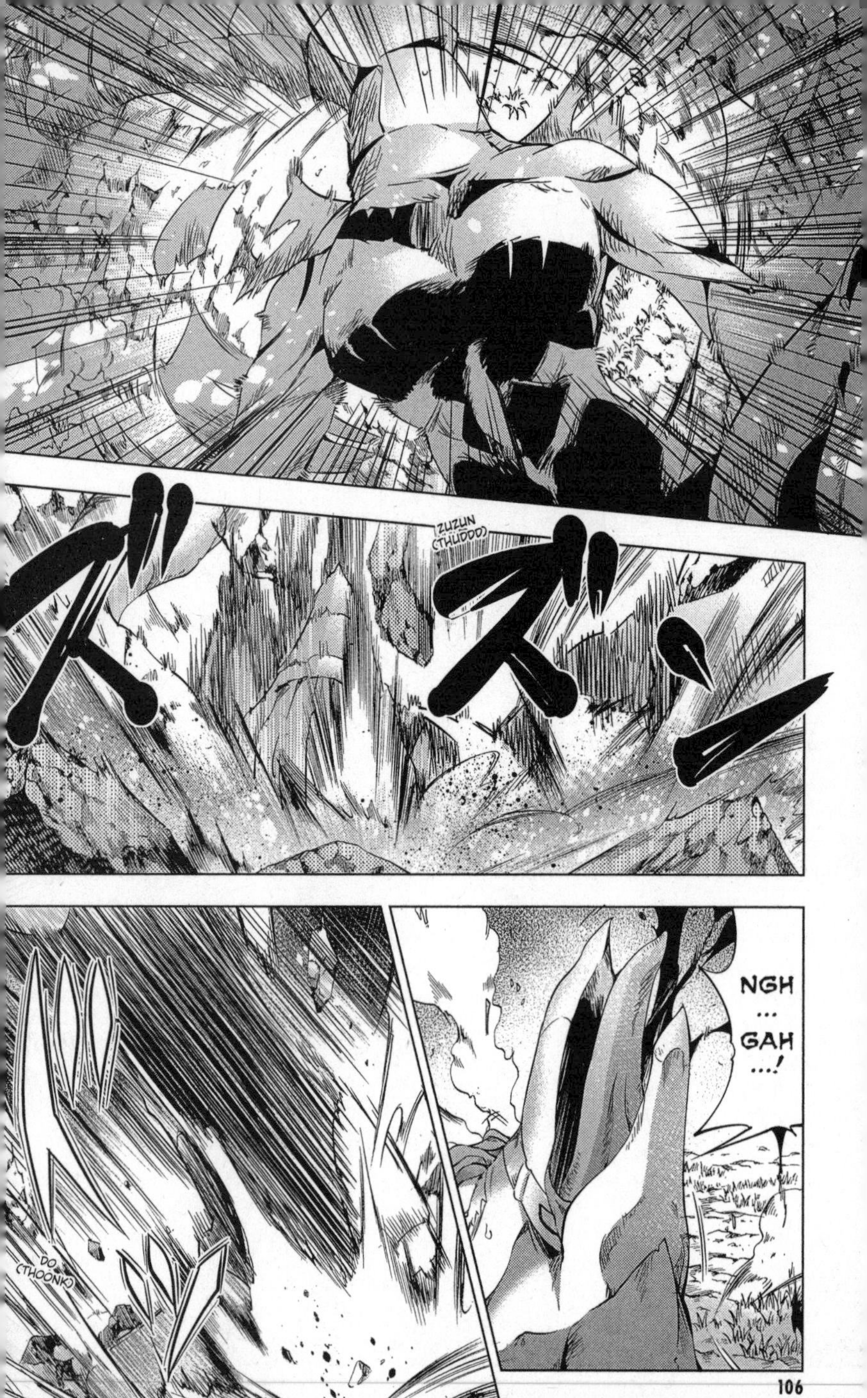
ZUZUN
(THUDDD)
NGH ... GAH ...!
DO
(THOONK)

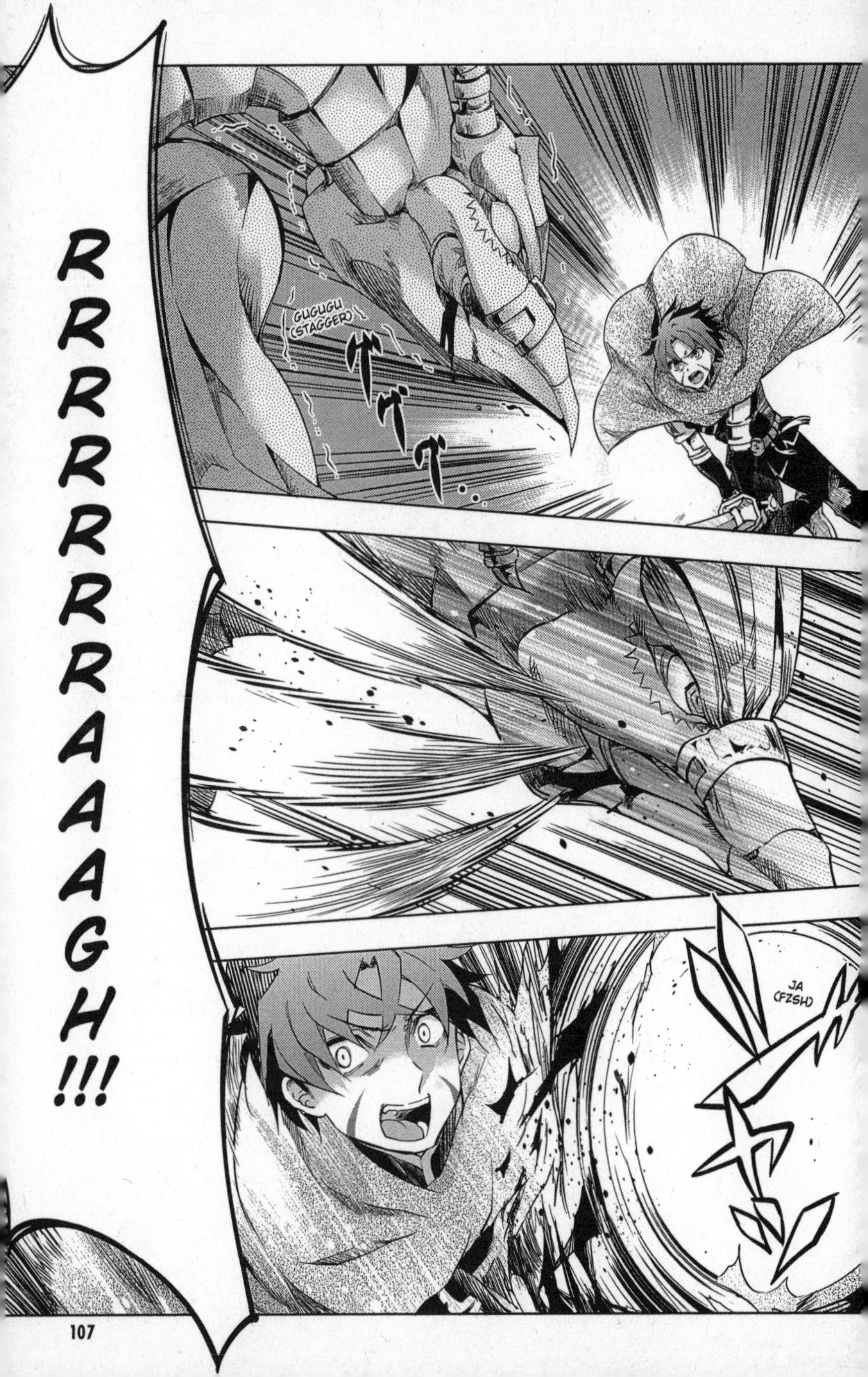
GUGUGU (STAGGER)
JA (FZSH)
RRRRRRAAAAGH!!!

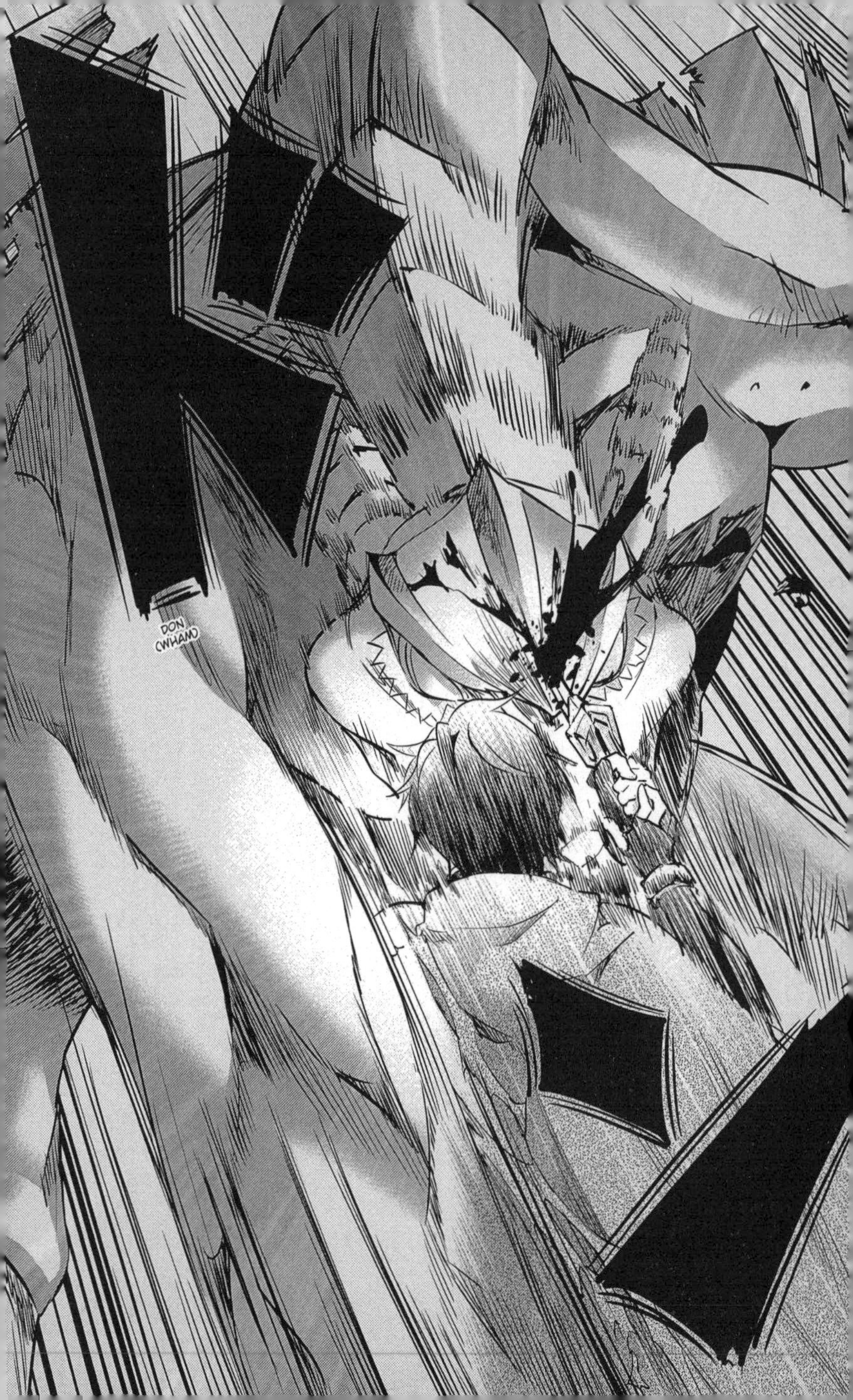
DON
(WHAM)

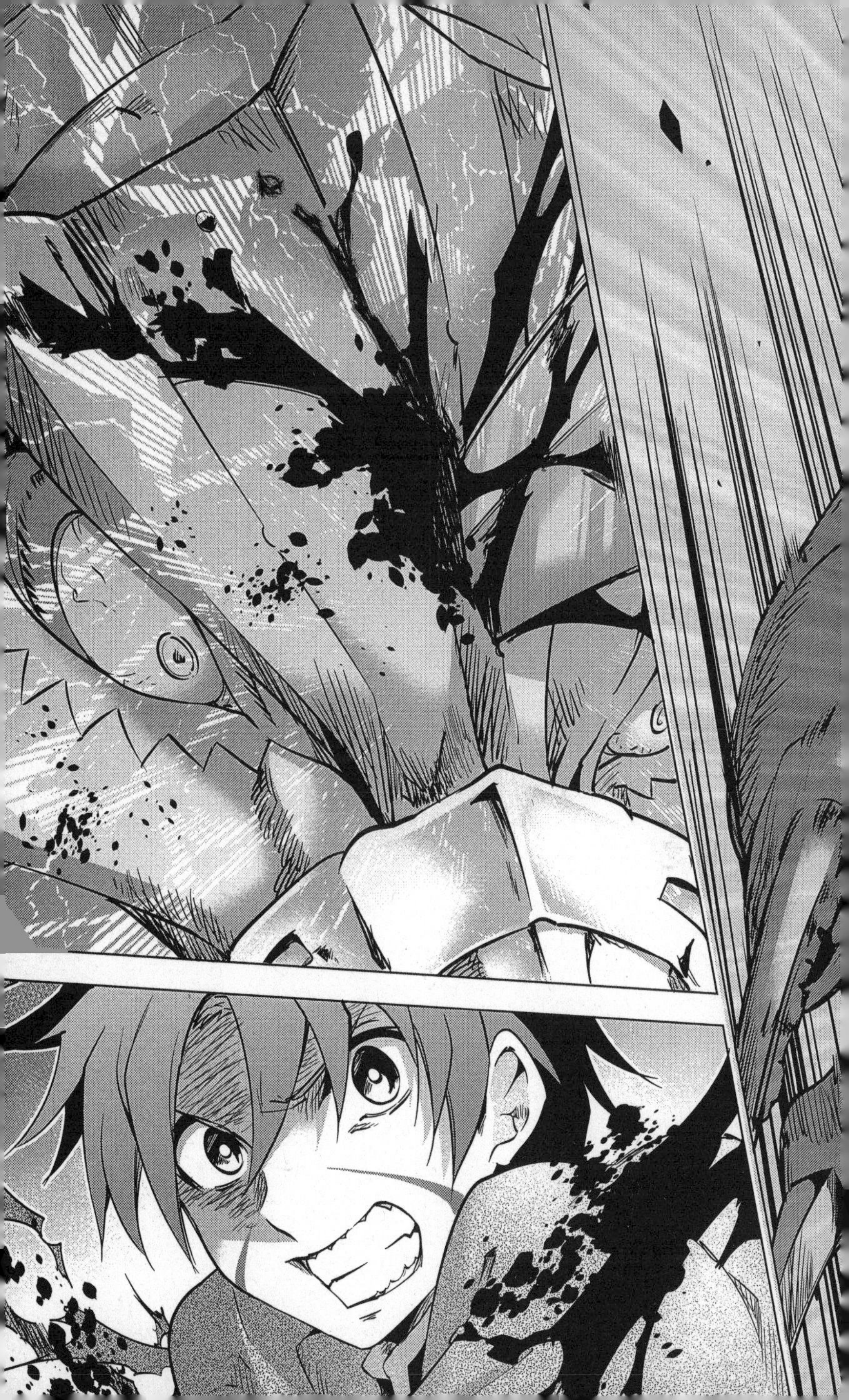

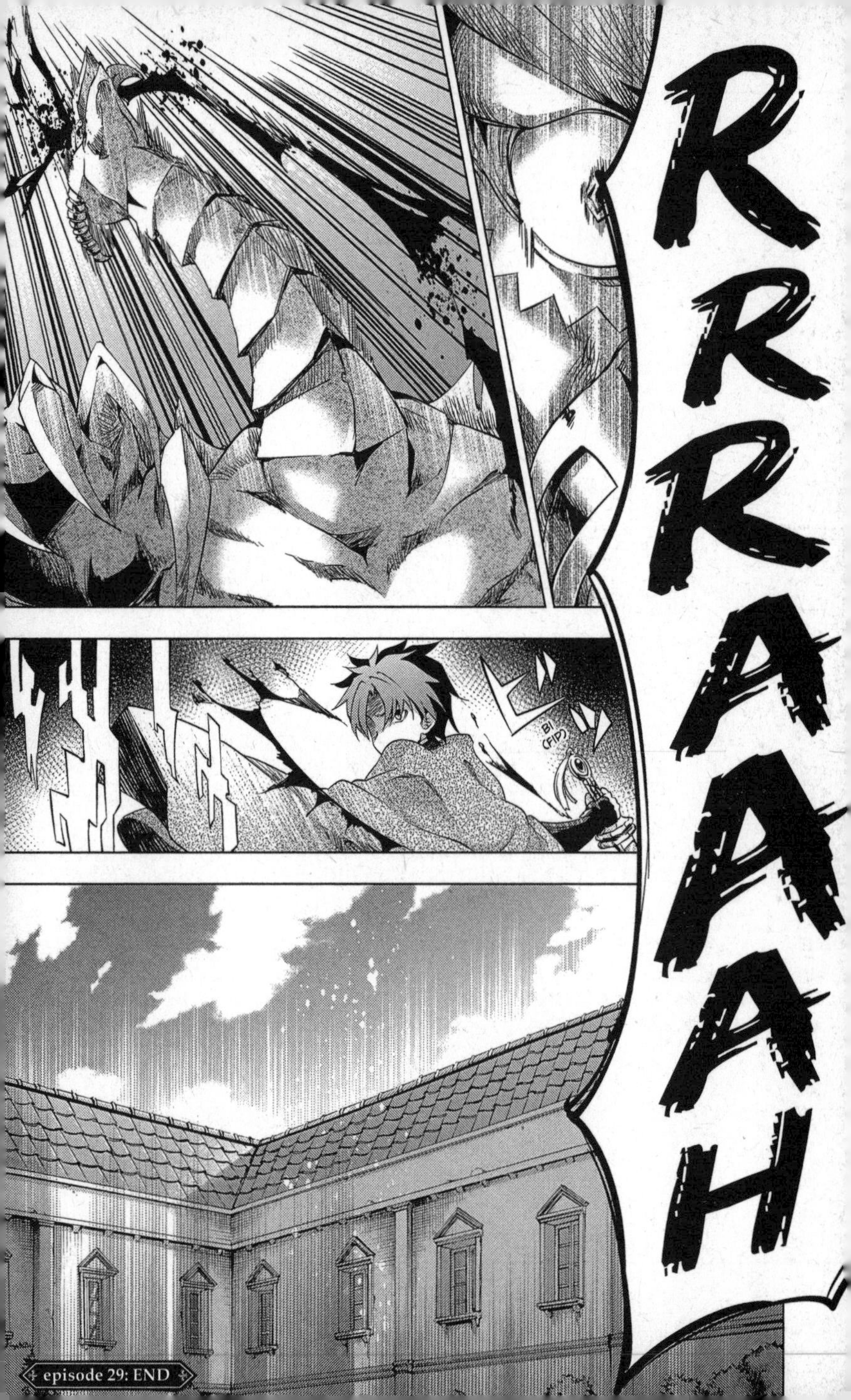
RRRAAAH
BI (FIP)
episode 29: END

CHAIKA: THE
COFFIN PRINCESS

episode 30: A Reason to Live

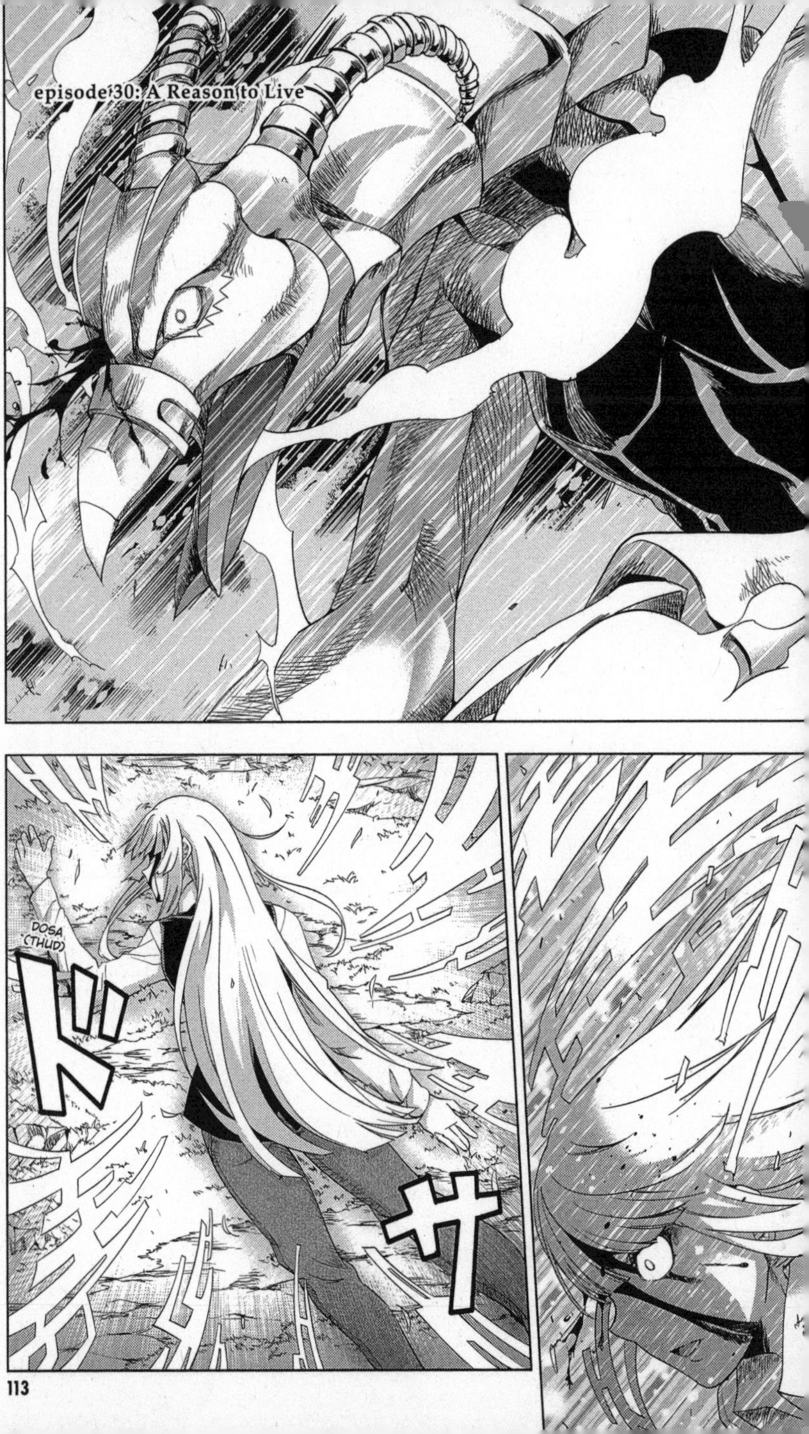
DOSA
(THUD)
ドサ

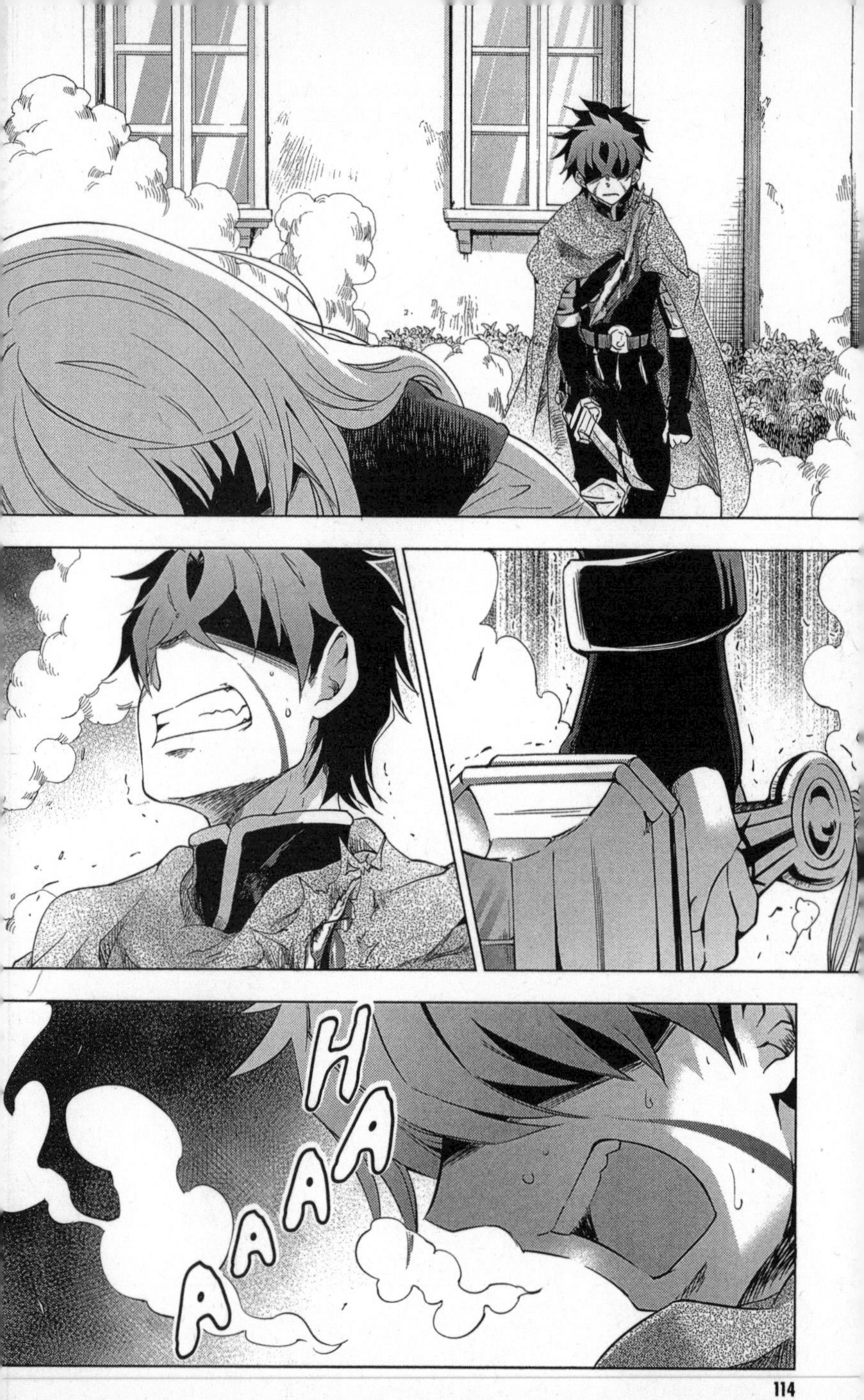
HAAAAA

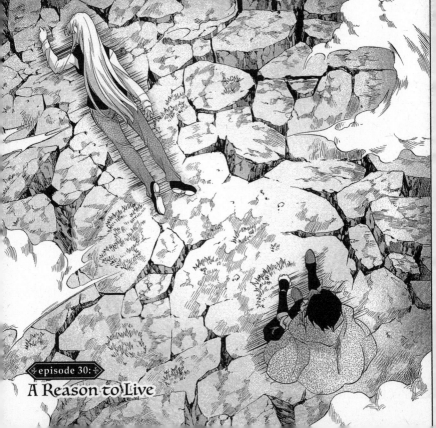

GASHA
(CLANK)

episode 30:
A Reason to Live

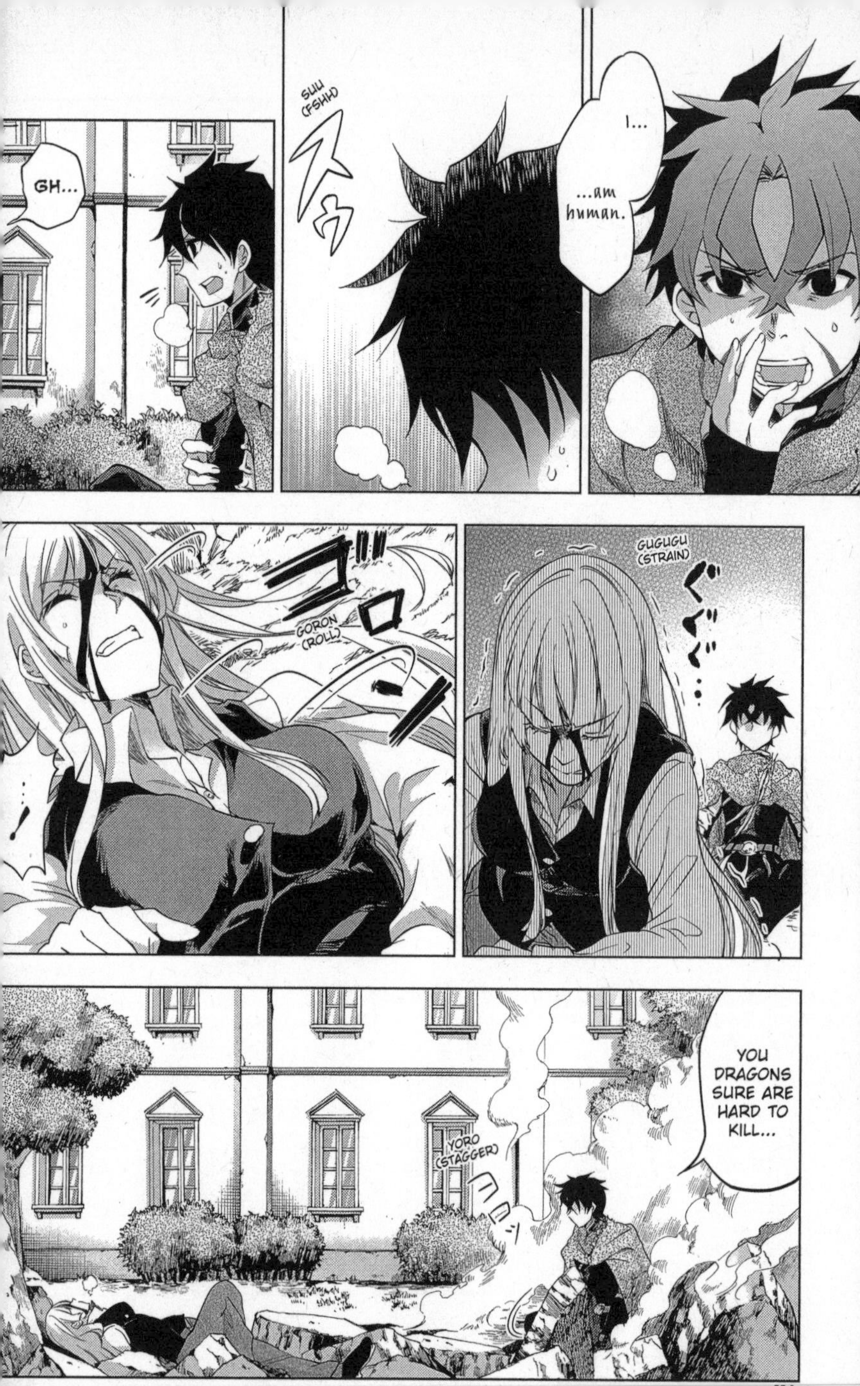
I...
...am human.
SUU (FSHH)
GH...
GUGUGU (STRAIN)
GORON (ROLL)
...!
YOU DRAGONS SURE ARE HARD TO KILL...
YORO (STAGGER)

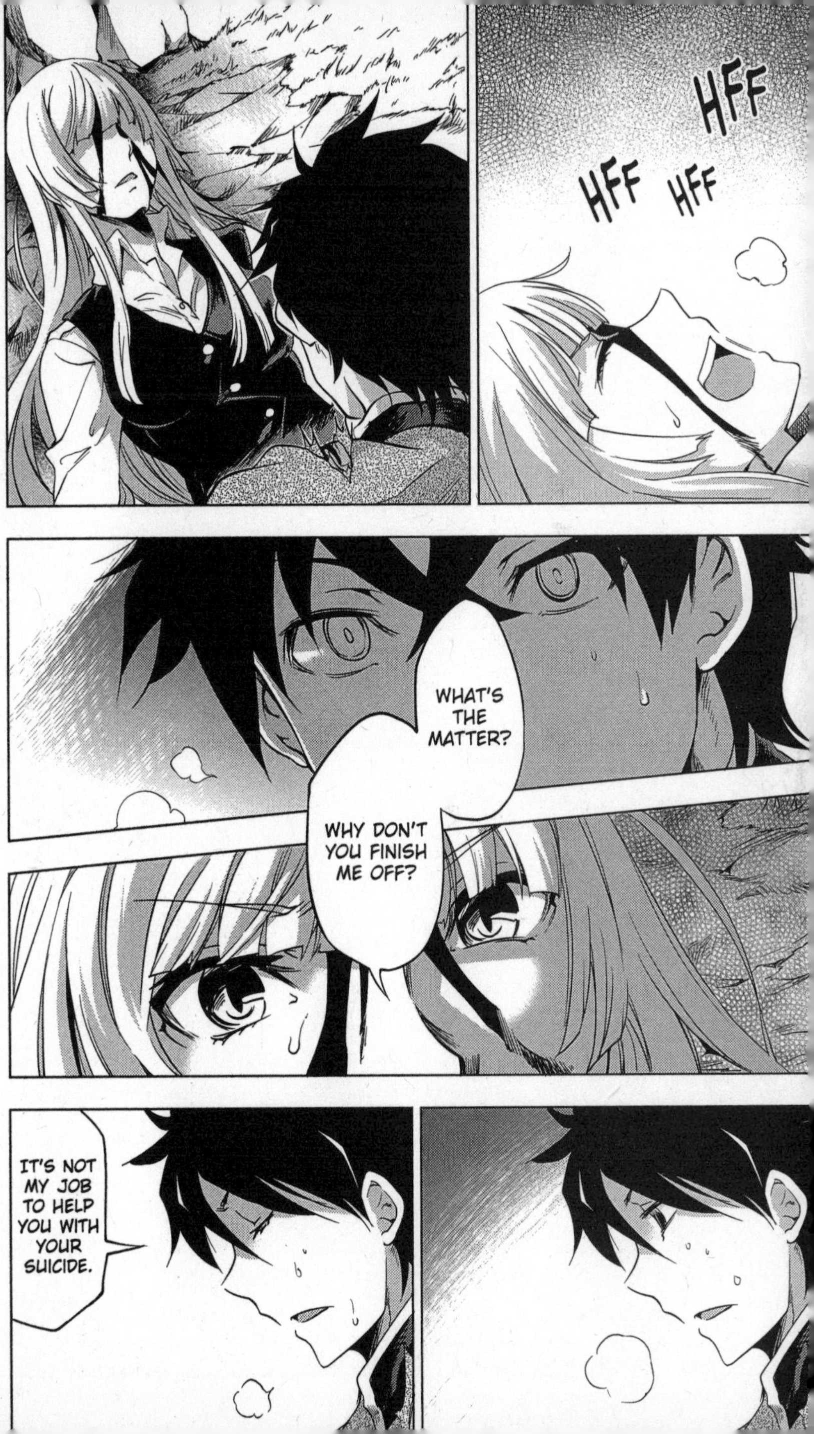
HFF
HFF
HFF
WHAT'S THE MATTER?
WHY DON'T YOU FINISH ME OFF?
IT'S NOT MY JOB TO HELP YOU WITH YOUR SUICIDE.

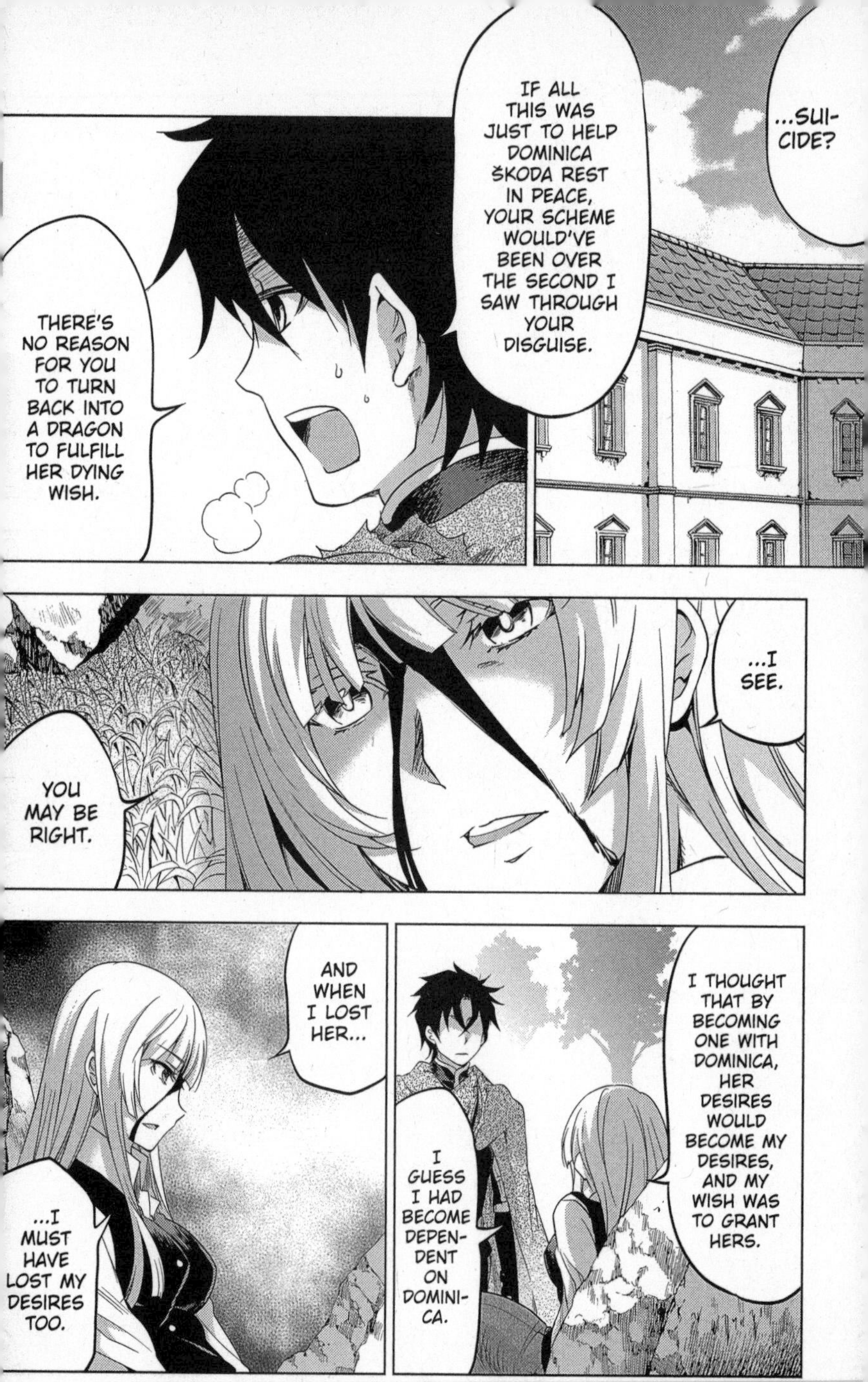

...SUI-CIDE?
IF ALL THIS WAS JUST TO HELP DOMINICA ŠKODA REST IN PEACE, YOUR SCHEME WOULD'VE BEEN OVER THE SECOND I SAW THROUGH YOUR DISGUISE.
THERE'S NO REASON FOR YOU TO TURN BACK INTO A DRAGON TO FULFILL HER DYING WISH.
...I SEE.
YOU MAY BE RIGHT.
I THOUGHT THAT BY BECOMING ONE WITH DOMINICA, HER DESIRES WOULD BECOME MY DESIRES, AND MY WISH WAS TO GRANT HERS.
I GUESS I HAD BECOME DEPEN-DENT ON DOMINI-CA.
AND WHEN I LOST HER...
...I MUST HAVE LOST MY DESIRES TOO.

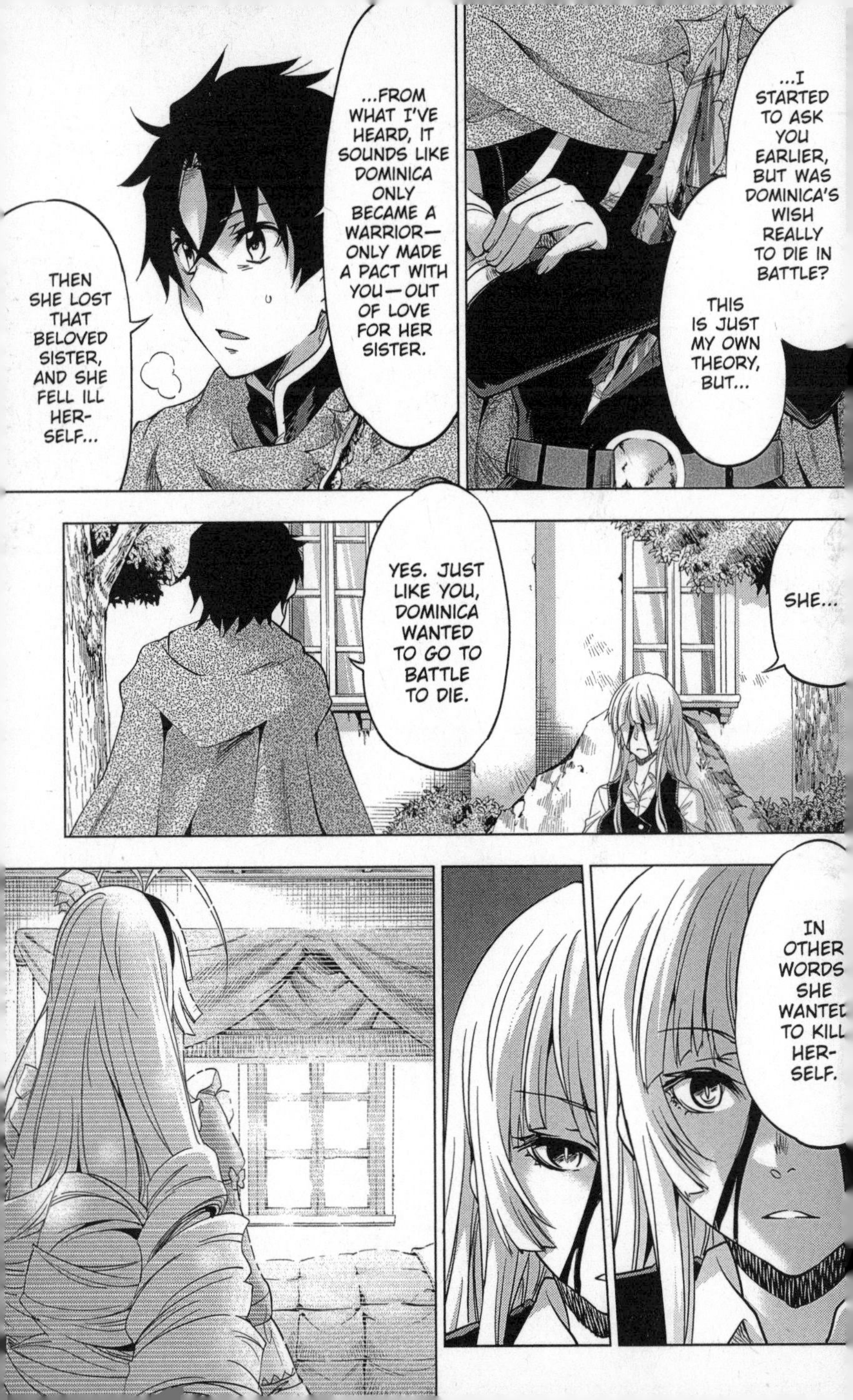
...I STARTED TO ASK YOU EARLIER, BUT WAS DOMINICA'S WISH REALLY TO DIE IN BATTLE?
THIS IS JUST MY OWN THEORY, BUT...
...FROM WHAT I'VE HEARD, IT SOUNDS LIKE DOMINICA ONLY BECAME A WARRIOR—ONLY MADE A PACT WITH YOU—OUT OF LOVE FOR HER SISTER.
THEN SHE LOST THAT BELOVED SISTER, AND SHE FELL ILL HER-SELF...
SHE...
YES. JUST LIKE YOU, DOMINICA WANTED TO GO TO BATTLE TO DIE.
IN OTHER WORDS SHE WANTED TO KILL HER-SELF.

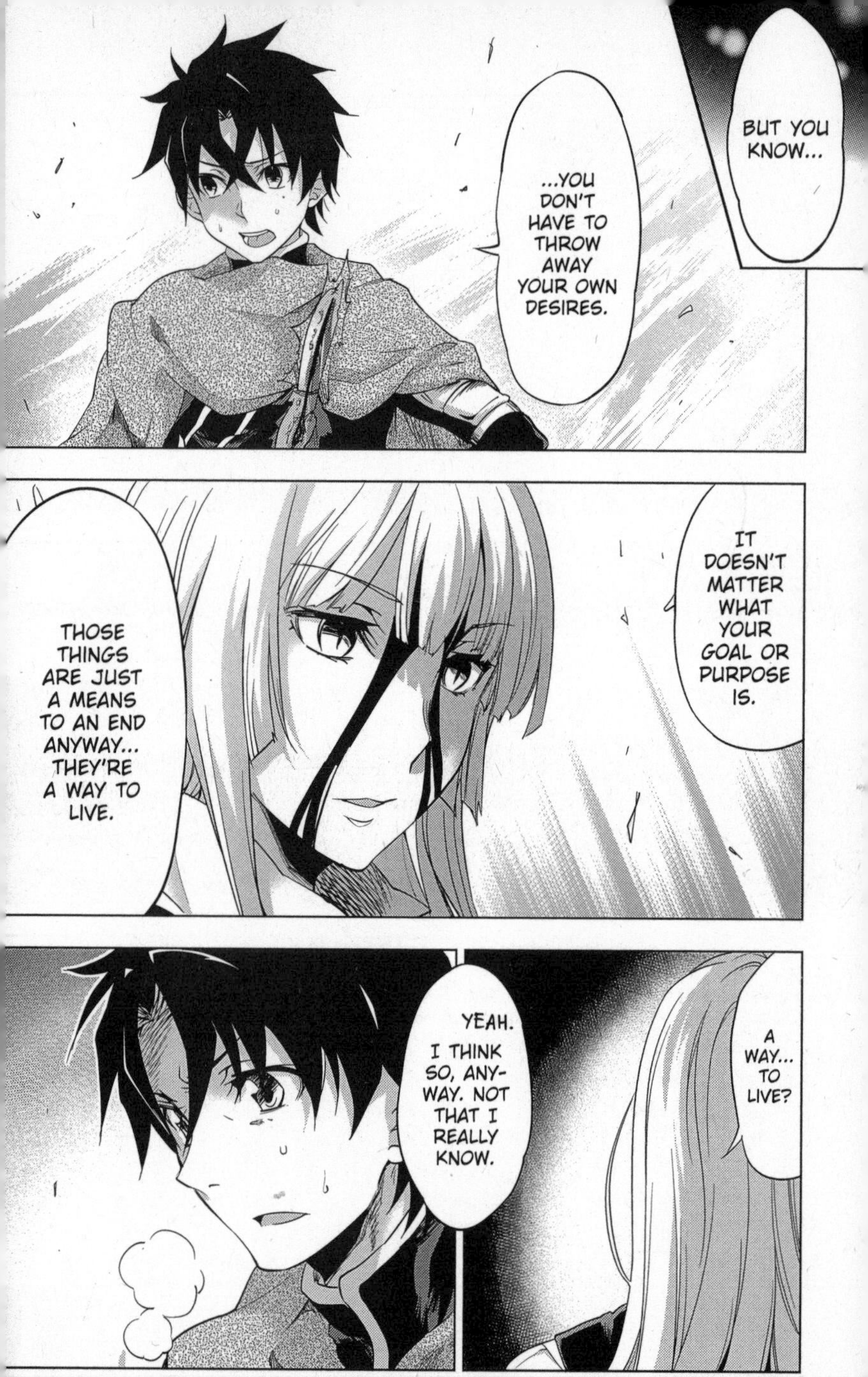
BUT YOU KNOW...
...YOU DON'T HAVE TO THROW AWAY YOUR OWN DESIRES.
IT DOESN'T MATTER WHAT YOUR GOAL OR PURPOSE IS.
THOSE THINGS ARE JUST A MEANS TO AN END ANYWAY... THEY'RE A WAY TO LIVE.
A WAY... TO LIVE?
YEAH.
I THINK SO, ANYWAY. NOT THAT I REALLY KNOW.

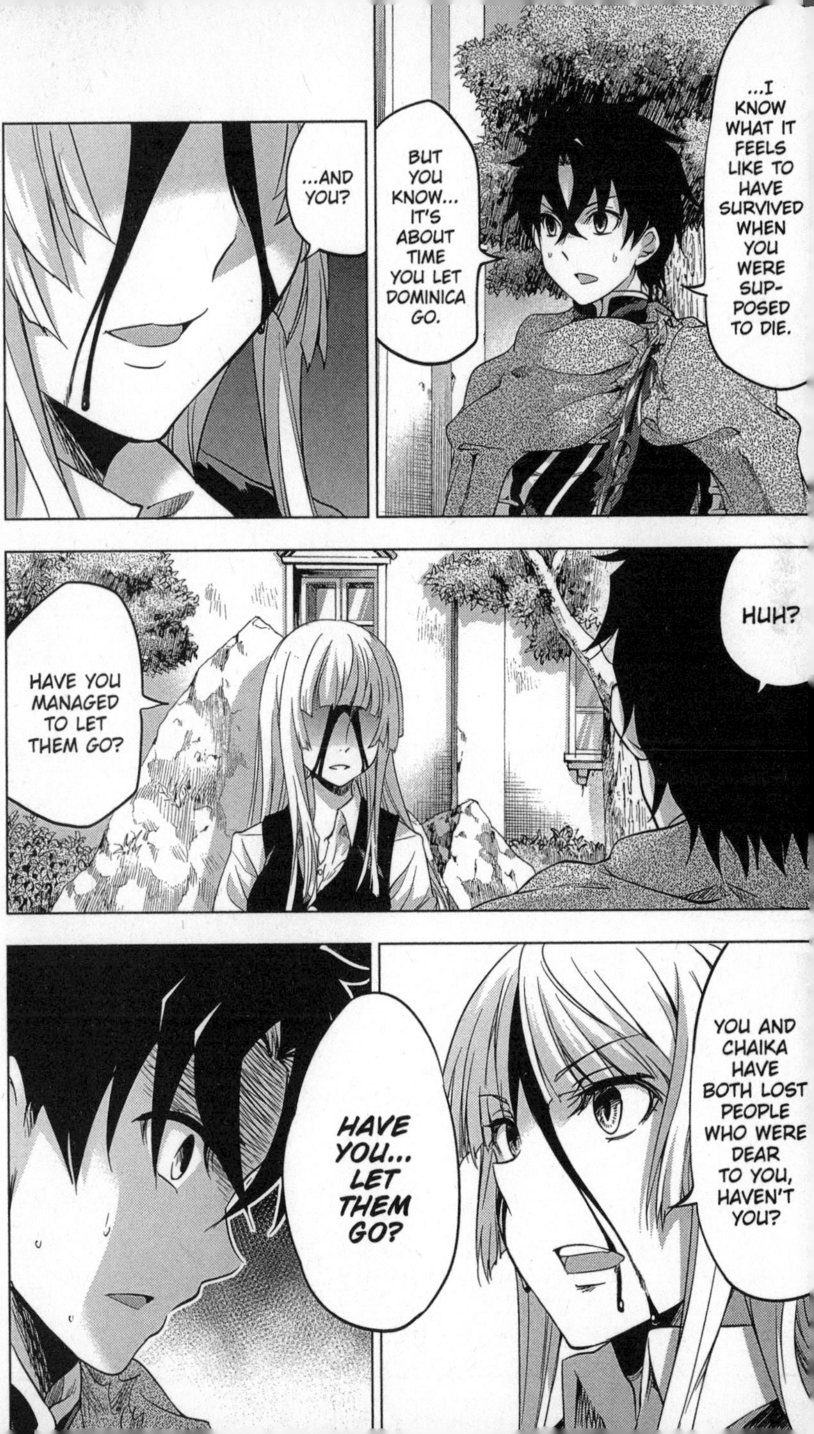
...I KNOW WHAT IT FEELS LIKE TO HAVE SURVIVED WHEN YOU WERE SUP-POSED TO DIE.
BUT YOU KNOW... IT'S ABOUT TIME YOU LET DOMINICA GO.
...AND YOU?
HUH?
HAVE YOU MANAGED TO LET THEM GO?
YOU AND CHAIKA HAVE BOTH LOST PEOPLE WHO WERE DEAR TO YOU, HAVEN'T YOU?
HAVE YOU... LET THEM GO?

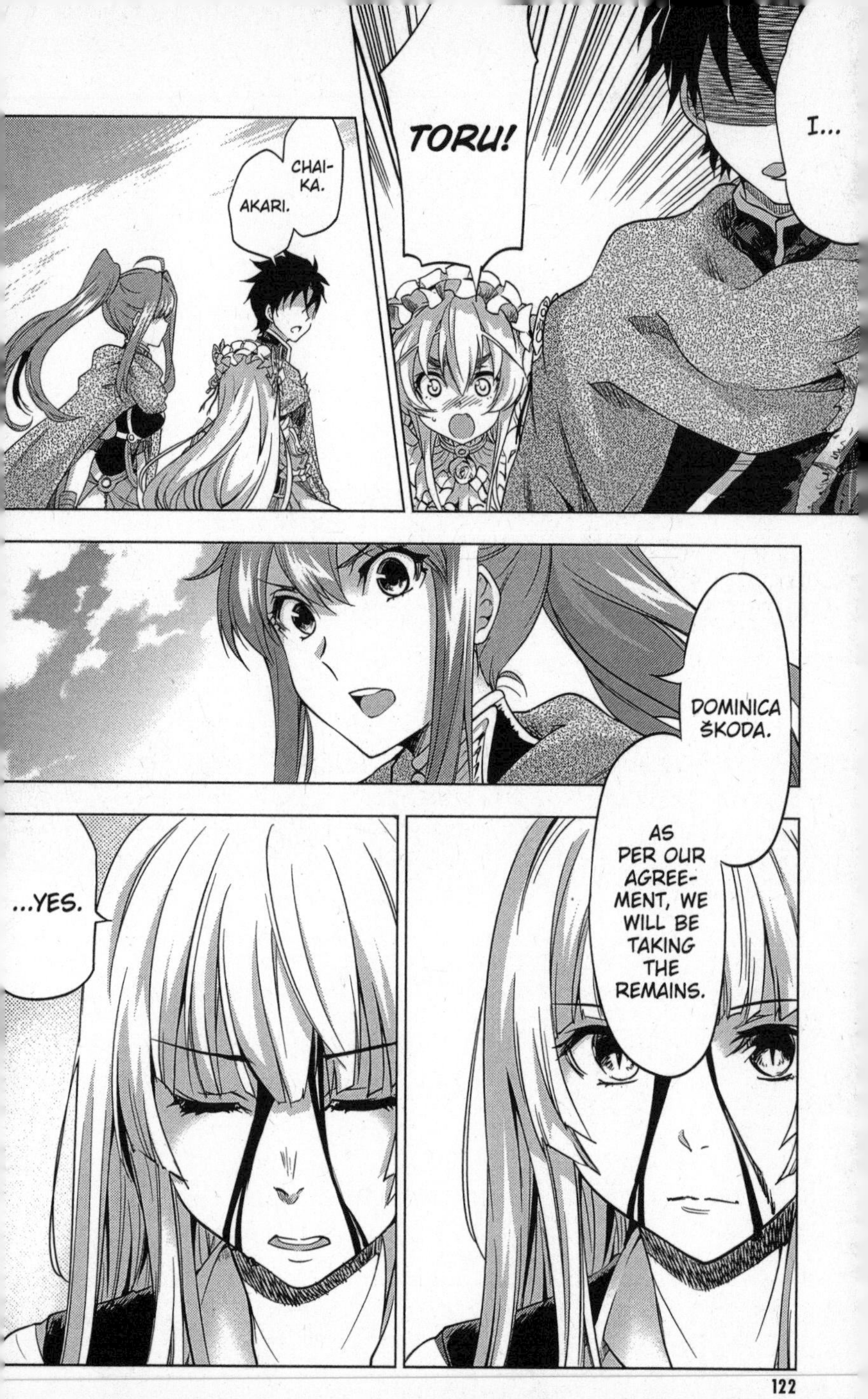
I...
TORU!
CHAI-KA. AKARI.
DOMINICA ŠKODA.
AS PER OUR AGREEMENT, WE WILL BE TAKING THE REMAINS.
...YES.

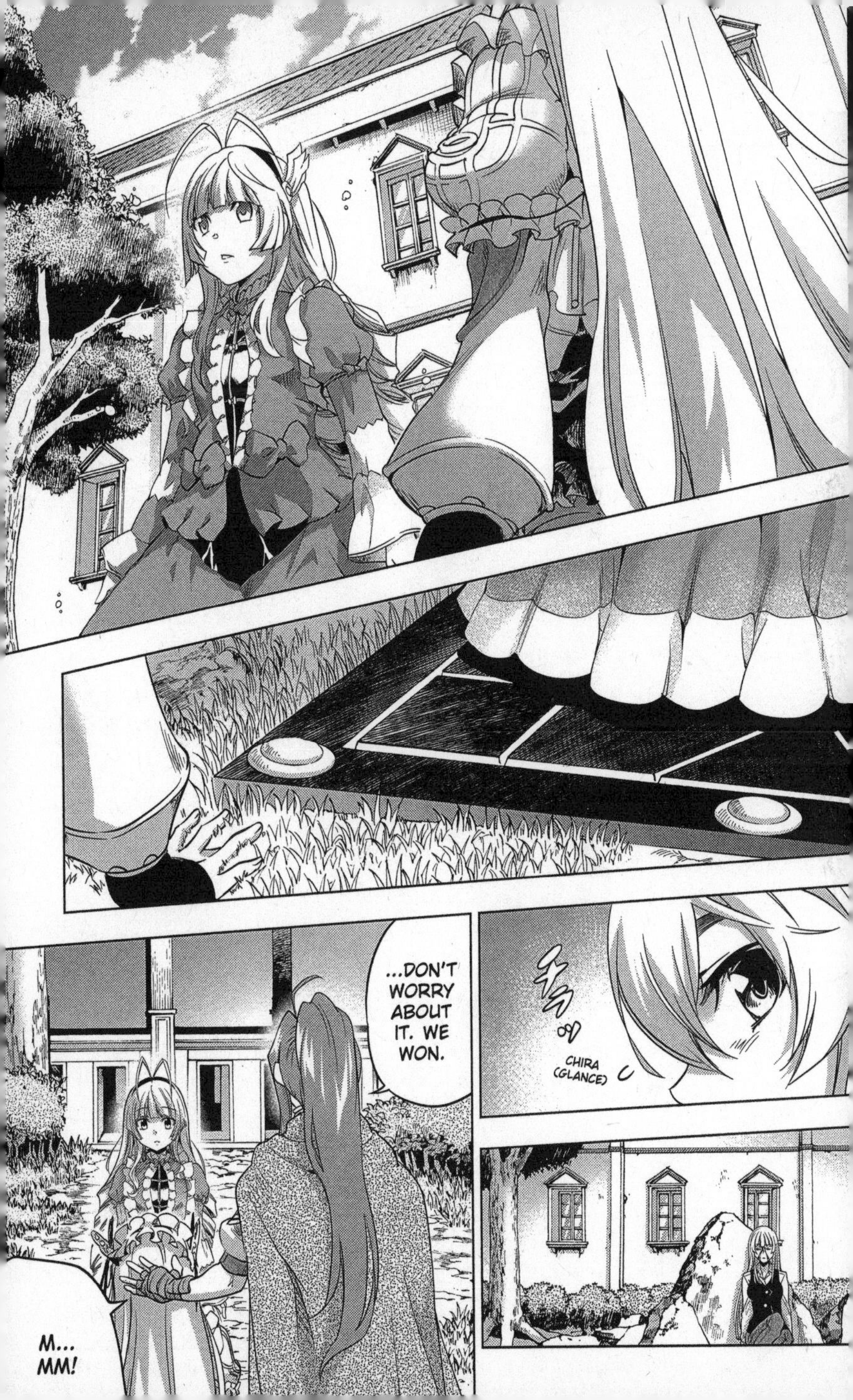
CHIRA (GLANCE)
...DON'T WORRY ABOUT IT. WE WON.
M... MM!

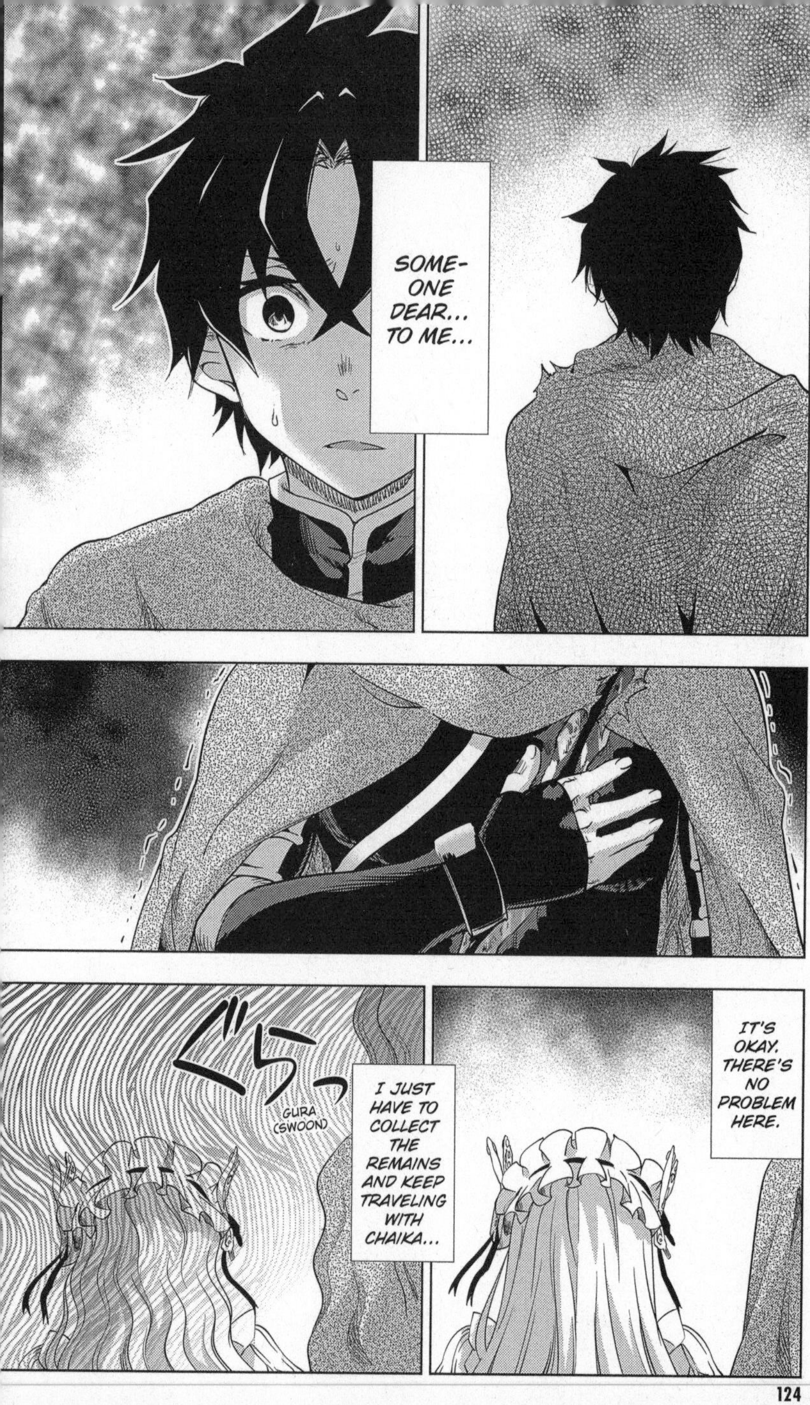
SOME-ONE DEAR... TO ME...
IT'S OKAY. THERE'S NO PROBLEM HERE.
I JUST HAVE TO COLLECT THE REMAINS AND KEEP TRAVELING WITH CHAIKA...
ぐらっ
GURA (SWOON)

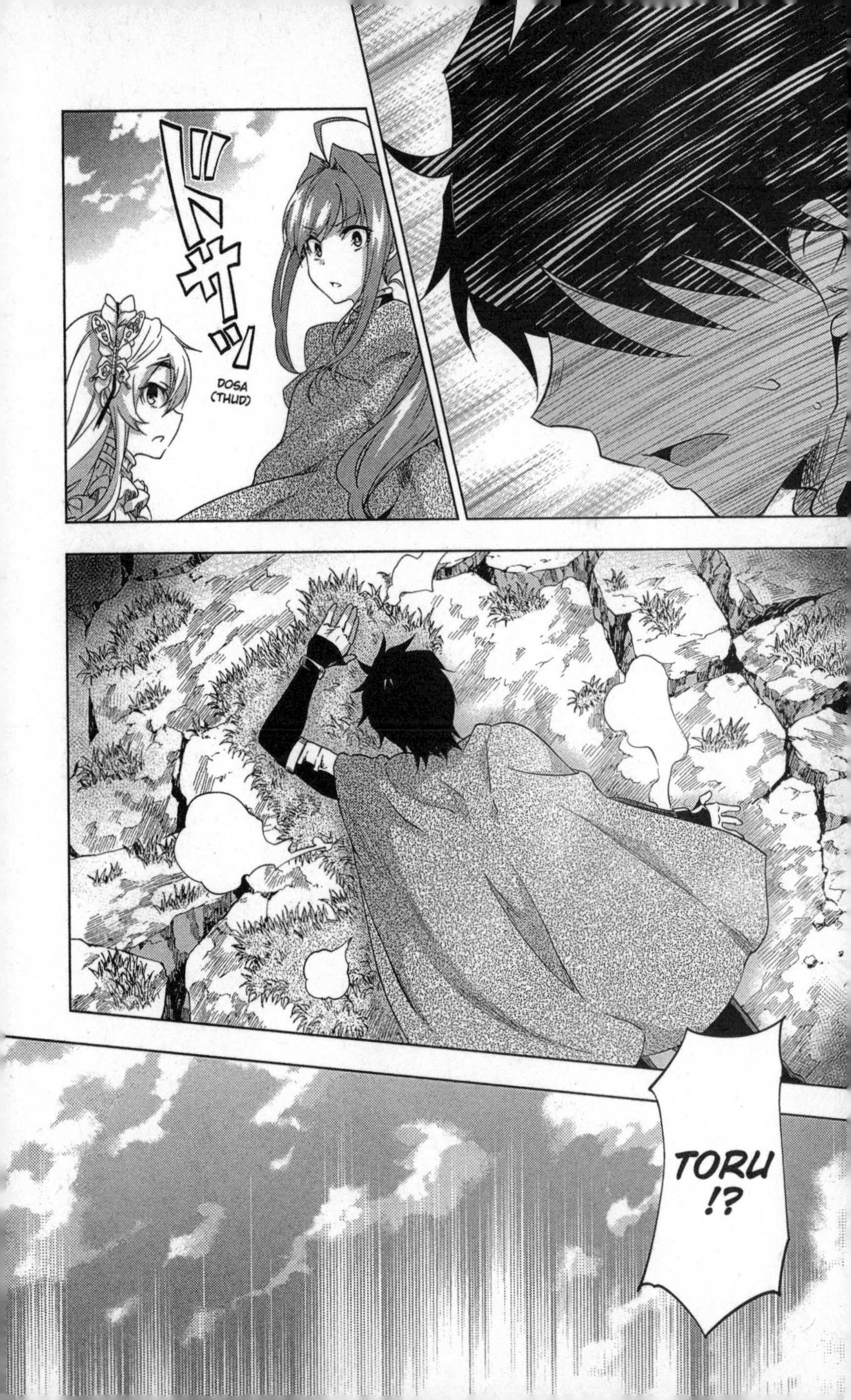
ドサッ
DOSA (THUD)
TORU !?

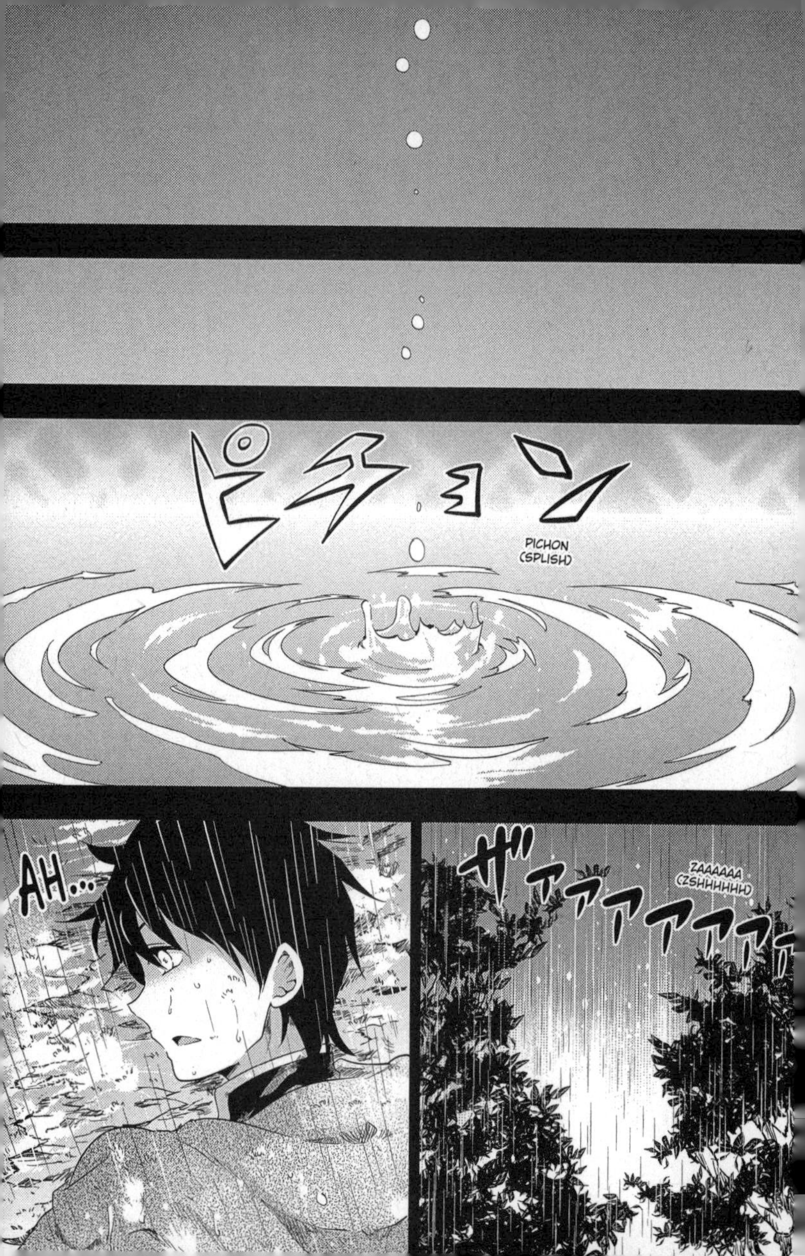
ピチョン
PICHON
(SPLISH)
ザァァァァァ
ZAAAAAA
(ZSHHHHHHH)
AH...

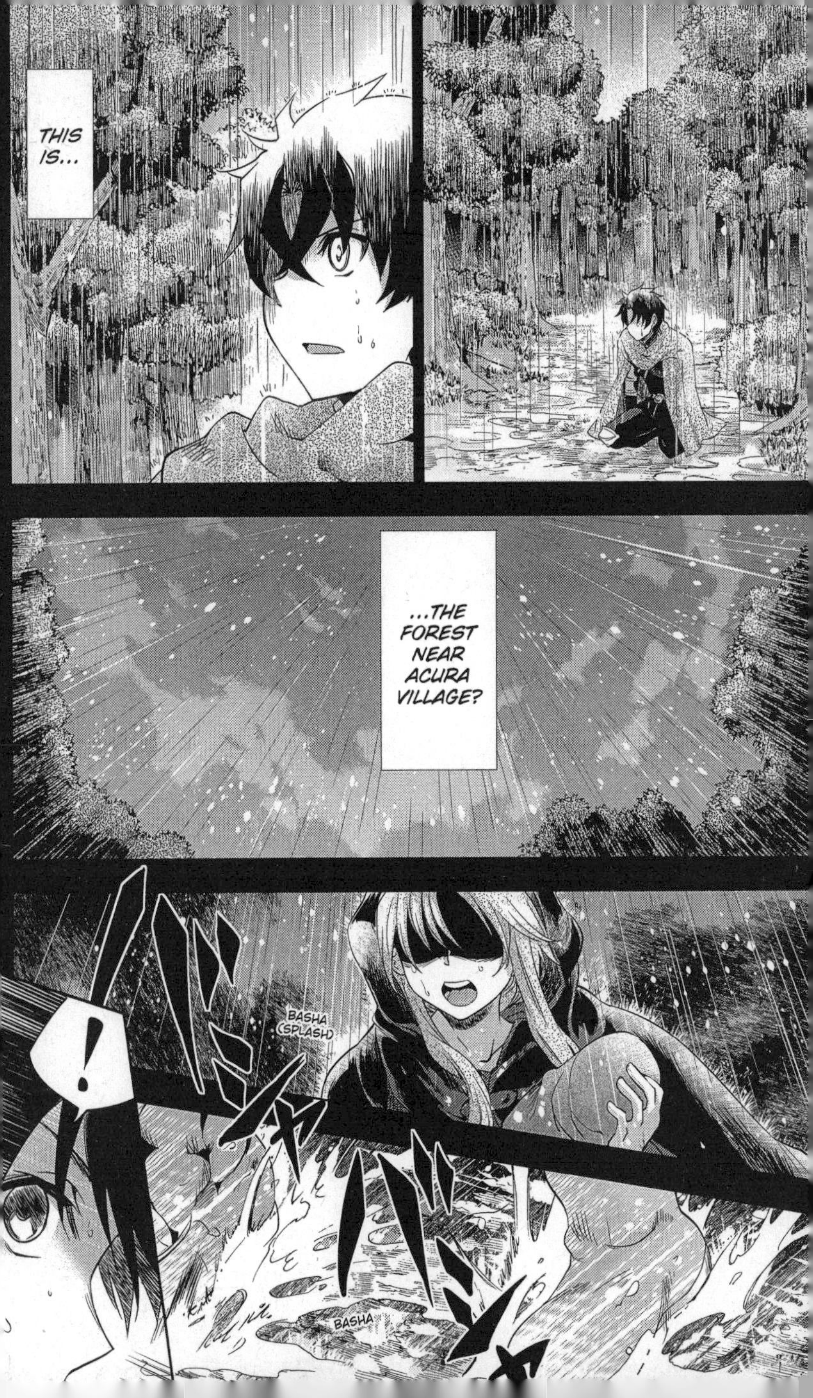
THIS IS...
...THE FOREST NEAR ACURA VILLAGE?
BASHA (SPLASH)
!
BASHA

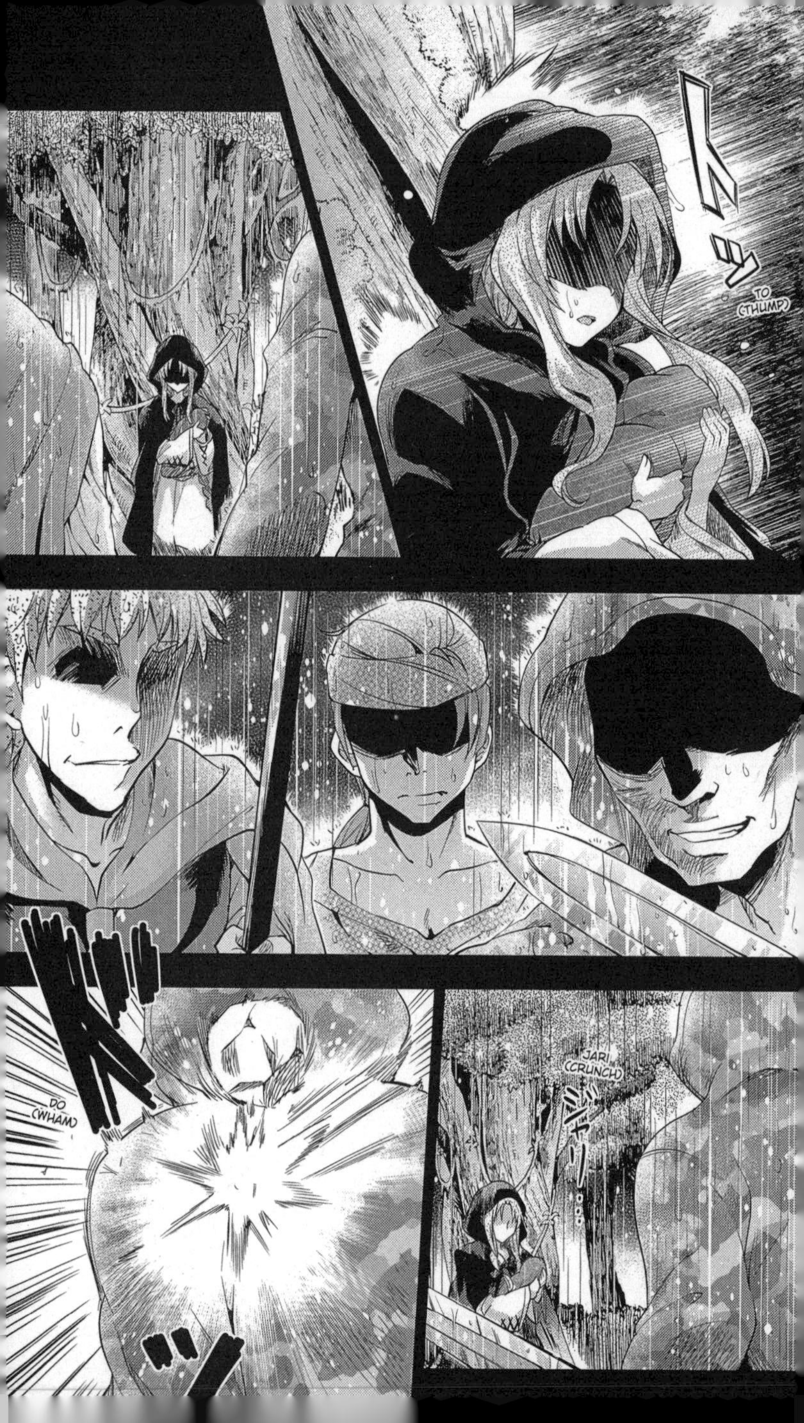
TO
(THUMP)
JARI
(CRUNCH)
DO
(WHAM)

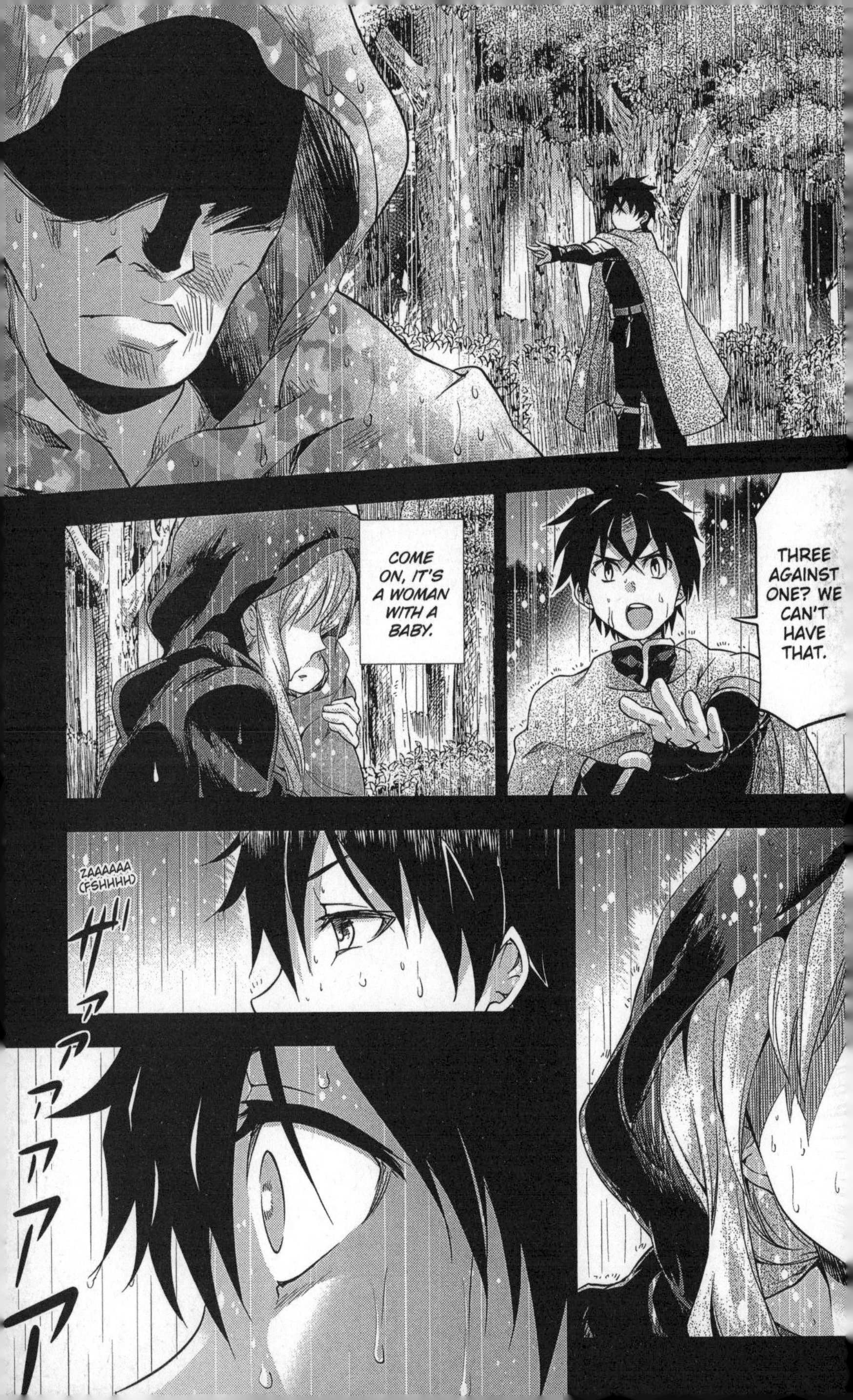
THREE AGAINST ONE? WE CAN'T HAVE THAT.
COME ON, IT'S A WOMAN WITH A BABY.
ZAAAAAA (FSHHHH)

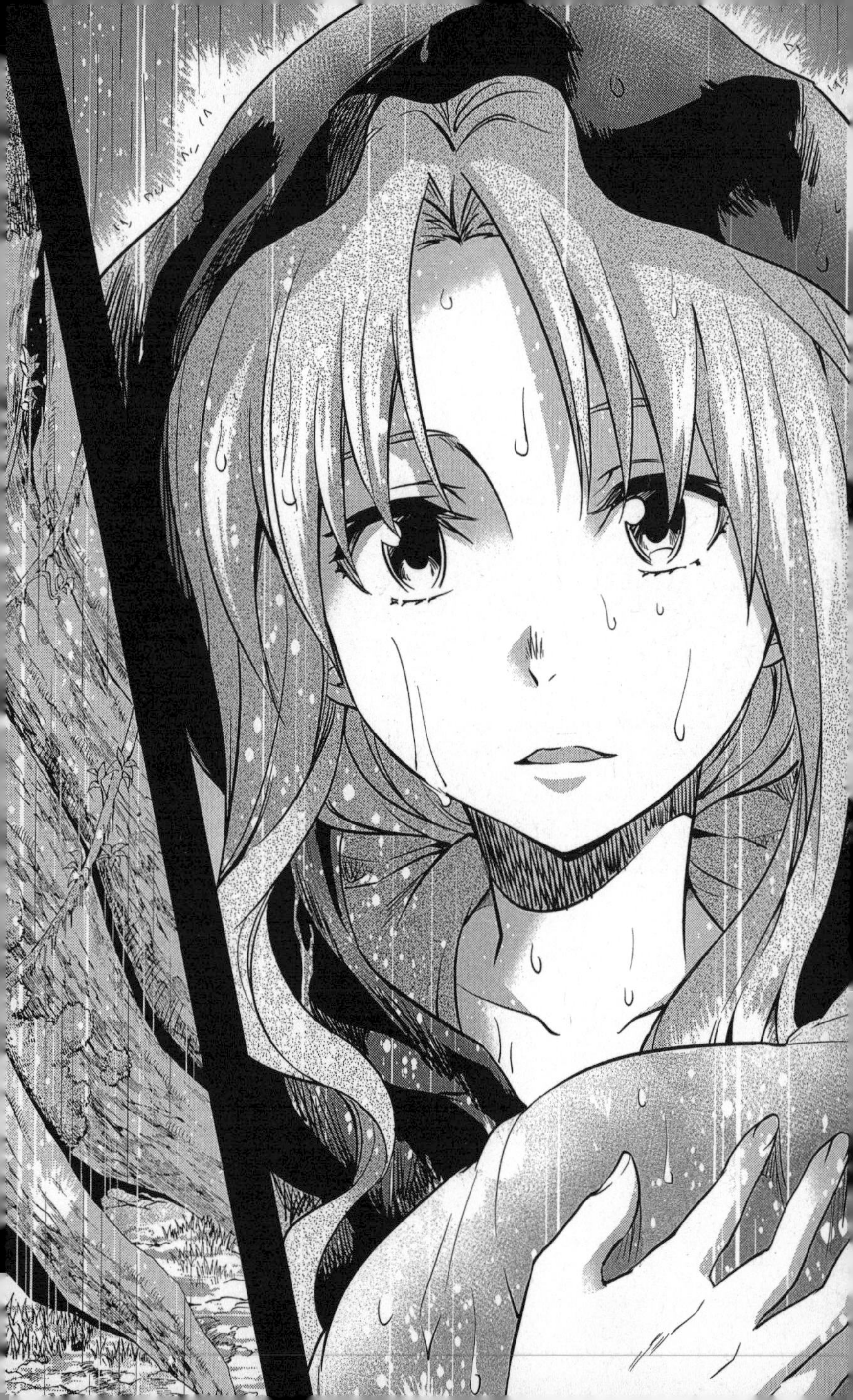

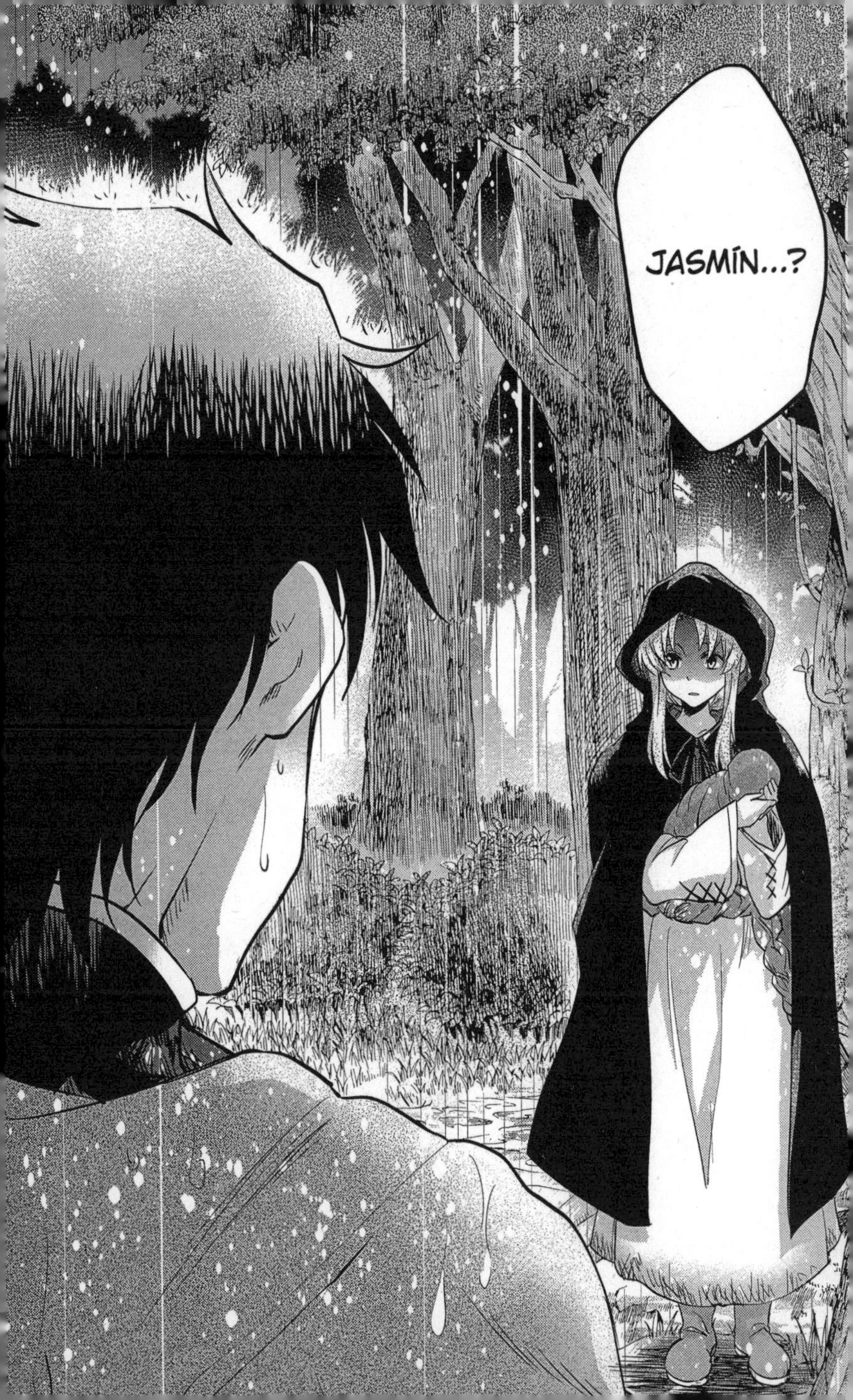
JASMÍN...?

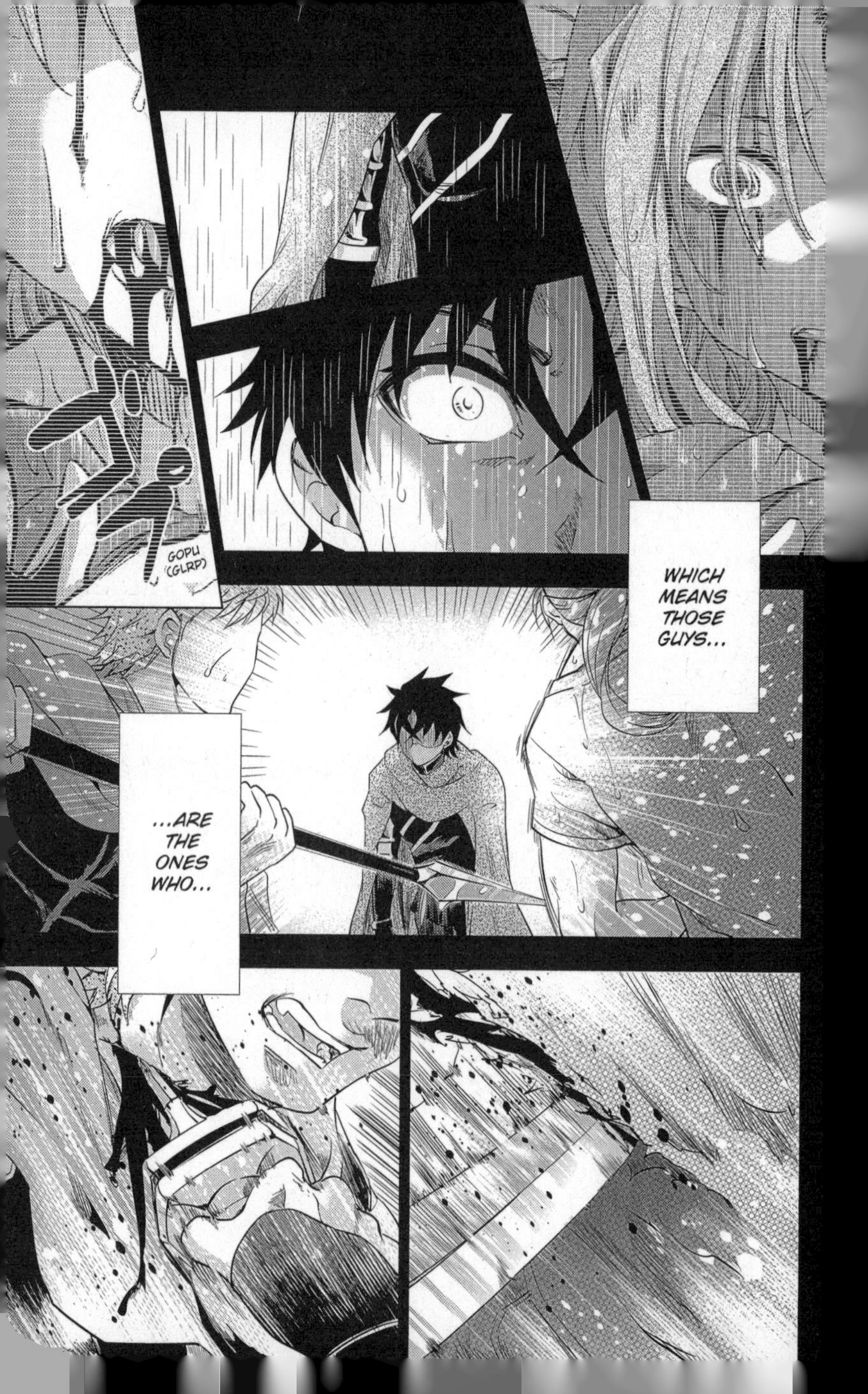
GOPU
(GLRP)
WHICH MEANS THOSE GUYS...
...ARE THE ONES WHO...

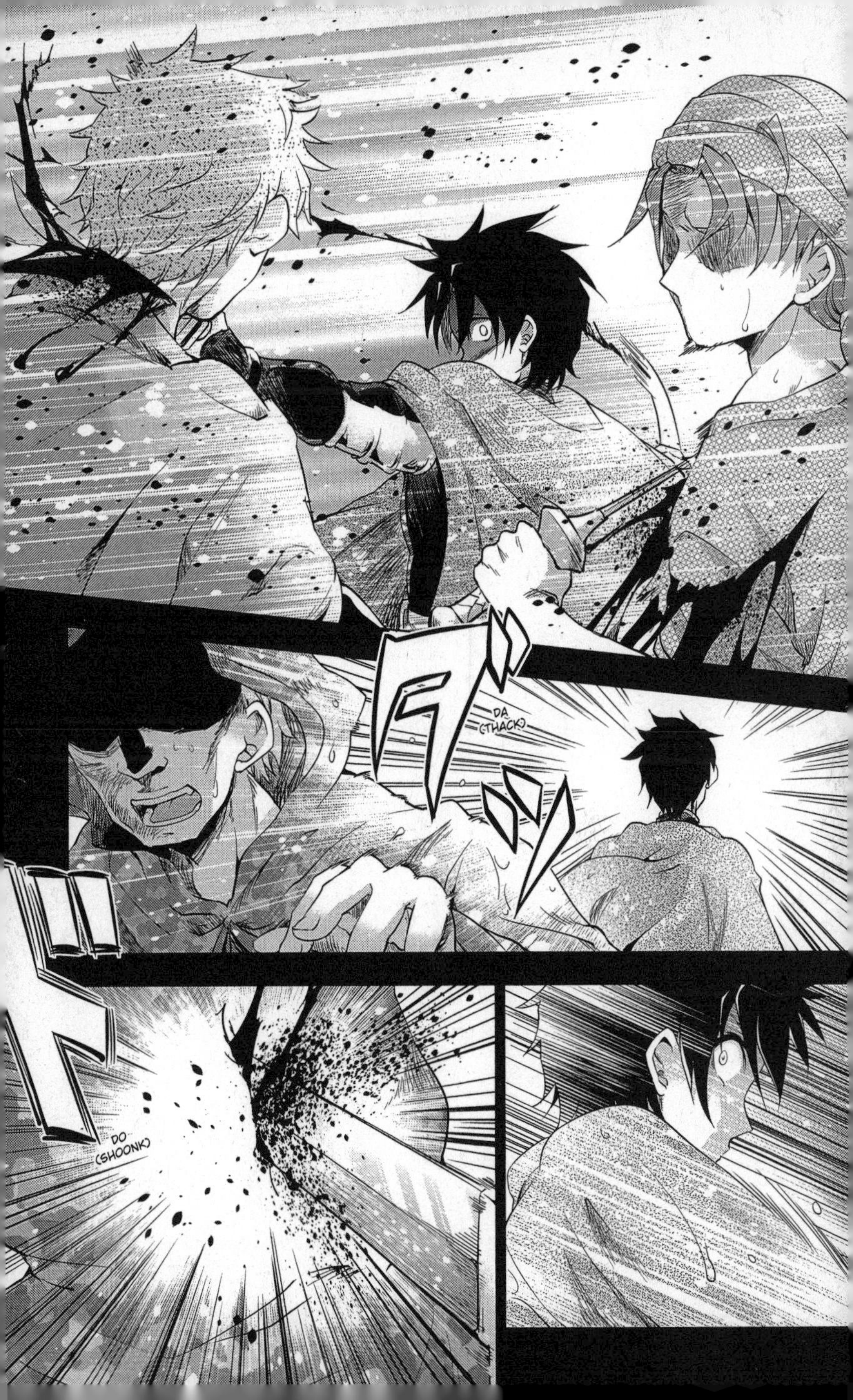
DA
(THACK)
DO
(SHOONK)

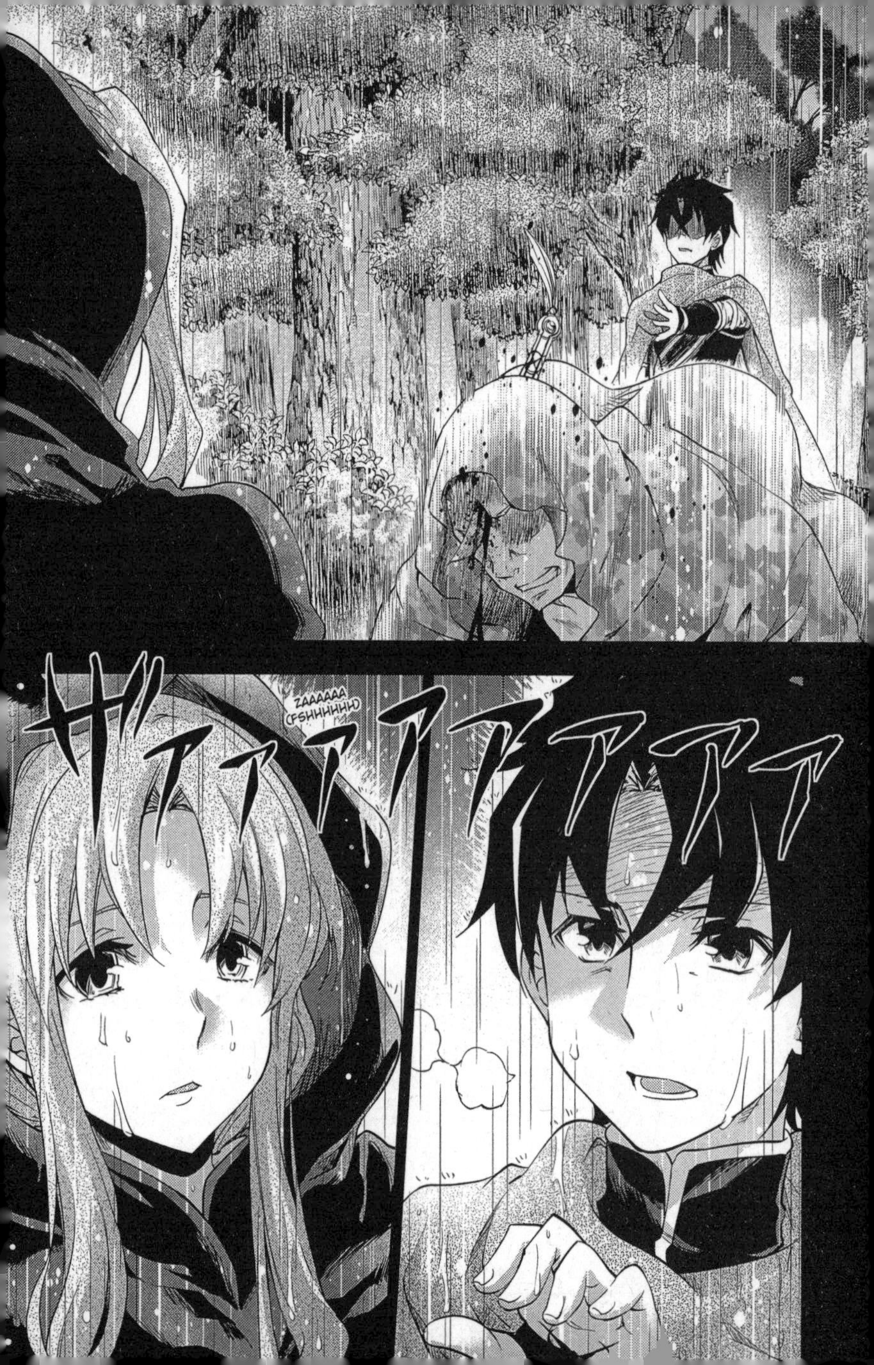
ザァァァァァァァァ
ZAAAAAA (FSHHHHHH)

CHAIKA: THE
COFFIN PRINCESS

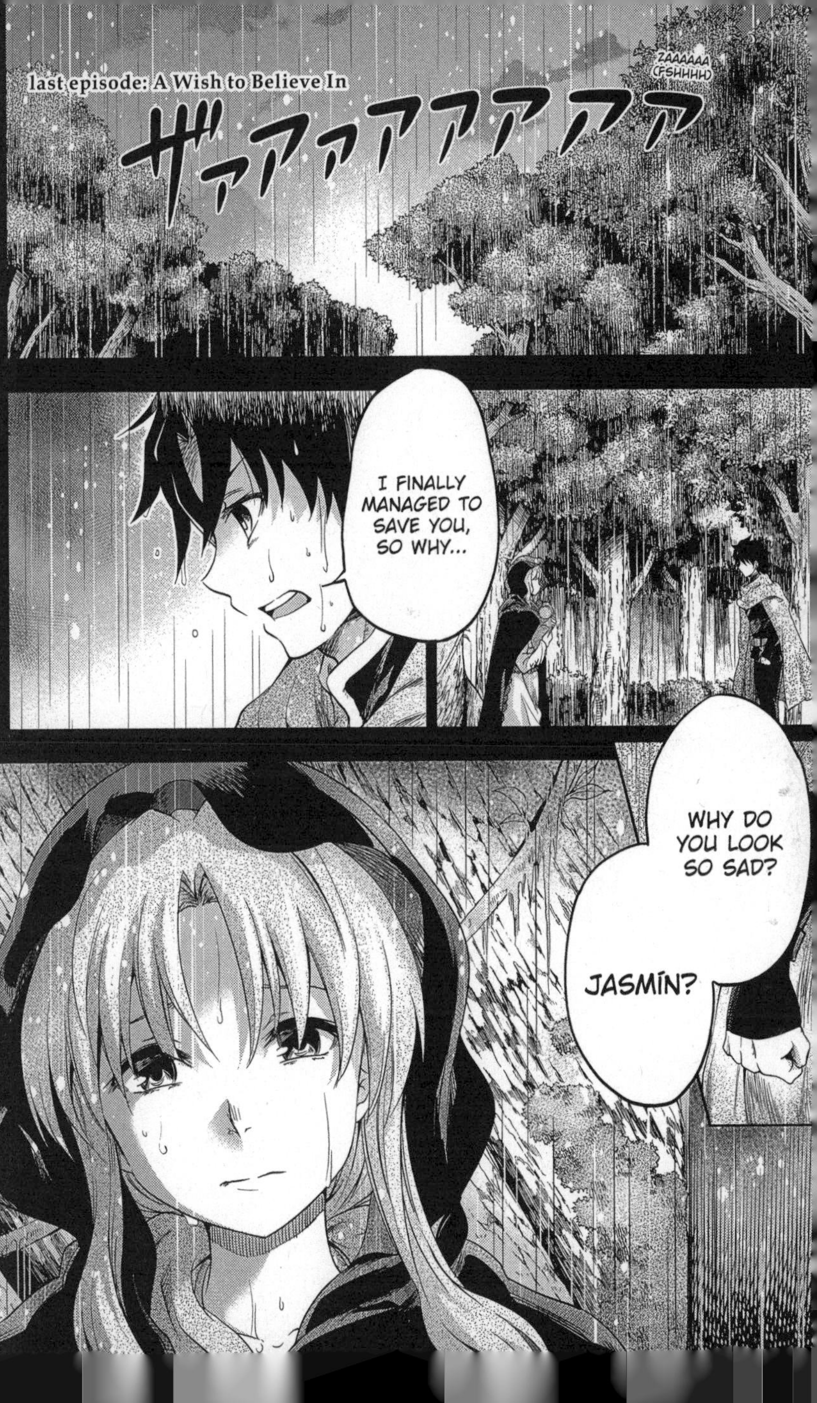
last episode: A Wish to Believe In
ZAAAAAA (FSHHHH)
ザァァァアアアア
I FINALLY MANAGED TO SAVE YOU, SO WHY...
WHY DO YOU LOOK SO SAD?
JASMIN?

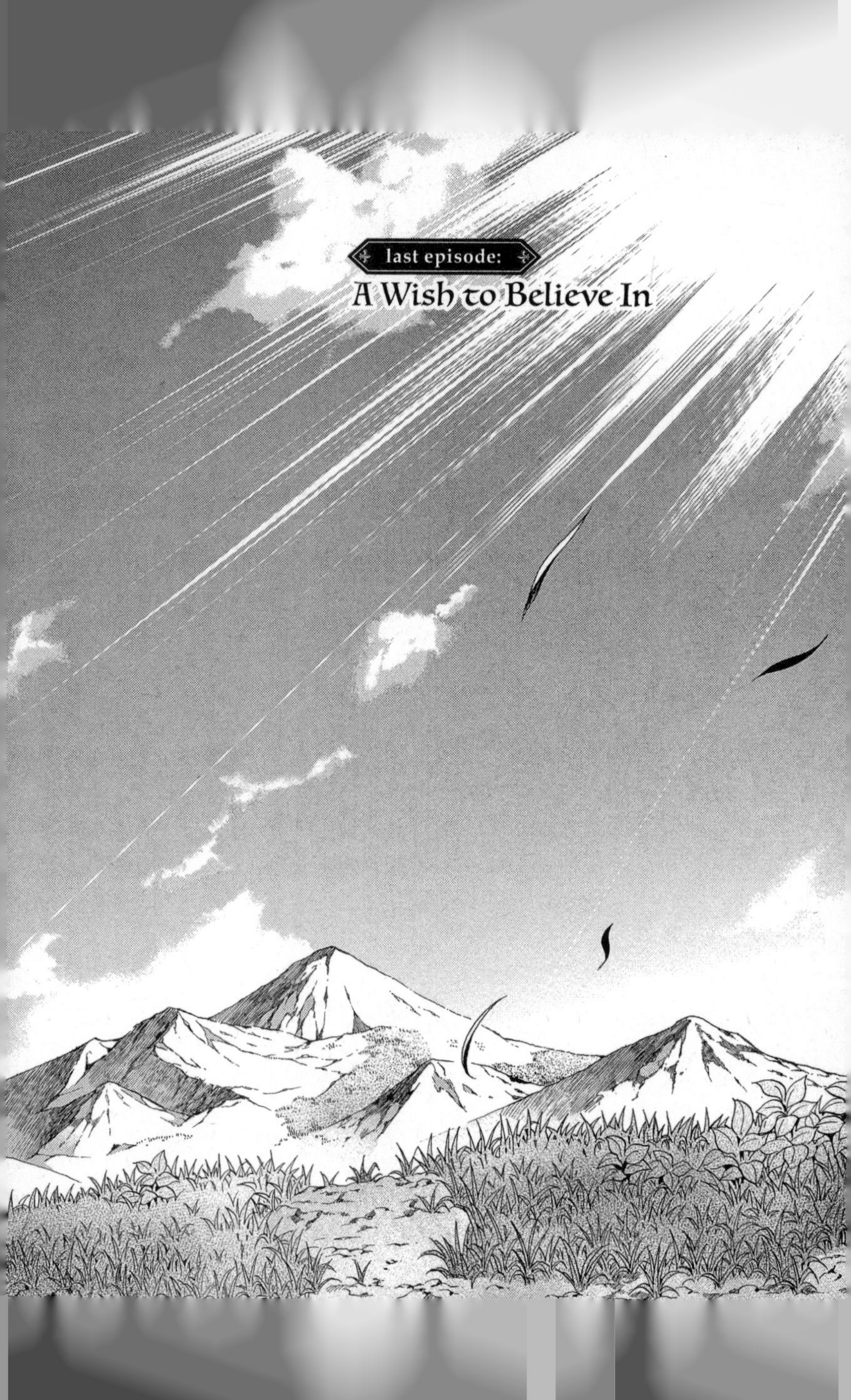
last episode:
A Wish to Believe In

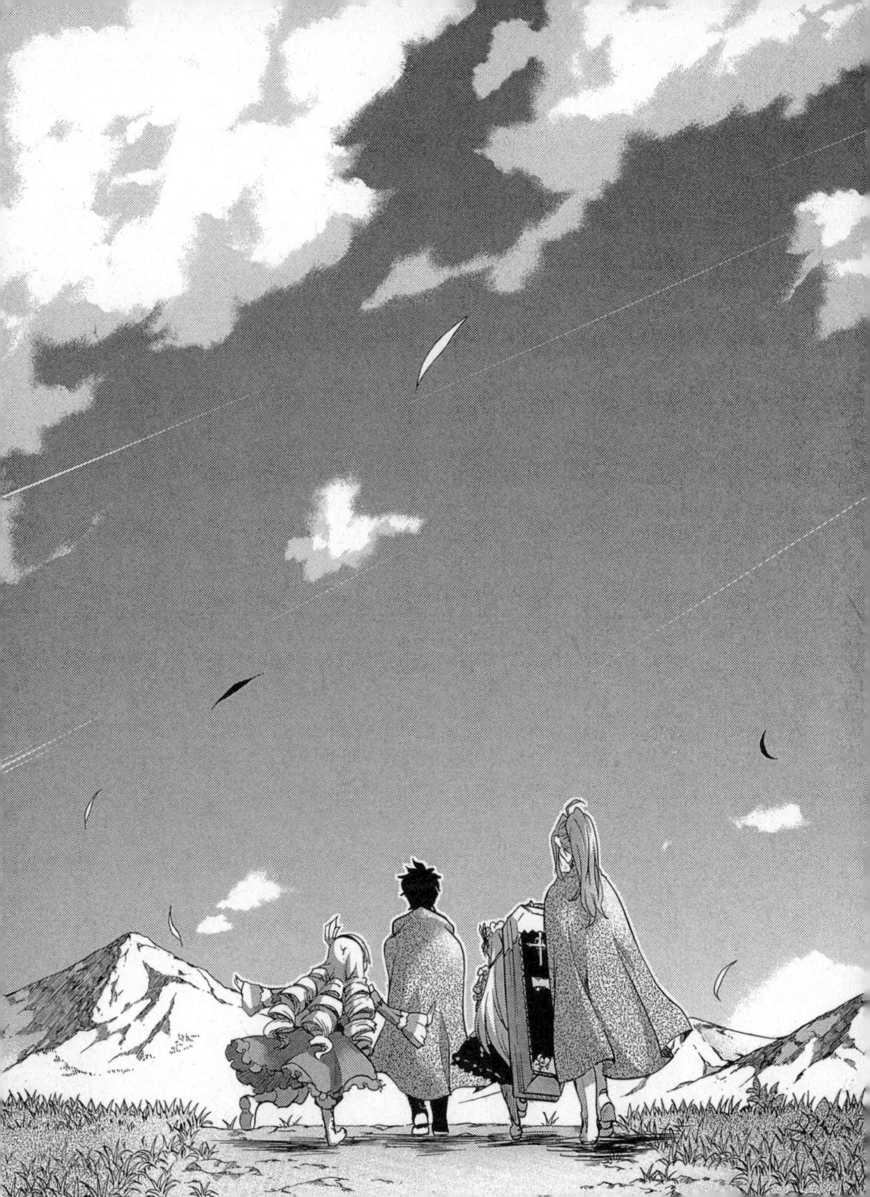

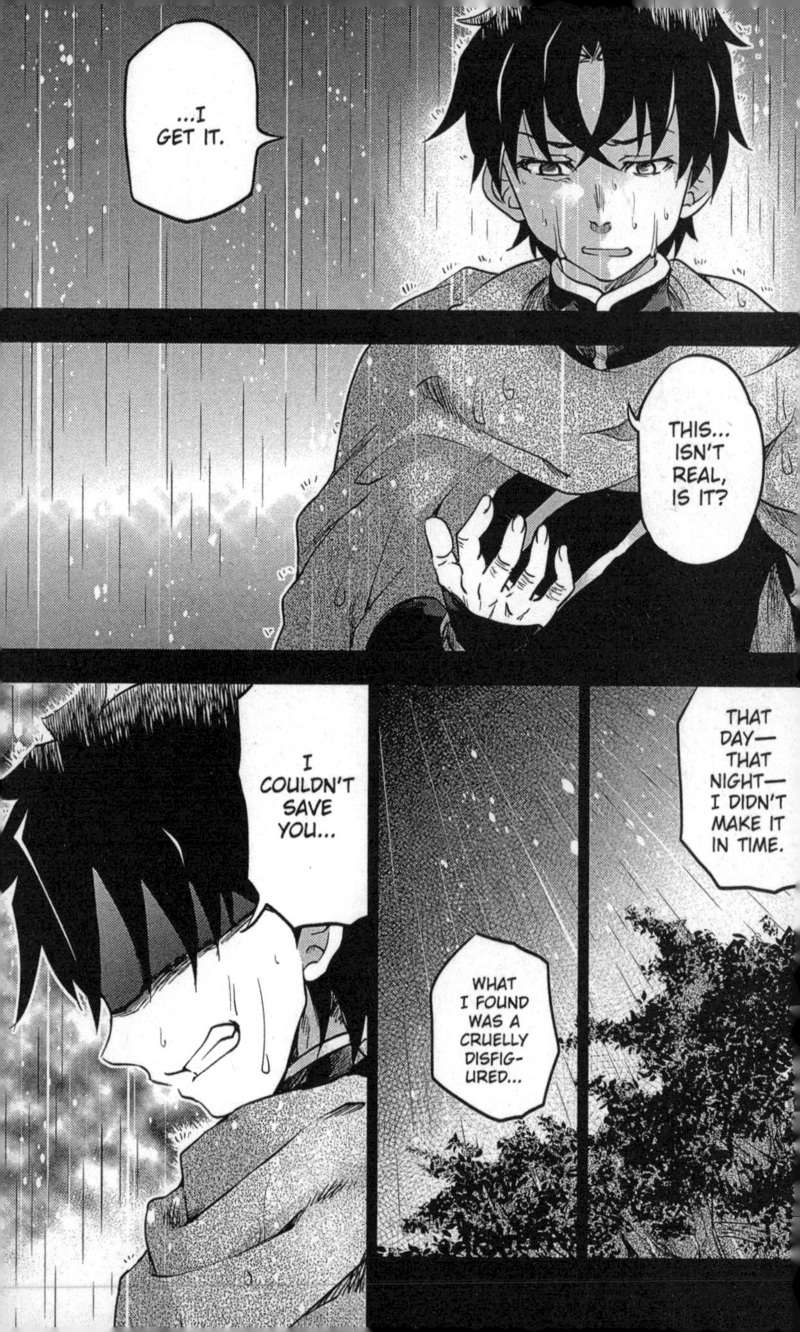
...I GET IT.
THIS... ISN'T REAL, IS IT?
THAT DAY—THAT NIGHT—I DIDN'T MAKE IT IN TIME.
WHAT I FOUND WAS A CRUELLY DISFIG-URED...
I COULDN'T SAVE YOU...

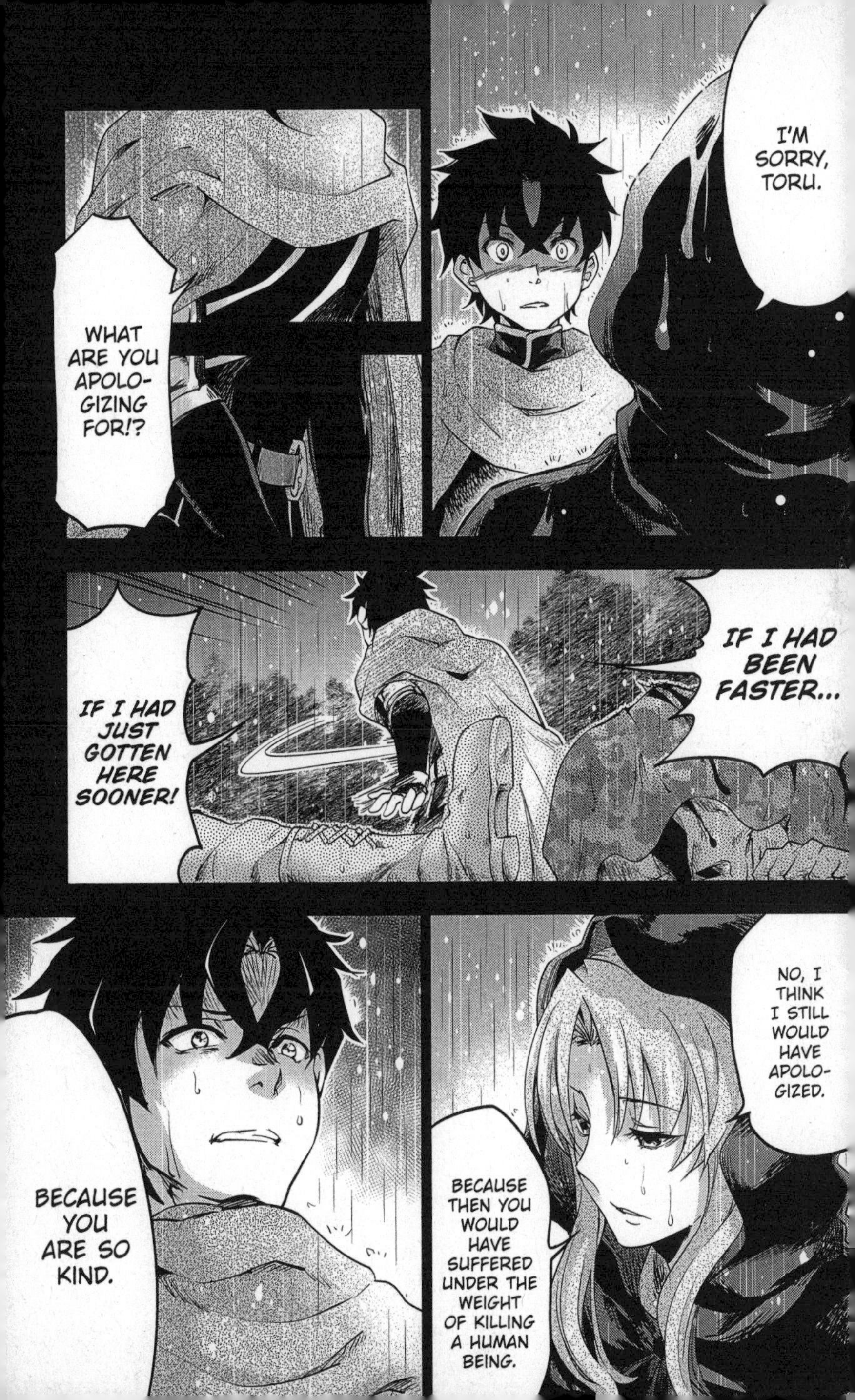
I'M SORRY, TORU.
WHAT ARE YOU APOLOGIZING FOR!?
IF I HAD BEEN FASTER...
IF I HAD JUST GOTTEN HERE SOONER!
NO, I THINK I STILL WOULD HAVE APOLOGIZED.
BECAUSE THEN YOU WOULD HAVE SUFFERED UNDER THE WEIGHT OF KILLING A HUMAN BEING.
BECAUSE YOU ARE SO KIND.

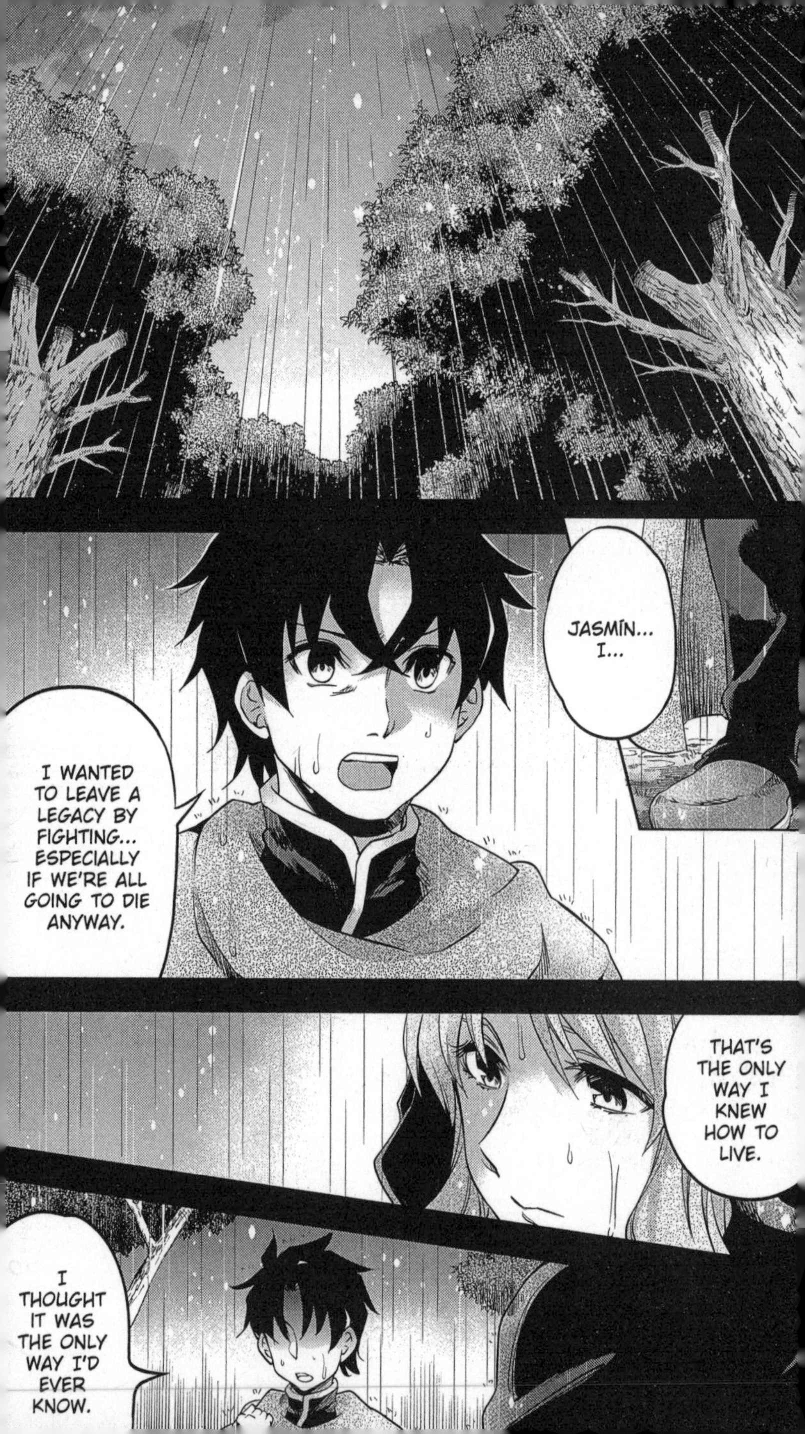
JASMÍN... I...
I WANTED TO LEAVE A LEGACY BY FIGHTING... ESPECIALLY IF WE'RE ALL GOING TO DIE ANYWAY.
THAT'S THE ONLY WAY I KNEW HOW TO LIVE.
I THOUGHT IT WAS THE ONLY WAY I'D EVER KNOW.

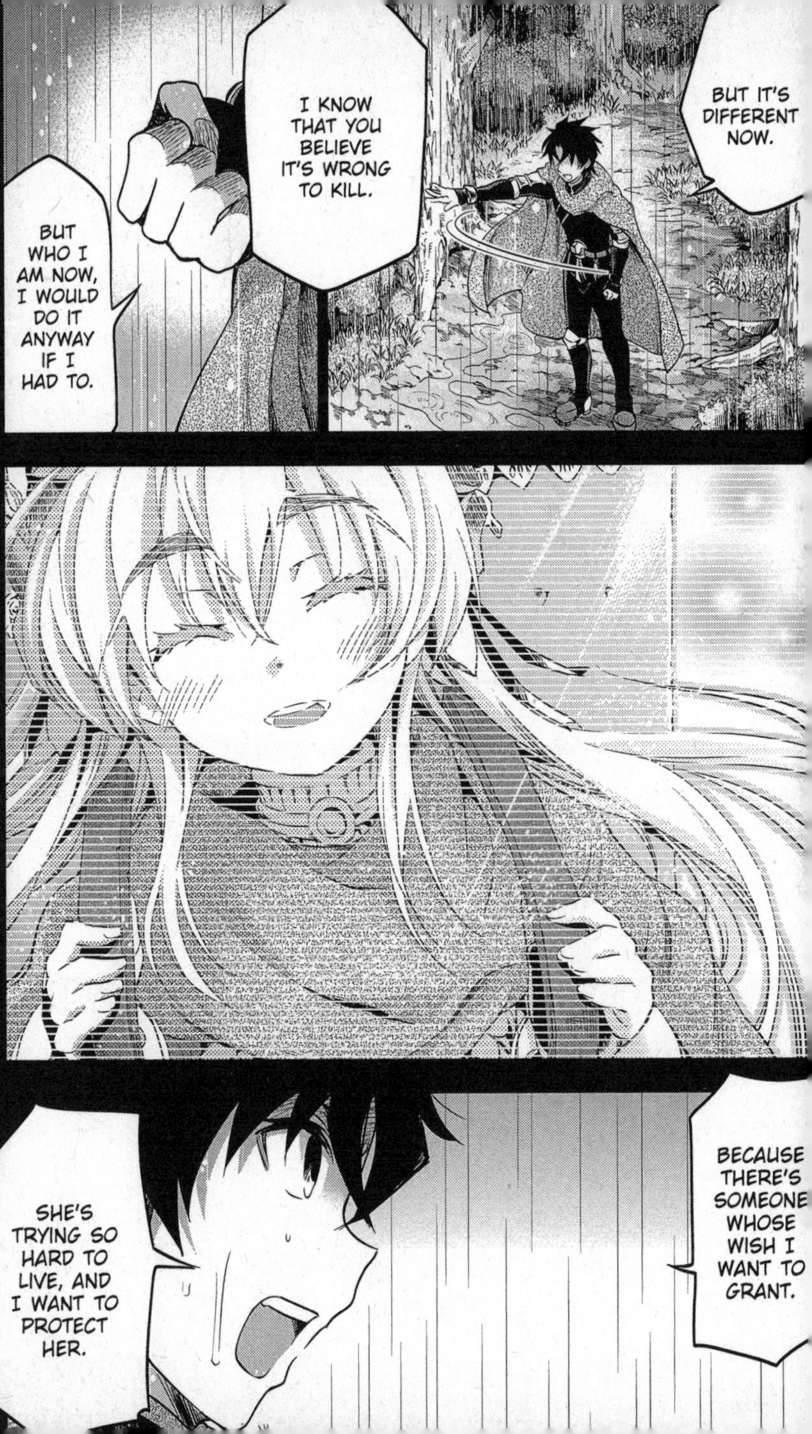
BUT IT'S DIFFERENT NOW.
I KNOW THAT YOU BELIEVE IT'S WRONG TO KILL.
BUT WHO I AM NOW, I WOULD DO IT ANYWAY IF I HAD TO.
BECAUSE THERE'S SOMEONE WHOSE WISH I WANT TO GRANT.
SHE'S TRYING SO HARD TO LIVE, AND I WANT TO PROTECT HER.

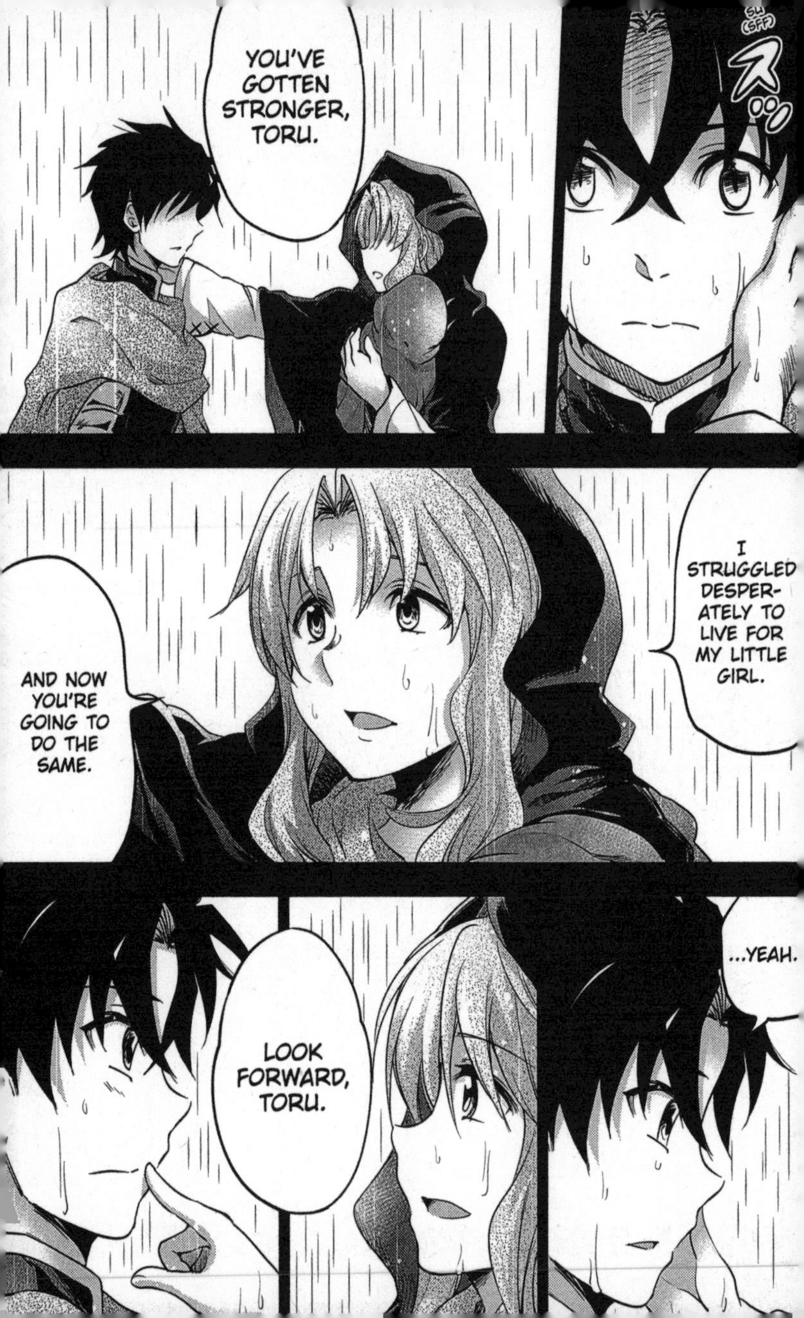
SU (SFF)
YOU'VE GOTTEN STRONGER, TORU.
I STRUGGLED DESPERATELY TO LIVE FOR MY LITTLE GIRL.
AND NOW YOU'RE GOING TO DO THE SAME.
...YEAH.
LOOK FORWARD, TORU.

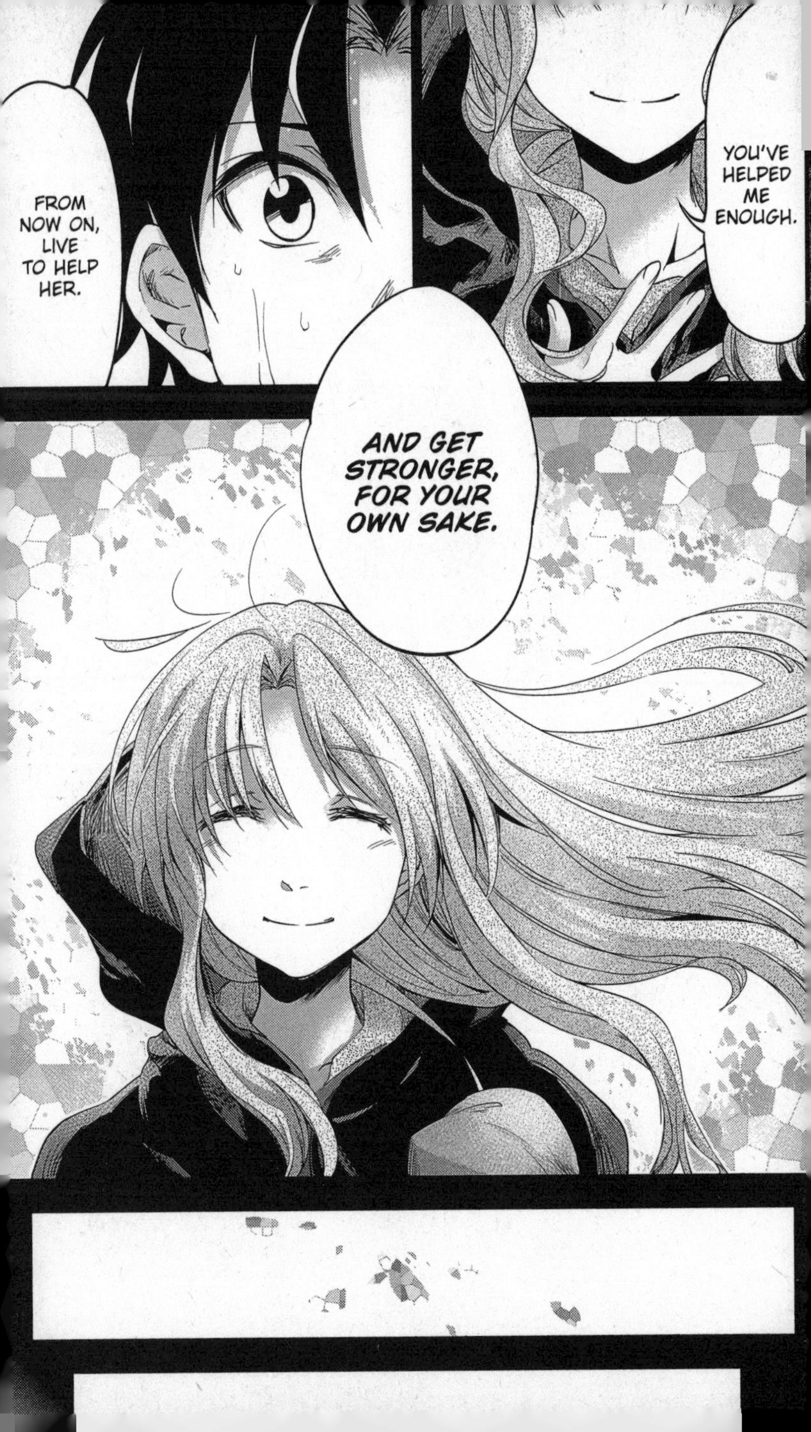
YOU'VE HELPED ME ENOUGH.
FROM NOW ON, LIVE TO HELP HER.
AND GET STRONGER, FOR YOUR OWN SAKE.

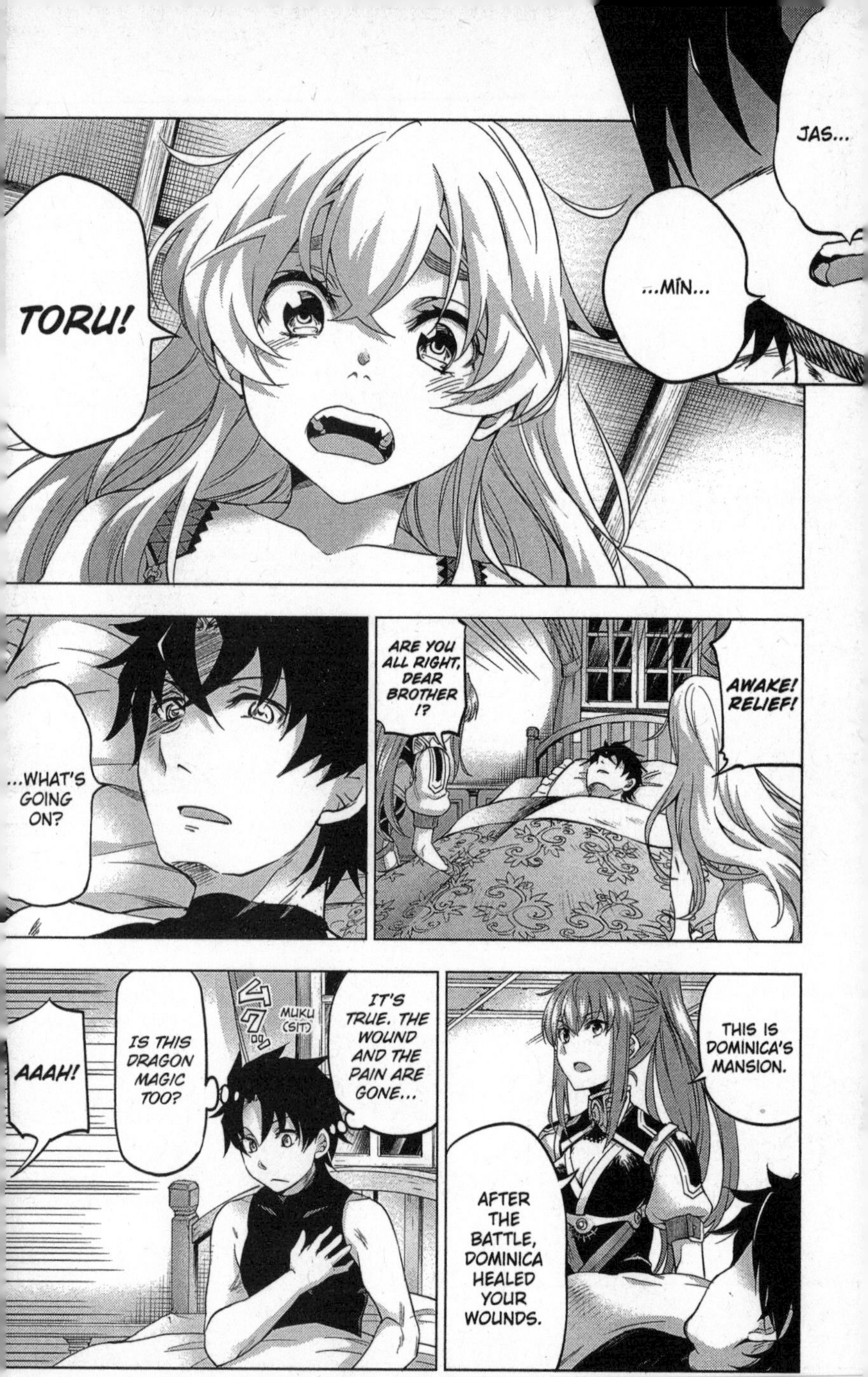
JAS...
...MÍN...
TORU!
AWAKE! RELIEF!
ARE YOU ALL RIGHT, DEAR BROTHER!?
...WHAT'S GOING ON?
THIS IS DOMINICA'S MANSION.
AFTER THE BATTLE, DOMINICA HEALED YOUR WOUNDS.
IT'S TRUE. THE WOUND AND THE PAIN ARE GONE...
MUKU (SIT)
IS THIS DRAGON MAGIC TOO?
AAAH!

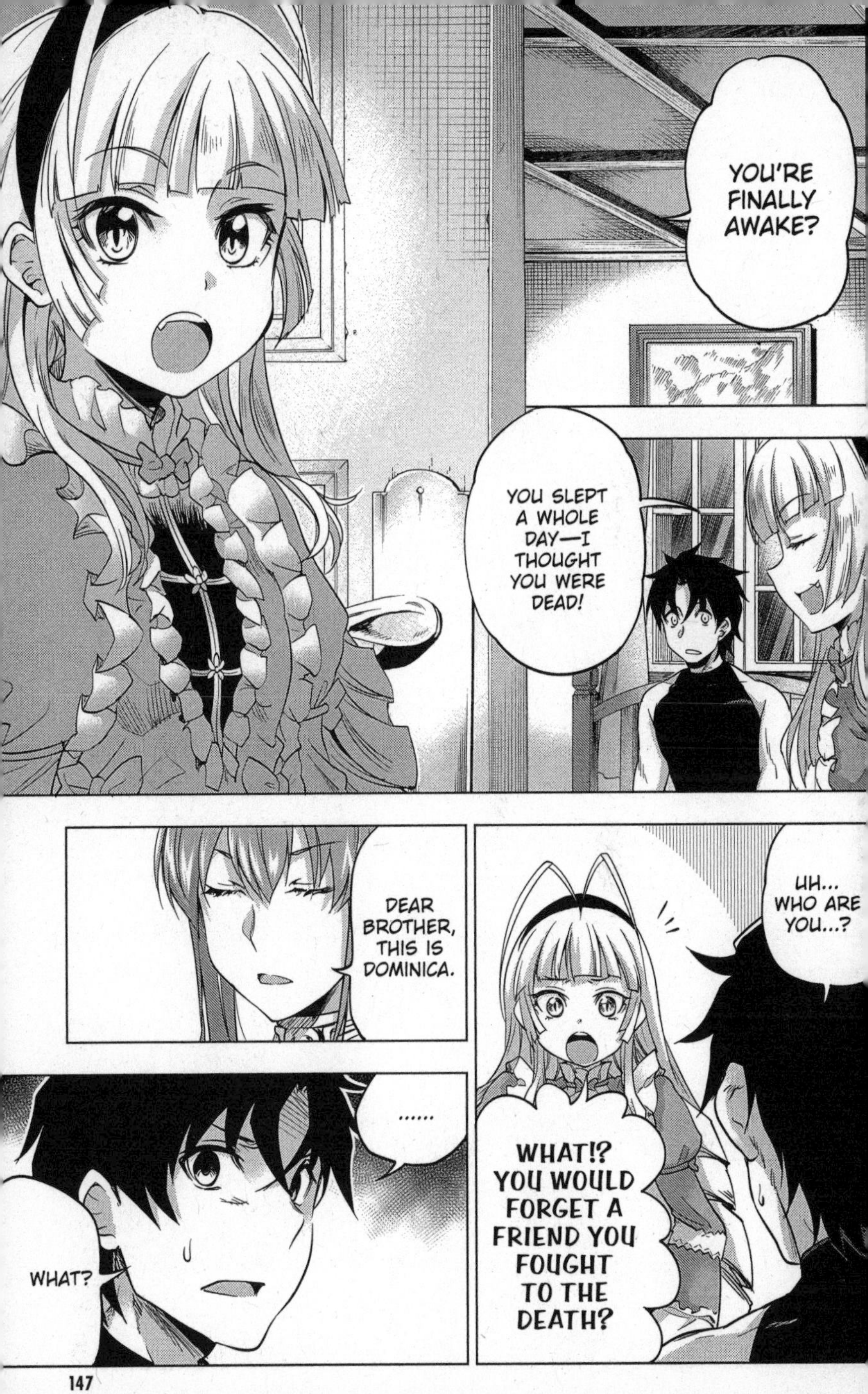
YOU'RE FINALLY AWAKE?
YOU SLEPT A WHOLE DAY—I THOUGHT YOU WERE DEAD!
UH... WHO ARE YOU...?
WHAT!? YOU WOULD FORGET A FRIEND YOU FOUGHT TO THE DEATH?
DEAR BROTHER, THIS IS DOMINICA.
......
WHAT?

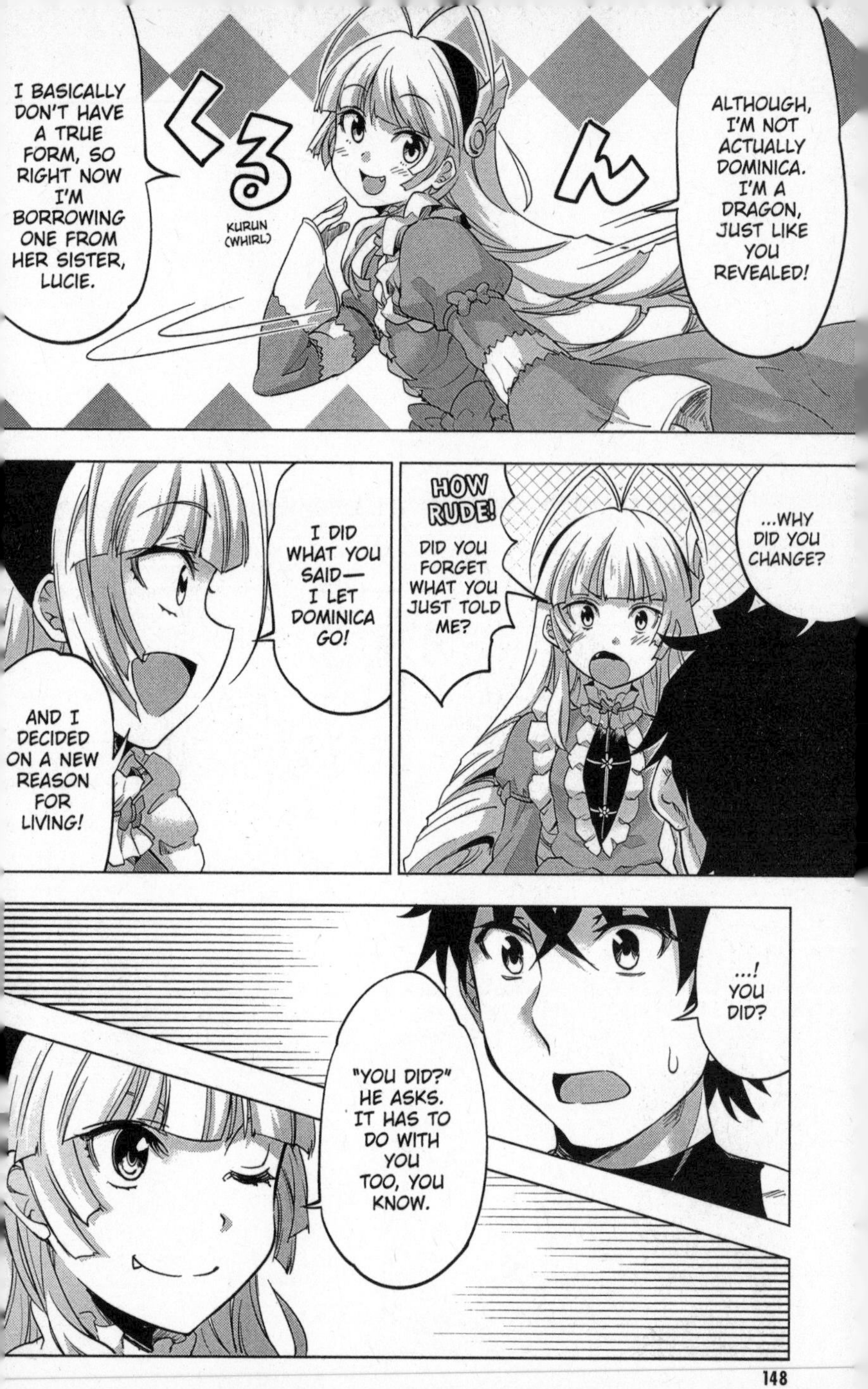
ALTHOUGH, I'M NOT ACTUALLY DOMINICA. I'M A DRAGON, JUST LIKE YOU REVEALED!
くるん
KURUN (WHIRL)
I BASICALLY DON'T HAVE A TRUE FORM, SO RIGHT NOW I'M BORROWING ONE FROM HER SISTER, LUCIE.
...WHY DID YOU CHANGE?
HOW RUDE!
DID YOU FORGET WHAT YOU JUST TOLD ME?
I DID WHAT YOU SAID— I LET DOMINICA GO!
AND I DECIDED ON A NEW REASON FOR LIVING!
...! YOU DID?
"YOU DID?" HE ASKS. IT HAS TO DO WITH YOU TOO, YOU KNOW.

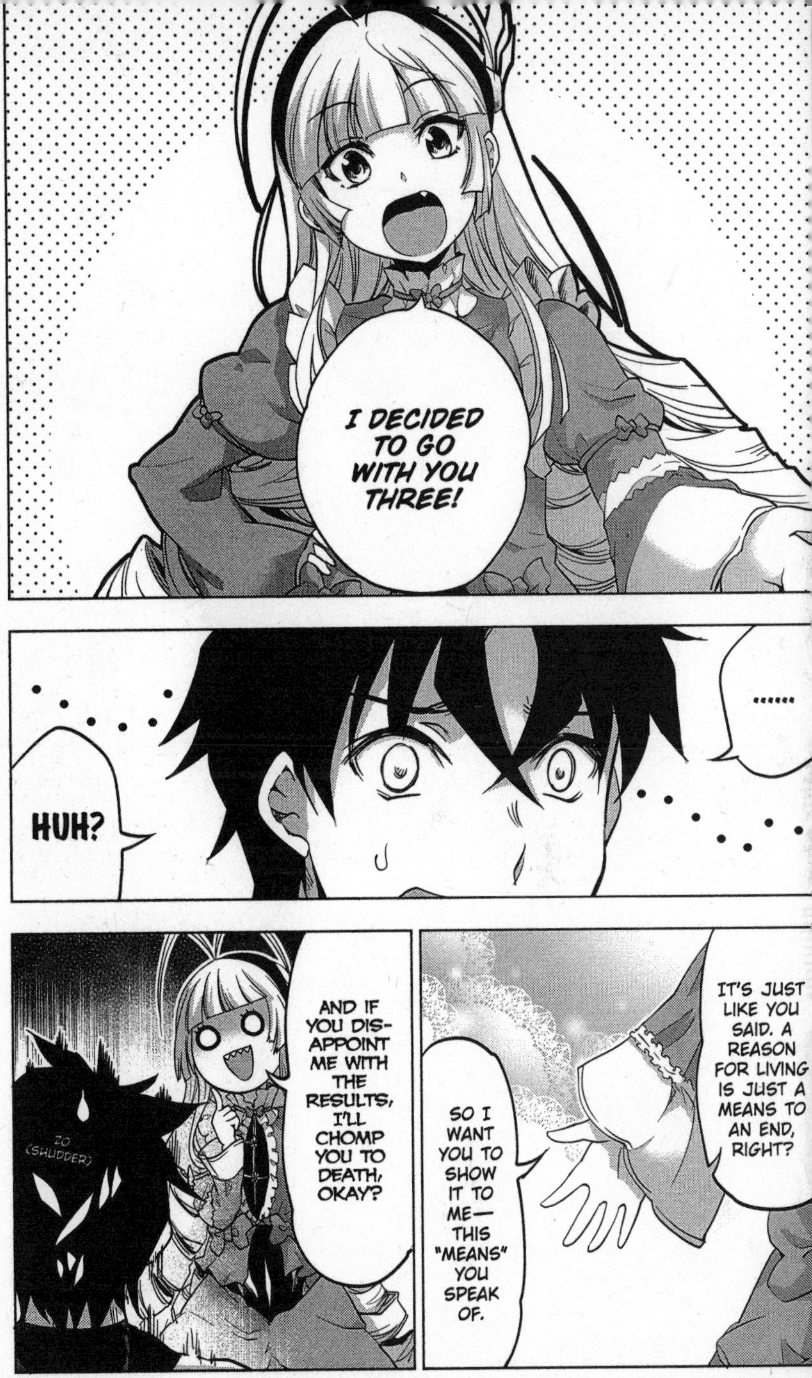
I DECIDED TO GO WITH YOU THREE!
......
HUH?
IT'S JUST LIKE YOU SAID. A REASON FOR LIVING IS JUST A MEANS TO AN END, RIGHT?
SO I WANT YOU TO SHOW IT TO ME— THIS "MEANS" YOU SPEAK OF.
AND IF YOU DIS-APPOINT ME WITH THE RESULTS, I'LL CHOMP YOU TO DEATH, OKAY?
ZO (SHUDDER)

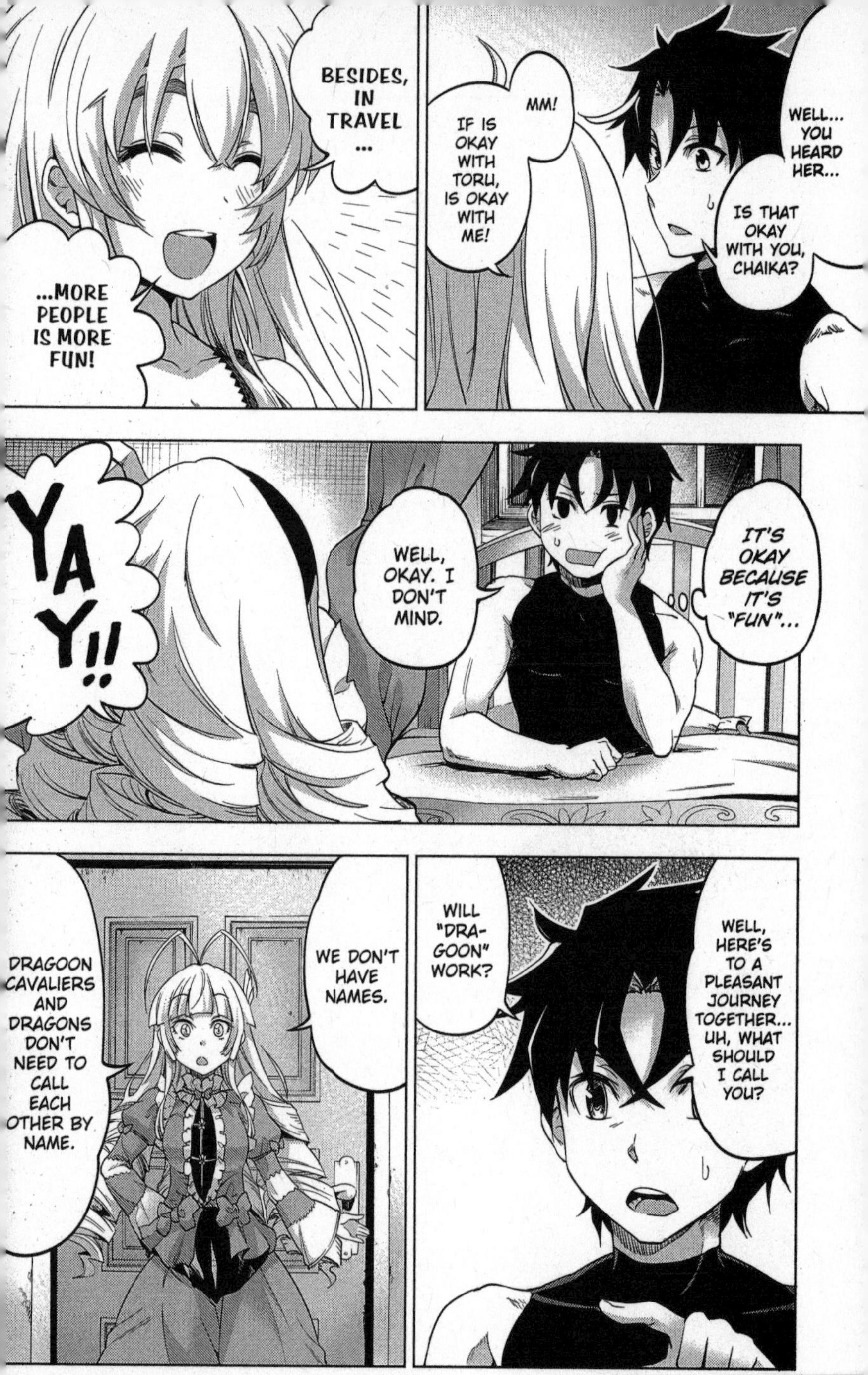
WELL... YOU HEARD HER...
IS THAT OKAY WITH YOU, CHAIKA?
MM!
IF IS OKAY WITH TORU, IS OKAY WITH ME!
BESIDES, IN TRAVEL ...
...MORE PEOPLE IS MORE FUN!
IT'S OKAY BECAUSE IT'S "FUN"...
WELL, OKAY. I DON'T MIND.
YAY!!
WELL, HERE'S TO A PLEASANT JOURNEY TOGETHER... UH, WHAT SHOULD I CALL YOU?
WILL "DRAGOON" WORK?
WE DON'T HAVE NAMES.
DRAGOON CAVALIERS AND DRAGONS DON'T NEED TO CALL EACH OTHER BY NAME.

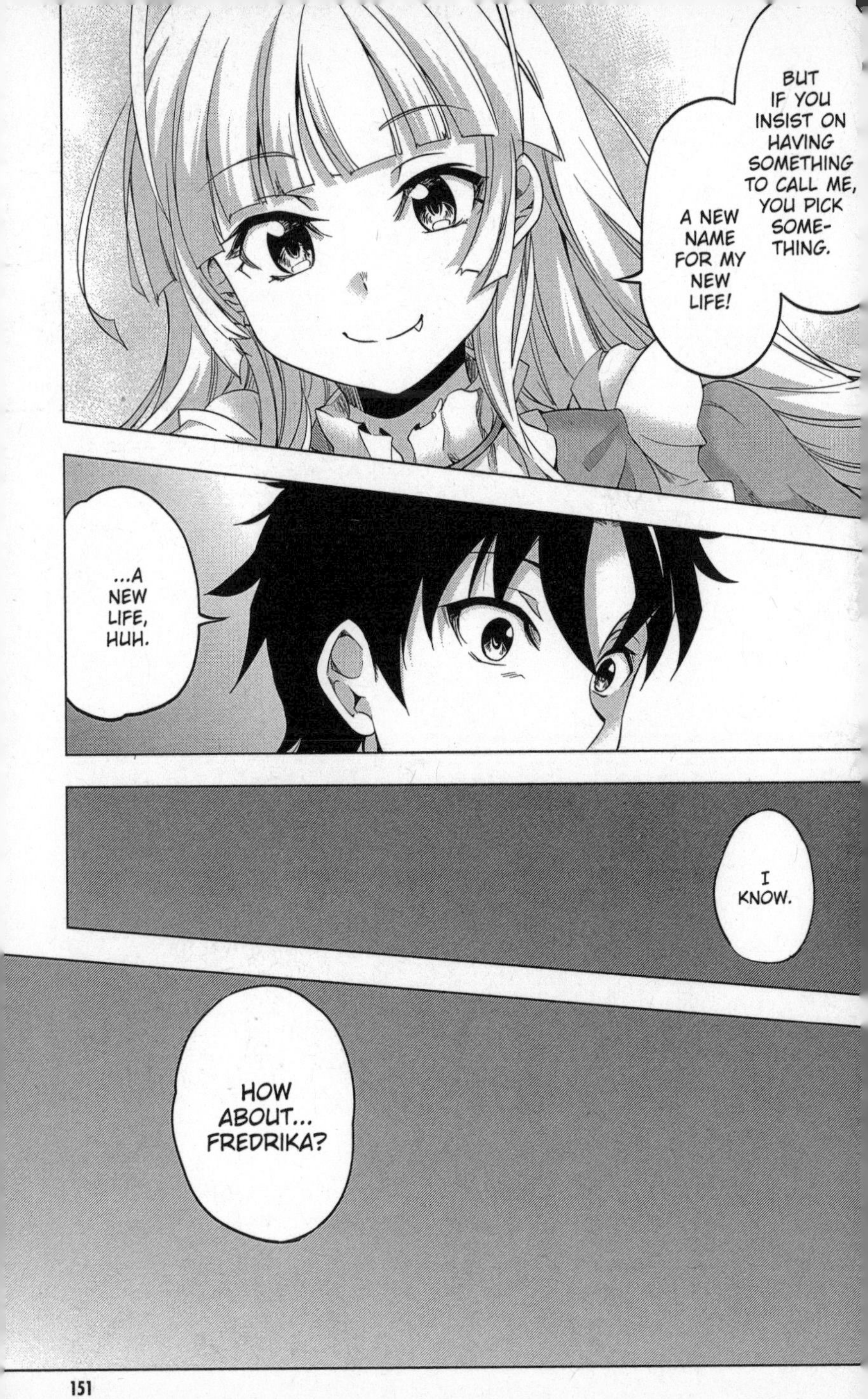
BUT IF YOU INSIST ON HAVING SOMETHING TO CALL ME, YOU PICK SOME-THING.
A NEW NAME FOR MY NEW LIFE!
...A NEW LIFE, HUH.
I KNOW.
HOW ABOUT... FREDRIKA?

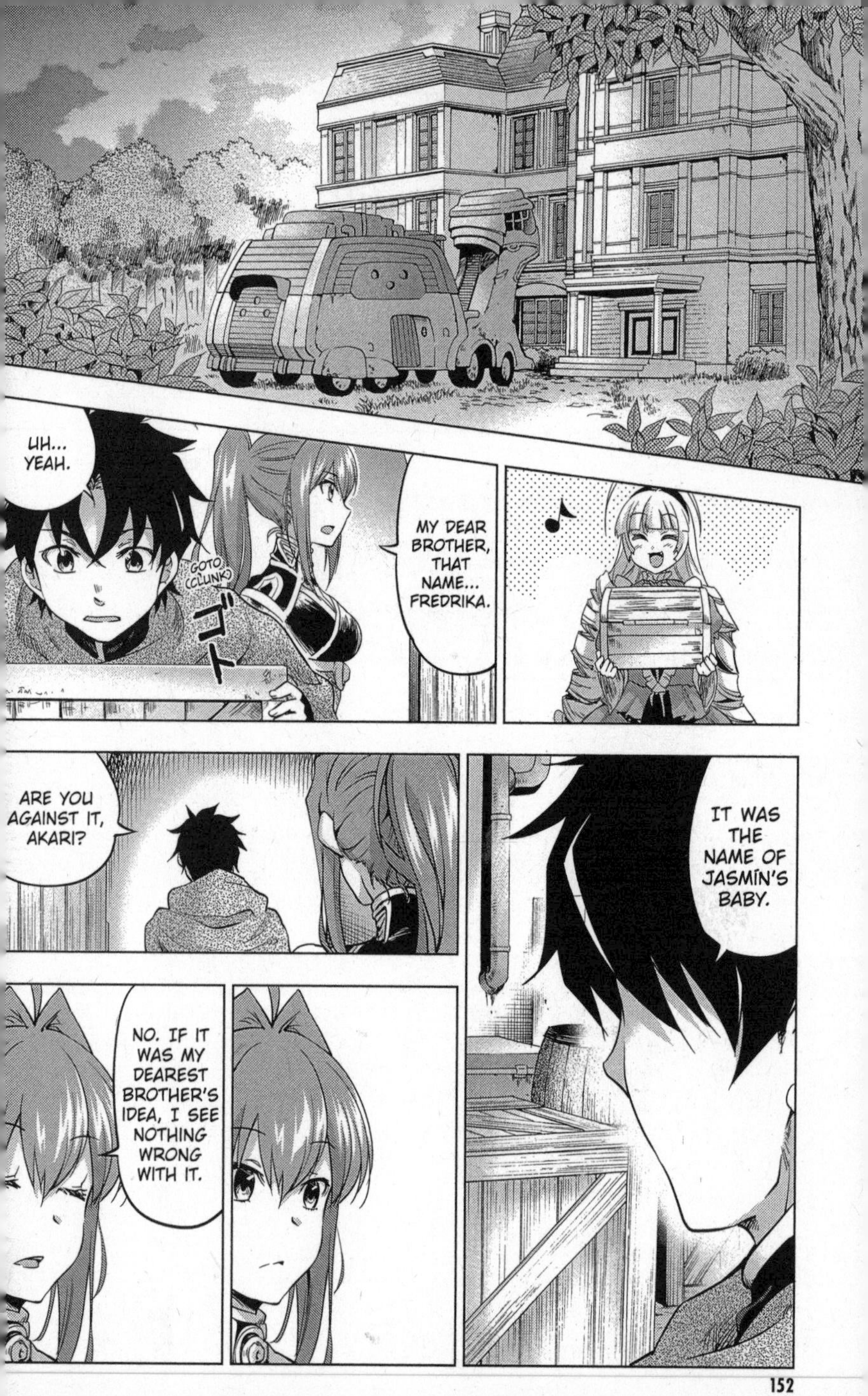
MY DEAR BROTHER, THAT NAME... FREDRIKA.
UH... YEAH.
GOTO (CLUNK)
IT WAS THE NAME OF JASMÍN'S BABY.
ARE YOU AGAINST IT, AKARI?
NO. IF IT WAS MY DEAREST BROTHER'S IDEA, I SEE NOTHING WRONG WITH IT.

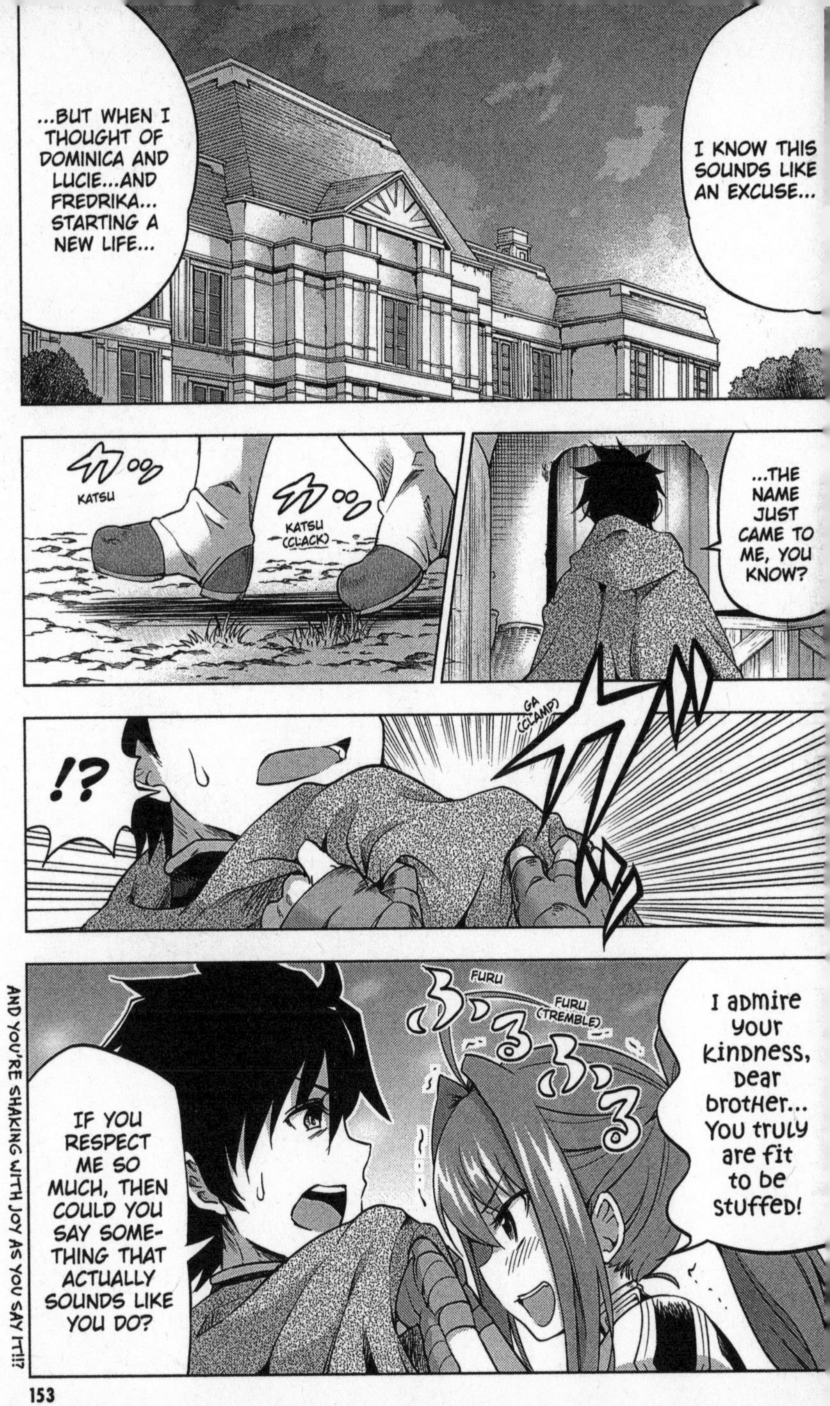
I KNOW THIS SOUNDS LIKE AN EXCUSE...
...BUT WHEN I THOUGHT OF DOMINICA AND LUCIE...AND FREDRIKA... STARTING A NEW LIFE...
...THE NAME JUST CAME TO ME, YOU KNOW?
KATSU
KATSU (CLACK)
GA (CLAMP)
!?
FURU
FURU (TREMBLE)
I admire your kindness, dear brother... You truly are fit to be stuffed!
IF YOU RESPECT ME SO MUCH, THEN COULD YOU SAY SOME-THING THAT ACTUALLY SOUNDS LIKE YOU DO?
AND YOU'RE SHAKING WITH JOY AS YOU SAY IT!!?

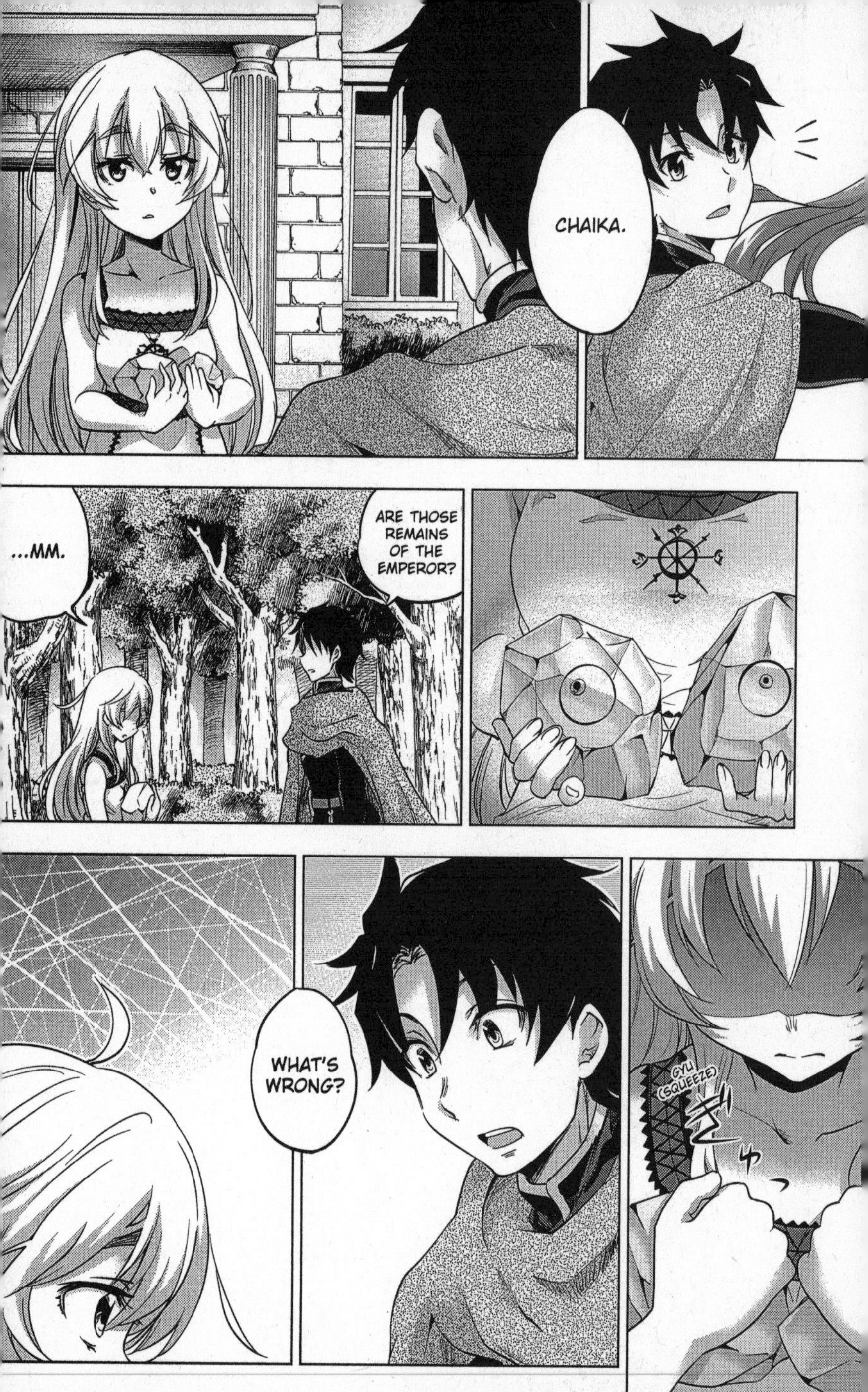
CHAIKA.
ARE THOSE REMAINS OF THE EMPEROR?
...MM.
GYU (SQUEEZE)
WHAT'S WRONG?

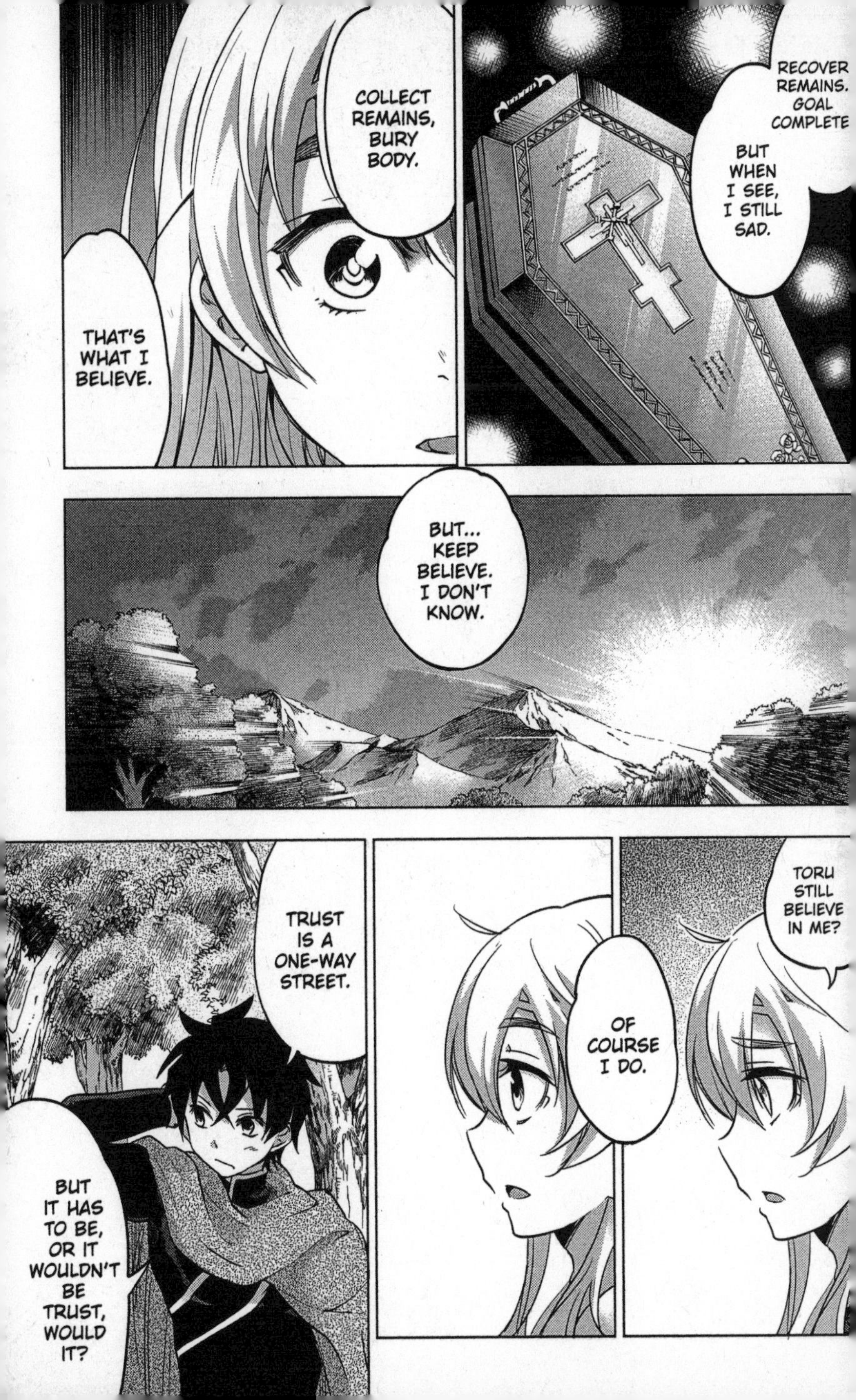
RECOVER REMAINS. GOAL COMPLETE
BUT WHEN I SEE, I STILL SAD.
COLLECT REMAINS, BURY BODY.
THAT'S WHAT I BELIEVE.
BUT... KEEP BELIEVE. I DON'T KNOW.
TORU STILL BELIEVE IN ME?
OF COURSE I DO.
TRUST IS A ONE-WAY STREET.
BUT IT HAS TO BE, OR IT WOULDN'T BE TRUST, WOULD IT?

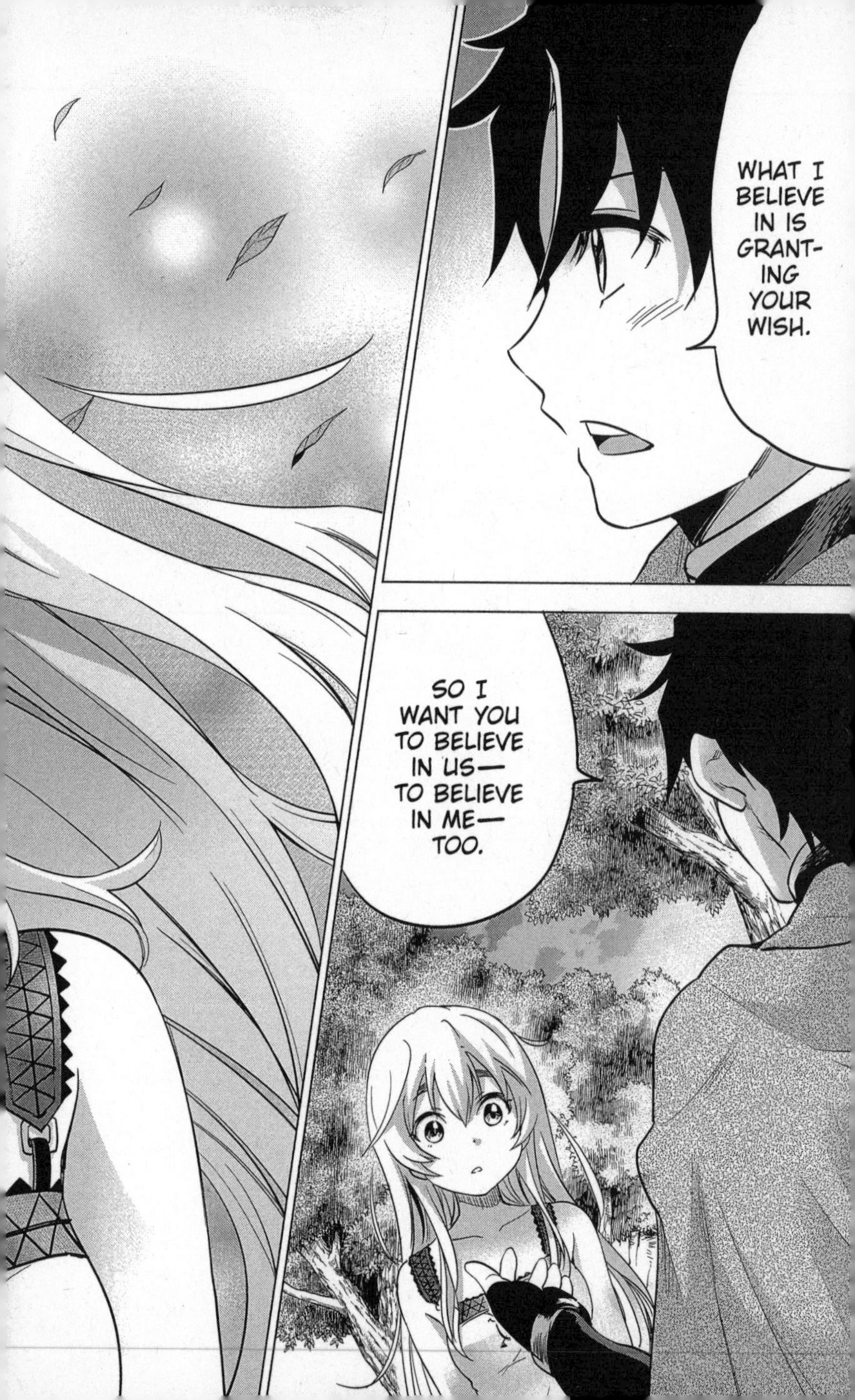
WHAT I BELIEVE IN IS GRANTING YOUR WISH.
SO I WANT YOU TO BELIEVE IN US— TO BELIEVE IN ME— TOO.

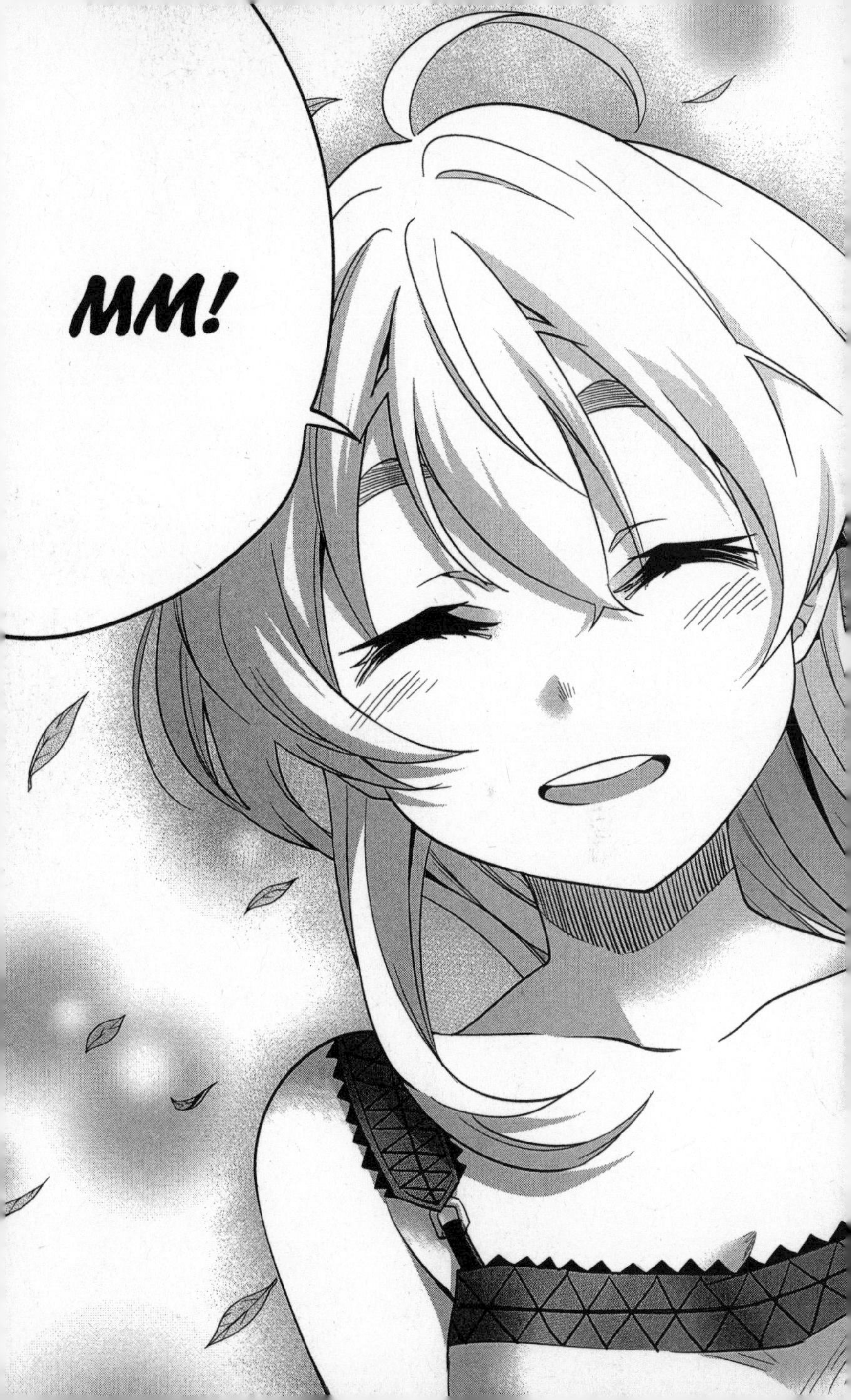
MM!

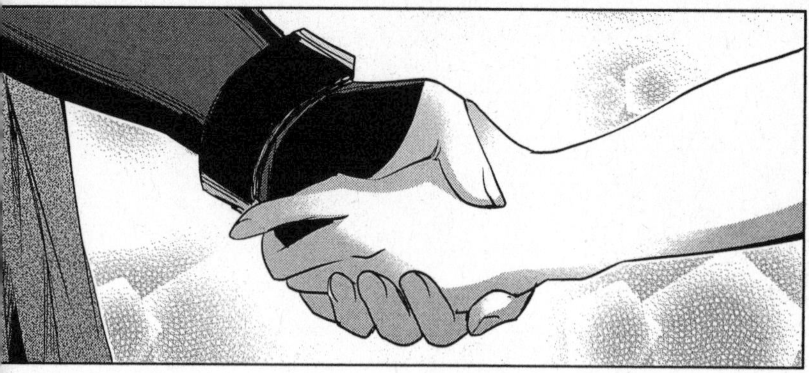

WHATEVER DIFFICULTIES LIE AHEAD...

...OUR JOURNEY IS ONLY JUST BEGINNING.

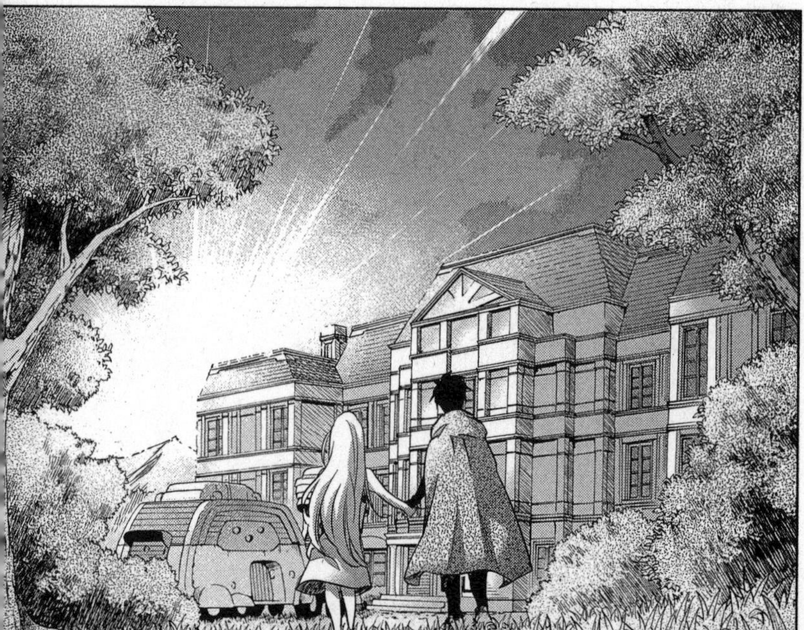
last episode: END

from Ichirou Sakaki

AND SO, THANK YOU FOR ALL YOUR HARD WORK ON THE MANGA VERSION OF *CHAIKA: THE COFFIN PRINCESS!*

IT BASICALLY FOLLOWS THE STORY AND MATERIAL OF THE ORIGINAL NOVELS, BUT EVEN THE CREATOR LOOKED FORWARD TO READING IT EVERY TIME. THAT'S PROBABLY BECAUSE, AS I WROTE BEFORE, SAKAYAMA-SENSEI'S UNIQUE (BUT STILL IN KEEPING WITH THE ORIGINAL CHARACTERS AND WORLD-BUILDING) INTERPRETATION WAS SO MUCH FUN. PERSONALLY, I FOUND IT A JOY TO SEE THE SAKAYAMA-SENSEI VERSION OF FREDRIKA (AND ALSO LUCIE) IN THE END.

ICHIROU SAKAKI

from Namaniku ATK

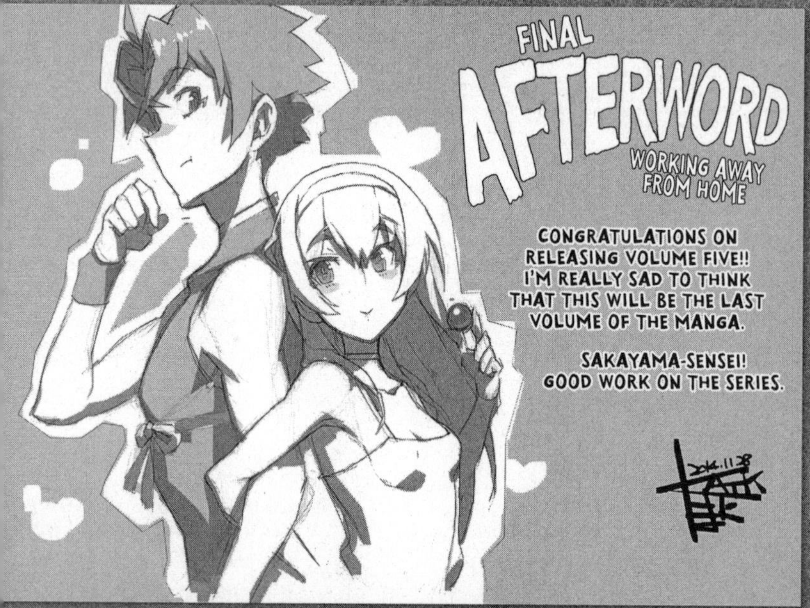
FINAL
AFTERWORD
WORKING AWAY FROM HOME
CONGRATULATIONS ON RELEASING VOLUME FIVE!! I'M REALLY SAD TO THINK THAT THIS WILL BE THE LAST VOLUME OF THE MANGA.
SAKAYAMA-SENSEI! GOOD WORK ON THE SERIES.

THANK YOU FOR BUYING VOLUME FIVE OF CHAIKA: THE COFFIN PRINCESS.

THIS IS THE LAST VOLUME OF CHAIKA: THE COFFIN PRINCESS. I THINK THE BOOK WILL GO ON SALE RIGHT AS THE SECOND SEASON OF THE ANIME IS ENDING.

NOW, SINCE THIS IS THE LAST VOLUME, I WILL INDULGE IN SOME DIGRESSION. THE TRUTH IS, WHEN THEY FIRST TALKED TO ME ABOUT DOING THE MANGA VERSION, THE PLAN WAS FOR IT TO END AT ABOUT TWO VOLUMES (TO COINCIDE WITH THE END OF THE ANIME). BUT PLANS KEPT CHANGING, AND THE NEXT THING I KNEW, IT HAD EXPANDED TO FIVE VOLUMES. (THAT'S ONE OF THE REASONS THE STORY MOVED SO SLOWLY.) EVEN I NEVER DREAMED I WOULD BE ALLOWED TO BE INVOLVED WITH CHAIKA FOR THREE WHOLE YEARS, AND IT WAS A GOOD EXPERIENCE.

SO NOW THE NOVELS, THE ANIME, AND THE MANGA ARE ALL ENDING AT THE SAME TIME. THIS IS THE END OF THE GRAPHIC NOVEL VERSION, BUT IF YOU ALL ENJOYED IT, THEN I'M HAPPY.

AND ONCE AGAIN, I WOULD LIKE TO THANK ICHIROU SAKAKI-SENSEI, NAMANIKU ATK-SENSEI, AND EVERYONE ELSE WHO HELPED WITH THIS WORK.

AND I HOPE WE CAN ALL MEET AGAIN IN A NEW SERIES.

THANK YOU VERY MUCH!

2014.12

茶菓山しん太

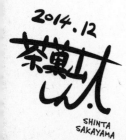

SHINTA SAKAYAMA

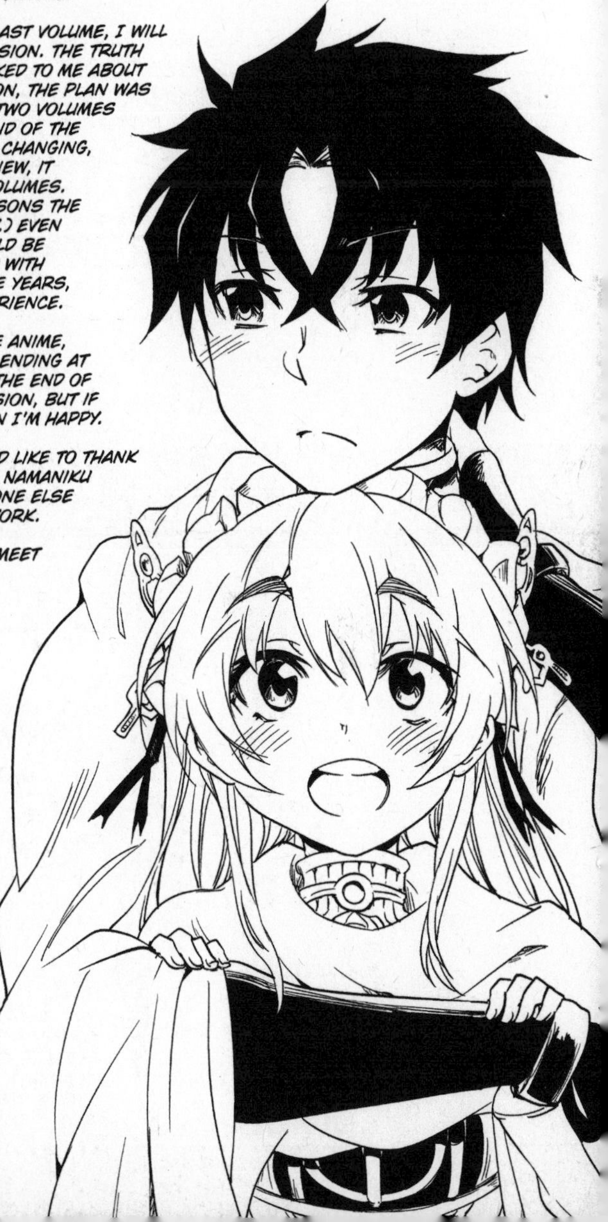

ENJOY EVERYTHING.

YOU SHOULD COME PLAY WITH YOTSUBA TOO!

Join Yotsuba as she delights in the
things many of us take for granted
in this Eisner-nominated series.

VOLUMES 1-13
AVAILABLE NOW!

Hello! This is YOTSUBA!

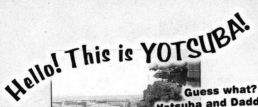

Guess what? Guess what?
Yotsuba and Daddy just moved here
from waaaay over there!

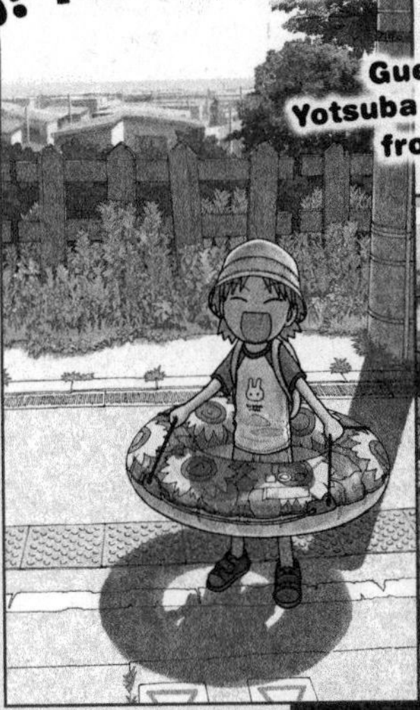

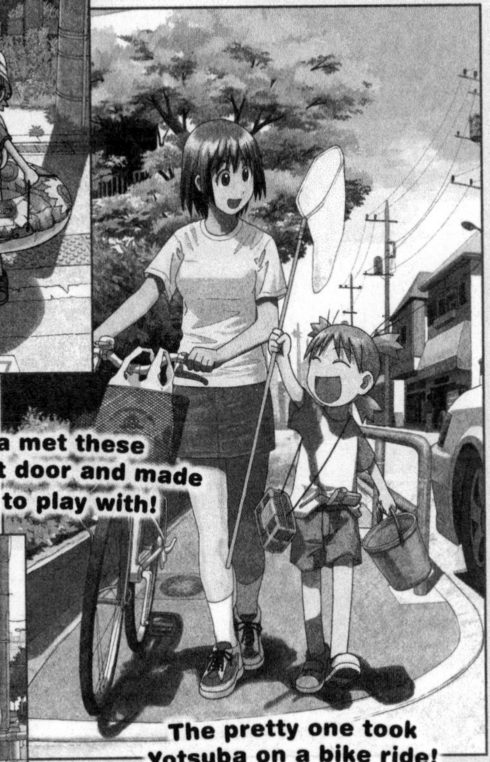

And Yotsuba met these
nice people next door and made
new friends to play with!

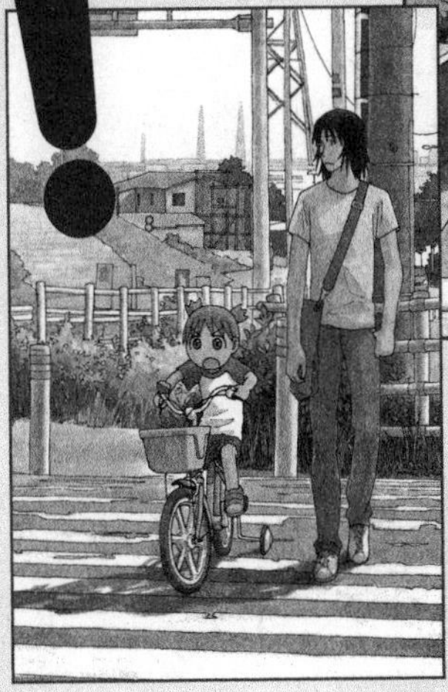

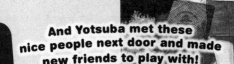

The pretty one took
Yotsuba on a bike ride!
(Whoooa! There was a big hill!)

And Ena's a good drawer!
(Almost as good as Yotsuba!)

And their mom always
gives Yotsuba ice cream!
(Yummy!)

And...
And...
OHHHH!

CHAIKA: THE COFFIN PRINCESS ❺

Original Story By: ICHIROU SAKAKI
Manga: SHINTA SAKAYAMA
Character Design: Namaniku ATK (Nitroplus)

Translation: Athena and Alethea Nibley
Lettering: Abigail Blackman

HITSUGI NO CHAIKA Volume 5
©Ichirou Sakaki,Nitroplus 2014
©Shinta SAKAYAMA 2014
First published in Japan in 2014 by KADOKAWA CORPORATION, Tokyo.
English translation rights arranged with KADOKAWA CORPORATION, Tokyo through TUTTLE-MORI AGENCY, INC., Tokyo.

English translation © 2016 by Yen Press, LLC

Library of Congress Control Number: 2014504622

ISBNs: 978-0-316-27234-6 (paperback)
       978-0-316-43372-3 (ebook)

10 9 8 7 6 5 4 3 2 1

BVG

Printed in the United States of America